Talking With the Spirits

ETHNOGRAPHIES FROM BETWEEN THE WORLDS

Edited by

Jack Hunter and David Luke

DAILY GRAIL PUBLISHING

Talking With the Spirits: Ethnographies From Between the Worlds

ISBN: 978-0-9874224-4-6

Daily Grail Publishing
Brisbane, Australia
publications@dailygrail.com
www.dailygrail.com

Cover image: A medium trancing the Underworld deity Tua Ya Pek on a tour of temples in Singapore to pay respects to deities in famous temples. The light tube was attached to a battery fitted to his belt, and he lit himself up when he got to temples. The medium next to him is trancing a deity called Jigong, a Twelfth century Buddhist monk who, when tranced through mediums, usually arrives drunk. Photograph by Fabian Graham.

CONTENTS

A performer in a troupe accompanying a deity statue on a tour of the borders of their territory during a procession in Taiwan. Photograph by Fabian Graham.

Talking With the Spirits: Ethnographies from Between the Worlds

David Luke & Jack Hunter

The usual advantage of an anthology of collected essays over an authored text is the diversity of opinion, perspective and scholarship that can be garnered, and this book is no exception. However, not only is this a collection of *Ethnographies from Between the Worlds*, in the ontological and spiritual sense, it is also a collection of ethnographies from between the worlds of ordinary social activity, as mediumship is a pursuit that locates itself at the awkward to get to crevices and junctions of life and society, offering a service somewhere between spiritual guidance, bereavement counselling, paranormal insight, life coaching, fortune telling, healing activity, religious practice and performance spectacle. It is often hidden away in private shows, shrines and even garden sheds, and yet is ancient and ubiquitous across cultures. That ubiquity is also apparent here in this tome, given the range of ethnographies from across the worlds as well as between them, with most continents represented by our adventurous and earnest ethnographers, and indeed many countries too, whether Kenya, Brazil, Cuba, Taiwan, Singapore, Hong Kong, Canada, the US or the UK. There is even ethnography from that most transnational of locations, cyberspace.

Such a range of nationalities provides a rich cross-cultural perspective across the chapters, and even within some chapters (Emmons, Graham), allowing for discernment to emerge on what might be universal or near-universal features of mediumship, such as, for example, the role of a control spirit and the use of an altered state of consciousness, respectively. There is a wide range of culturally mediated differences too, with mediumship appearing in many guises from the quotidian online readings of cyber psychics (Ryan) to the quixotic and exotic displays of self-mortification in the Chinese mediumistic theatres of pain (Graham). But it's all too easy to assume that such cultural differences betray geographical trends, with Europe typically being the preserve of the lightest of trances and the least elaborate performances, Africa and the Americas tending towards the deeper dynamic bodily incorporation of spirits, and Asia as the bastion of self-mortification and high theatricality. Yet, in recent years, the rise of enormous cults like Maria Lionza in Venezuela that practice self-mortification trance mediumship (Ferrándiz, 1996), and the recent return of physical mediumship across Europe (Hunter, Bowie) makes such observations as shaky as the digits of the Navaho hand trembler. Nevertheless, some parallels are perceptible – Cuban spirits relish cigars and alcohol as fuel (Espirito Santo), as much as Chinese spirits feed on the pain and self-mortification of Taiwanese warrior mediums (Graham).

The twelve separate essays in this book also present a range of different subject backgrounds and approaches, including transcultural psychiatry, psychology, parapsychology, religious studies, sociology and, of course, anthropology. Yet despite these different backgrounds all these approaches share a common subject matter – mediumship – and a common methodology. The method that binds all these narratives, true to the title of the book, is ethnography, primarily interviews and participant observation – such fieldwork being the main tool of the essays in this collection – and on occasion (Emmons) these methods have been augmented by the use of surveys too. Additionally, all have textual support from the literature, to varying degrees, and for at least one (Gilbert) biographical texts *are* the data. The advantage of such multi/mixed methods (Emmons) is not just in the richness of the data and the triangulation of the observations, but in the depth of understanding and insight that comes from a long stew within a specific domain, exemplified in the longitudinal, cross-cultural, emically-etically balanced, career-long perspective of a researcher like Charles Emmons. Indeed, Emmons' deep ethnographic approach to participant observation even goes beyond participating as a consumer of mediumship, a client, and extends as far as actually training and practicing as a medium himself (Emmons, 2001), a move which, thankfully, is being somewhat emulated by more novice researchers in the field, such as Spiritualist medium researcher Elizabeth Roxburgh (2010). True to the spirit of Gielser's (1984) call for a multi-method approach in the anthropological study of ostensibly paranormal phenomena, one chapter in this book is also dedicated to the empirical (i.e., parapsychological) research of mediumship conducted in Brazil (Maraldi *et al.*).

Ultimately, despite the various fields and research domains that the researchers come from, the commonality of method and subject matter here corrals the disparate approaches into the intellectual intersection now emerging under the banner of *paranthropology*. Stemming from the 1970s' revolution in the field of anthropology, a consequence of the rift that emerged between those researchers sympathetic to apparent parapsychological phenomena and those against (see Long, 1977; Angoff & Barth, 1974), the *anthropology of consciousness* was born, but ultimately moved away from parapsychology (Schroll & Schwartz, 2005) and is now being reinvigorated with the growth of the paranormal-focused paranthropology (Hunter, 2009, 2012; Luke, 2010). The term paranthropology itself was originally proposed by Roger Wescott (1977) in the first wave of interest in this emerging sub-discipline, but was immediately superseded by *transpersonal anthropology* (see Laughlin, 2012) and then the anthropology of consciousness (Luke, 2010). The term has since been renewed by Jack Hunter (2010) who, in 2010, began publishing the ongoing periodical *Paranthropology: Journal of Anthropological Approaches to the Paranormal*. Ethnographies of the ostensibly paranormal, including accounts of spirit mediumship, are at the core of Hunter's vision of this re-emerging and re-invigorated sub-discipline (Hunter, 2011) and so this book truly embodies the spirit of paranthropology, as much as the spirits are embodied by the mediums under the microscope within.

The essence of paranthropology is also echoed in the phenomenological approach to mediumship in the various chapters of this book, which often tend to duck the thorny issues of belief and skepticsm and the various ontological obstacles that can hinder access to core experience. In Hunter's chapter, for example, we find that the research 'seeks to take the first-hand experiences of fieldwork informants seriously, at face-value,' and that 'the experience itself has validity and that such beliefs are not to be lightly brushed aside as necessarily irrational or unfounded.' And we observe that Hunter's (2009) entreaty to treat the subject matter 'as if' it is real has been borne out elsewhere too, or at the very least the opinions and views of the informants and host cultures have been respected and collected with care, like precious cargo not just superstitious folly.

For instance, in her chapter Hannah Gilbert promotes an agnostic sociological position, somewhat passively sidestepping the need to find validation for the alleged paranormality of mediumship, whereas Fiona Bowie takes a more active approach to striking a balance by finding the razor's edge pivot between a clear critical perspective and the open-minded cultural insider view. A calling to be simultaneously both *acad-emic* and *acad-etic* perhaps. At the same time, to redress a somewhat imbalanced view historically, Bowie warns us of the beliefs that masquerade as critical scientific perspectives but which are rather more pseudo-sceptical than genuinely sceptical. A warning, as Sheldrake (2010) reminds us, to beware falling foul of science delusions and instead to free the spirit of enquiry.

And yet, while for most contributors to this volume the issue of evidence for the paranormal is generally superseded by honestly mapping the phenomenological terrain of mediumship in these disparate cultures, stashes of astonishing events and observations can be found stowed here and there, or sometimes even stockpiled (Emmons, Graham, Maraldi *et al.*). Indeed, it is worth noting that in addition to the huge amounts of ethnographic literature on the varied practice and experience of spirit mediumship there is also a wealth of experimental data, going back over a century, which appears to suggest that, with certain mediums at least, there may be some form of information and energy transfer taking place that cannot be accounted for by normal means (see Gauld, 1982; Braude, 1997, 2003; Beischel & Schwartz, 2007; Beischel, 2008 for useful overviews of some of this literature). Whether this data provides evidence for the survival of consciousness after death or for some form of psi phenomenon, however, is an ongoing debate in parapsychology (Braude, 1992; Rock, Beischel & Cott, 2009). The gathering of supportive evidence for the paranormal is also a feature of the many narratives of mediums, and may be expressed in the form of mental mediums' delivery of accurate information, physical manifestations – as with the Felix Group (Bowie) and Bristol Spirit Lodge (Hunter) – or demonstrations of extraordinary physiological feats (Graham).

Such a range of apparently paranormal manifestations speaks to the variety of mediumships being researched, with everything from cyber psychics (Ryan), through European platform mental mediums (Gilbert) and private physical mediums (Bowie, Hunter), traditional African healers (Stöckigt), Latin American Spiritists (Espirito Santo, Schmidt, Maraldi *et al.*) and North American Spiritualists (Emmons, Meintel), to psychedelic possession practitioners (Luke) and Chinese warrior mediums (Graham). It is also apparent that this broad range of mediums also express a spectrum of different states of consciousness too, such that the differing styles are dependent upon differing degrees of depth of what might be called *trance*, notwithstanding idiosyncratic differences between individual mediums within a particular tradition. Such trance states may be light, or even absent in the case of mental mediumship, or deep in the case of those engaging in more dynamic and physical behaviour. This apparent continuum includes features such as awareness of surroundings, anaesthesia, amnesia, a change in mannerisms, voice, and personality, and even seizure (Graham, Espirito Santo). This latter experience of seizure is also taken as a sign of mediumistic potential among pre-trained mediums and has echoes in the initiatory stages of shamanism, which is also often characterised by the journey of the wounded healer – a self-initiation through the conquest of illness (Eliade, 1972). Indeed, the parallels and overlaps with mediumship and shamanism are intimately threaded throughout the chapters in this collection.

As a final note of observation it is clear that as much as these different mediumships utilise different depths of trance, so too is there a multiplicity of terms used to describe this phenomenon, sometimes tending to distort rather than define the processes at hand. For instance, while all the chapters refer to mediumship as a voluntary process, many opt to use the term possession (for example, Bowie, Emmons, Graham, Stöckigt), connotative of involuntary spirit embodiment, be that spirit possession or possession trance, in distinction to the term preferred by many practitioners, especially those in Latin Amercica, *incorporation* (see Espirito Santo, Meintel, Schmidt), connotative of a voluntary spirit embodiment (Luke). Others, still, use no such term at all (Gilbert) or merely refer to trance (Ryan), whereas others simultaneously use multiple terms (Espirito Santo, Hunter, Luke, Schmidt), often in an attempt to tease the different uses apart.

The perplexing diversity of the use of such terms is nowhere better illustrated than in the chapter by Schmidt, which demonstrates how demonic possession is assigned by Brazilian evangelists to what is termed incorporation by Afro-Brazilian practitioners, and yet the evangelists themselves are engaging in what might be called spirit possession or mediumship by an outside observer. The situation is far from simple and the complex and sometimes contradictory use of terminology represents both conflicts between mediumistic groups and cultural constructions surrounding the continuum of experiences coalescing about spirit embodiment, for want of a better term. Hopefully anthologies such as the one here will help illuminate and alleviate the issues involving terminology and the connotations arising out of it. It is hoped too that this volume offers the reader a unique and diverse séance-side seat at the ongoing parley between mediums and spirits.

References

Angoff, A. & Barth, D. (1974). *Proceedings of an international conference: Parapsychology and anthropology.* New York: Parapsychology Foundation.

Beischel, J. & Schwartz, G. (2007). Anomalous information reception by research mediums demonstrated using a novel triple-blind protocol. *Explore: The Journal of Science and Healing, 3,* 23-27.

Beischel, J. (2008). Contemporary methods used in laboratory-based mediumship research. *Journal of Parapsychology, 71,* 37-68.

Braude, S.E. (1992). Survival or super-psi? *Journal of Scientific Exploration, 6* (2), 127-144.

Braude, S.E. (1997). *The limits of influence: Psychokinesis and the philosophy of science.* New York: University Press of America.

Braude, S. (2003). *Immortal remains: The evidence for life after death.* Oxford: Rowman & Littlefield.

Eliade, M. (1972). *Shamanism: Archaic techniques of ecstasy.* Princeton, NJ: Princeton University Press. (Originally published in French in 1951).

Emmons, C. (2001). On becoming a spirit medium in a "rational society." *Anthropology of Consciousness, 12* (1), 71-82.

Ferrándiz, F. J. (1996). *The body and its senses: The spirit possession cult of Maria Lionza in contemporary Venezuela.* Berkeley, CA: University of California.

Gauld, A. (1982). *Mediumship and survival: A century of investigations.* London: Granada Publishing Ltd.

Giesler, P. (1984). Parapsychological anthropology: I. Multi-method approaches to the study of *psi* in the field setting. *Journal of the American Society for Psychical Research, 78* (4), 289-330.

Hunter, J. (2009). Anthropology and the paranormal: Approaches to the investigation of paranormal beliefs and practices. *Anomaly: Journal of Research into the Paranormal, 46,* 24-36.

Hunter, J. (2010). Anthropology and the paranormal: What's the point? *Paranthropology: Journal of Anthropological Approaches to the Paranormal, 1* (1), 2-3.

Hunter, J. (2011). Reflecting on paranthropology. *Paranthropology: Journal of Anthropological Approaches to the Paranormal, 2* (3), 14-17.

Hunter, J. (2012) Anthropology and the paranormal. In J. Hunter (Ed.), *Paranthropology: Anthropological approaches to the paranormal* (pp. 20-42). Bristol: Paranthropology.

Laughlin, C.D. (2012). Transpersonal anthropology: What is it, and what are the problems we face in doing it? In J. Hunter (Ed.) *Paranthropology: Anthropological Approaches to the Paranormal* (pp. 69-98). Bristol: Paranthropology

Long, J.K. (1977). *Extrasensory ecology: Parapsychology and anthropology.* Metuchen, NJ. Scarecrow Press.

Luke, D. (2010). Anthropology and parapsychology: Still hostile sisters in science? *Time & Mind: The Journal of Archaeology, Consciousness and Culture, 3* (3), 245-266.

Rock, A. J., Beischel, J., & Cott, C. C. (2009). Psi vs. survival: A qualitative investigation of mediums' phenomenology comparing psychic readings and ostensible communication with the deceased. *Transpersonal Psychology Review, 13,* 76-89.

Roxburgh, E. C. (2010). *The psychology and phenomenology of spiritualist mental mediumship.* Unpublished doctoral thesis, The University of Northampton, UK.

Schroll, M.A. & Schwartz, S.A. (2005). Whither psi and anthropology? An incomplete history of SAC's origins, its relationship with transpersonal psychology and the untold stories of Castaneda's controversy. *Anthropology of Consciousness, 16* (1), 6-24.

Sheldrake, R. (2012) *The science delusion: Freeing the spirit of enquiry.* London: Coronet.

Wescott, R. W. (1977). Paranthropology: A nativity celebration and a communion commentary. In J. K. Long (Ed.), *Extrasensory ecology: Parapsychology and anthropology* (pp. 331-347). Metuchen, NJ: Scarecrow Press.

Physical medium Kai Muegge with ectoplasm during a séance in Cassadaga, NY USA.
Photograph by Shannon Taggart.

BELIEVING IMPOSSIBLE THINGS: SCEPTICISM AND ETHNOGRAPHIC ENQUIRY

FIONA BOWIE

Alice laughed: 'There's no use trying,' she said;
'one can't believe impossible things.'
'I daresay you haven't had much practice,' said the
Queen. 'When I was younger, I always did it for half
an hour a day. Why, sometimes I've believed as many
as six impossible things before breakfast.'

Alice in Wonderland

Whether we identify with Alice or the White Queen may well rest on the semantics of the word 'impossible.' If something is impossible it is by definition illogical to believe in it, but one person's impossible may not be the same as another's.[1] Views of how the world works and how it is expected to behave vary across cultures and over time, as well as during the life course of an individual. We are shaped by our culture, including language, religion and ideology, our intellectual environment, family and friends, and by our own direct experience and reflection upon it. Western academic culture is a child of the Enlightenment, and although it contains within it many approaches, disciplines and points of view, there is a

strongly hegemonic belief in a form of reductionist materialism
(Hanegraaf, 2012) with well policed borders designed to keep
at bay 'magical' and illogical forms of thought. I use the term
'belief' advisedly as this is an ideological and not a rational or
scientific position (Sheldrake, 2012). In anthropological studies
this ideology is manifested in the urge to explain away or provide
a rational account of the supposedly irrational beliefs of others,
whether through a sociological, psychological or biological
reductionism. Taking an emic or insider view of what one studies
is permitted as reportage, but the ethnographer is expected to
make clear his or her intellectual distance from the illogical,
improbable and fanciful beliefs and explanations of others. The
taunt that the researcher is 'going native' is to question his or her
intellectual and scientific credibility (with concomitant damage
to their career prospects).[2]

But do we really need to choose between a rather rigid
form of Western scientific materialism and the relativistic free-
for-all that comprise the beliefs and practices of most of the
world's populations? Can we combine the virtues of Western
Enlightenment thinking with its disciplined examination
of evidence and rejection of superstition and credulity, with
a more expansive and all-embracing world-view that allows
for seemingly 'impossible things'? Can we find an approach
that retains academic rigour while also admitting that not all
reality is immediately apprehensible and visible? There seems to
be plenty of actual evidence that the world does not work on
strictly Newtonian principles, and we might therefore admit the
possibility that alternative explanations might have some validity.[3]

Aaron Joshua Howard (2013, p.2) is not alone in critiquing
the distancing project of much anthropology as a form of
signification that 'hearkens back to the oppression and hegemony
that legitimated the expansion of Western imperialist rule' while
reinstating 'the primitive versus civilized dualism upon which
this reign depended.' Howard calls for an anthropological study

of religion that allows for the possibility of supernatural realities, 'an allowance for a transcendence that cannot be solely attributed to humanistic origins' (ibid. p.1). Methodologically this involves an open dialogue with one's research subject and subjects (Bowie, 2013), and the refusal to close down any particular line of enquiry prematurely, or to predetermine the nature of experience. It allows for the possibility that others know and understand the world in ways that may seem unlikely, but which may nevertheless be legitimate, or contain seeds of a reality beyond the norms of our everyday experience. A Western positivist education, with its critical scepticism, can serve us well in examining evidence rather than ignoring or excluding uncomfortable data. It can allow the same generosity to people who talk of dialogues with the dead or possession by spirits as to physicists who talk of particle entanglement and unimaginable distances between galaxies, of fields of conscious energy and universal information systems. Attempts to unify the data of religion, parapsychology and physics may not convince everyone, but all these disciplines are evolving, and often seem to be forging a common, or at least mutually hospitable, language.[4] One reason given for ignoring supposedly anomalous data is that we do not have an explanation for a phenomenon (however unevenly and selectively this dictum is applied in science and medicine). The quality and quantity of research in fields such as biology, parapsychology and physics, among others, however, does appear to be steadily narrowing the gap between conventional science, the findings of parapsychology and religious belief.[5]

Anthropologists have often reported, or even more often experienced but not reported, so-called anomalous events that are consistent with the world-view of the people they study, but at odds with a Western positivist framework. Edith Turner's sighting of a visible spirit form leaving a sick woman after a healing ceremony in Zambia is well known (Turner, 1992), as is Paul Stoller's life-threatening encounter with sorcery in Niger

(Stoller and Olkes, 1987). These personal experiences may be transformative, undermining a view of the world in which such things simply don't happen. More often they seem to be relegated to a separate category of 'things without obvious explanation that happen in the field,' which are not permitted to impinge unduly on the ethnographer – as with Evans-Pritchard's strange tale from the 1920s of seeing an unexplained light, interpreted by the Azande in the Southern Sudan as witchcraft, travelling to the hut of a man who was found dead the following morning (1976). Evans-Pritchard rationalized that it could have been a man carrying a torch, but does not appear very convinced by this explanation. When such experiences happen in far-away places, and can at least be understood within a coherent cosmology of a non-Western 'other' they are not too threatening, and might even be expected. When African, Native American or other non-Western anthropologists write of spirits, powers and forces that intrude into their lives and shape reality, this too is tolerated within academia. They have, after all, been shaped by such cultural beliefs and practices, even if 'benefiting from' a Western education.[6] What happens, however, when anomalous events are reported from within Western societies? The only acceptable academic approach seems to be to explain them away or more or less subtly dismiss them and ridicule those who 'believe in' such impossible things. Simon Coleman found that even researching something as mainstream as Christian Evangelicals in Sweden was enough to rouse suspicions in Cambridge anthropological circles that he might somehow become one of them (and by implication lose academic credibility), a reaction that he would almost certainly not have had if he had studied Christianity in Africa or Asia (Bowie, 2003).[7]

This raises methodological questions concerning the nature of evidence, the role of experience and the persistence of scepticism and denial among scholars when faced with a challenge to their worldview. In this chapter I review some of the possible reasons for dismissing uncomfortable and 'impossible' data. The context is a discussion of physical mediumship in a contemporary Western setting. In many ways physical mediumship – the production of physical phenomena, from moving objects within a room, producing noises and voices, spirit lights, apports (objects that appear or disappear from the séance room), to full physical materializations, usually through the use of ectoplasm, should be one of the most straightforward 'impossible things' to verify, or to expose as fraudulent. Physical mediumship is repeatable in strictly controlled settings, and many of the best physical mediums working today are, like their Nineteenth and Twentieth Century predecessors, willing to undergo repeated and uncomfortable procedures, such as routinely being searched, bound and gagged before going into trance, in order to deflect accusations of fraud and trickery.[8]

Grounds for Belief in 'Impossible Things': Evidence from Physical Mediumship

The claim that 'extraordinary claims require extraordinary proof' has variously been attributed to Marcello Truzzi, Carl Sagan and even David Hume. The idea that proceeding by assertion is insufficient and that the burden of proof rests with those who challenge a dominant paradigm is not in itself particularly controversial, although it is worth pointing out that most currently accepted scientific understandings of the world were at one time rejected by the establishment as improbable and lacking evidence (Friedlander, 1995; Silvers, 2003). What qualifies as an extraordinary claim is also relative, based on ideology as much as observation, changing radically over time. Having said that, for many Westerners in the Twenty First Century claims concerning an extra-physical or 'paranormal' realm qualify as extraordinary. What counts as proof, however, is contested and it becomes evident that for some 'professional' sceptics evidence is not really the issue as the boundaries of what is accepted and what is rejected have been established *a priori*. The admission of evidence becomes irrelevant.

Anthropological investigation is not immune from this approach, but as a discipline that methodologically seeks to understand the 'native's point of view' it is at least in theory open to new information that adds to our understanding of the world and of what it means to be a human being within it. The phenomenological method in religious studies, the interpretive turn in anthropology, and postmodernist approaches in general, are shy of making ontological claims. To entirely bracket out questions of 'truth' or 'reality' can, however, appear as a form of ethnocentrism rather than liberal open-mindedness. Behind the refusal to engage with another's reality often lies a confident assertion in the implicit rightness of one's own (usually Western positivist) interpretation of the world. I have argued elsewhere (Bowie, 2013) that we need to seek a balance between a critical appreciation of the data before us, using whatever analytical tools may be at our disposal, and an ability to suspend judgment and try to experience the world through the hermeneutical lens of those we seek to understand. The outcome will always be a provisional, positioned and, one hopes, dialogical understanding of the phenomenon and people we are studying.

Physical mediumship

Physical mediumship challenges many of the taboos of Western society. It offends religious traditions that are nervous of the occult, and falls foul of Biblical prescriptions of the avoidance of mediums, witches and psychics (Leviticus 19:31, 20:27; I Chronicles 10:13-14). Mediums are generally motivated by ethical concerns, primarily in helping to alleviate the distress of bereavement by helping people contact their loved ones who have died. Removing the fear of death by 'proving' the continued existence of the soul or of the individual personality is another often quoted reason for engaging in mediumship. Curiosity about life's great questions, and more prosaically a desire to expand our understanding of the boundary between Newtonian laws of matter and psychic realities also play a part in physical mediumship. In some cases there is a pedagogical element, as in the conversations described by Di Nucci and Hunter (2009) between a spirit known as Charlie and sitters at the Bristol Spirit Lodge, or between the spirit of William Cadwell, materialized by physical medium David Thompson, and sitters at Thompson's séances.

Those who practice physical mediumship and those who attend physical mediumship séances do not necessarily see themselves as performing a religious act, and there is not the same association between physical mediumship and formal religion that we see in Christian Spiritualist churches, where the predominant mode of engaging with spirits is through mental or clairvoyant mediums (Skultans, 1974; Wilson, 2013). The Society for Psychical Research (SPR), with its headquarters in London, UK, has since its inception in 1882 sought 'to examine without prejudice or prepossession and in a scientific spirit those faculties of man, real or supposed, which appear to be inexplicable on any generally recognised hypothesis.' This has often included detailed studies of physical and mental mediums, with the results published in their *Proceedings* and *Journal*, both of which reproduce this statement of intent. As the members of the SPR include a roll call of distinguished mathematicians, physicists, medics and statesmen, their scientific investigations and subsequent reports are also intended to be within the scientific arena. This has been a red flag to those who, for various reasons, wish to contest the notion that the claims of physical mediumship have any basis in reality. I will briefly discuss the nature of physical mediumship and its claims, and then look at some of the cultural and psychological reasons that might account for the rejection of these claims and the evidence on which they are based, by those who describe themselves, and are sometimes pejoratively described by others, as sceptics.

Physical mediumship is a broad term used to designate the production of physical phenomena by a medium, usually entranced, with the help of the energy of a group of 'sitters' and a spirit team. A key feature of physical mediumship that distinguishes it from mental mediumship - in which the medium is generally the only person who sees, hears or receives impressions from the spirit world, is that the phenomena produced are objective:

> that is to say, they are to all intents and purposes based on reality – everybody present is able to see, hear and feel such manifestations as they occur, and the phenomena themselves can be recorded on audio tape or photographed under favourable conditions for posterity, thus proving that the experience is not the result of over-active imagination (Foy, 2007:vii).

Robin Foy, quoted above, was one of the four core members of the Scole Experimental Group, who conducted a five year study into the possibility of communication with discarnate intelligences at the Foy's home in Scole, Norfolk, in the early 1990s. Over 99 different types of physical phenomena were recorded, with different mediums. These included some of the more traditional features of the séance room such as the production of moving lights in a darkened room, independent movement of an aluminium 'trumpet,' a variety of sounds, water being splashed on sitters, sudden and dramatic changes in temperature, voices with distinct personalities who could hold an intelligent conversation, the production and disappearance of objects such as coins and crystals (apports), the formation of apparently solid objects, such as flowers, which would then disappear again, ectoplasmic limbs, the impression of pictures on blank film and electronic voice communications. The complexity of the phenomena produced built up gradually over time as the spirit team and sitters worked together to improve communication, and find new technologies to aid it (Solomon 1999).

Advanced forms of mediumship

Some mediums can produce physical phenomena, such as apports, without going into a trance (such as the Brazilian medium Amyr Amiden), and trance is often a feature of mental mediumship. Lady Cynthia Sandys, for example, would go into a light trance when writing 'letters' from her spirit communicators. Some of the most dramatic forms of mediumship occur when a physical medium, almost invariably in a deep trance, is able to produce a substance known as ectoplasm. Ectoplasm is said to be made up of physical substances from the medium's body, which can be manipulated energetically by experienced spirits. Initially a trance medium may display transformations, visible in red light, during which an ectoplasmic energy layer over the medium's face is manipulated by the spirits to change the appearance of the face. The spirits may speak though the medium's vocal cords, changing the tone and character of the voice. A further stage of development involves the production of an ectoplasmic 'voice box,' enabling the spirits to speak from anywhere in the séance room. A further development includes the use of much larger quantities of ectoplasm to fashion limbs or complete bodies, which can appear solid and interact with sitters, before dissolving back into the medium's body. The production of full manifestations is relatively rare (and risky for the medium), requiring many years of training and patience by the medium and a regular group of sitters.[9] During séances with trance mediums a range of other physical phenomena are also said to take place.

Unbelievable as mediumship and the goings-on of the séance room may sound, both mental and physical mediums have been studied and subject to tests for fraud for over a century.

The Masssachusetts housewife and trance medium, Leonora Piper (1859-1950) was studied intensively for twenty-five years (Tymn, 2008; 2013). While in trance Mrs Piper was taken over by a number of 'controls,' in particular a spirit who described himself as a French doctor called Phinuit. The control acts as a partner to the medium, and has to enter an equivalent 'trance' state from the 'other side' in order to speak through the medium. When not possessing the medium directly, the control acts as a gatekeeper for other spirits who are permitted to enter and use the medium's body. Mrs Piper by all accounts had her off-days, but was also capable of offering substantial evidential information to sitters that could not be explained by cold-reading (guesswork), telepathy, prior research or general knowledge (Tymn, 2013). The doctor, psychologist and philosopher of religion, who also founded the American Society for Psychical Research, William James (1842-1910), called Leonora Piper his 'white crow,' that is the exception that disproves the general rule.

Physical trance mediums who produce ectoplasm that can be used by spirits to create solid bodies, or partial bodies, have routinely been strip searched, sometimes sewn into special clothes, bound and gagged before and during the séance. The séance room is routinely searched and independent observers asked to check it for hidden devices. In other words, the possibility that the phenomena of the séance room are the product of a magician's conjuring trick is generally eliminated. While no doubt extremely uncomfortable for the medium, such precautions are accepted both to rule out fraud for the medium's own protection, and to convince sitters of the reality of the communications from the other side.[10]

The Felix Experimental Group

There appear to be developments in physical mediumship as the technology and experience of both investigators and mediums on the one hand and spirit teams and discarnate communicators on the other, increase over time. The Scole Experimental Group had access to photographic and recording technology, for instance, that was not available to earlier researchers. The Felix Experimental Group (FEG) founded by trance medium Kai Muegge in 2004 in Frankfurt, Germany, has had remarkable success in not only enabling spirit forms to manifest using ectoplasm from the medium's body, but photographing the process in red light conditions (http://felixcircle.blogspot. co.uk). Academic researcher, Professor Stephen Braude (recently retired head of philosophy at the University of Maryland),[11] has been investigating the FEG since 2010. According to a report on the Felix Circle website (above, accessed 2.10.2013), Braude and a team of four other investigators and a filmmaker, arranged a final controlled investigation of the FEG over the period of a week in an Austrian farmhouse in May 2013. The measures put in place to eliminate the possibility of fraud were similar to those I witnessed at a séance with trance medium David Thompson at Jenny's Sanctuary in England in August 2011.[12] The FEG account of the experiment[13] outlines the safety protocols followed, which included:

1. A location that had not been disclosed to the medium in advance and no additional sitters.
2. Full control by the scientists of a permanently locked séance room, and scrutiny of all preparations by the medium or his wife in the séance room.
3. Repeated checks and searches of the room, all objects brought into the room and people who entered the room. These included a full strip search of the medium, Kai M. and his wife Julia by Braude and a physician. The medium and his wife were kept separate before and after the strip search.
4. The medium was guided to the séance room by two controllers, one in front and one behind, while holding his hands in the air.

5. During the séance when full table levitation occurred the researchers kept full contact with the hands, knees and feet of both the medium and his wife.

6. When an oral apport was announced by the medium his mouth was checked with white light torch and bright red light, while his hands and feet were held.

7. When the medium announced the imminent appearance of an apport in midair above the table, his hands were held and checked repeatedly in red light.

8. The medium's body was checked by a physician during the production of ectoplasm.

Despite these controls, which because of the additional stress they caused the medium might be expected to reduce the likelihood of success, several paranormal events were observed and filmed in red light. These included apports into the séance room – a crystal the size of a finger and a large piece of copper, full table levitation, considerable amounts of ectoplasm from the medium's mouth that morphed into different forms, including rudimentary limbs, heads and faces, and which wrapped itself around the medium like a cocoon. As Braude (2007, p.12) has pointed out, it is one thing for magicians or others to claim that such phenomena are possible through magical performance, it is quite another to demonstrate that this is so under similarly carefully controlled conditions. To date this has never, to my knowledge, been attempted.

Fraudulent mediumship

All mediums I have heard or spoken to, whether mental or physical mediums, warn against the possibility of fraudulent mediumship, so one can only conclude that whether through innocent self-deception or intentional deceit, fraudulent practices can and do occur where the checks, such as those described above, are not in place. While it is hardly credible that a medium will sit for years with a small group of people to develop his or her mediumship – generally at great personal and financial cost, rather than for any obvious gain – with the intention of fooling the gullible, there does appear to be a temptation to cheat on occasion. The pressure on the medium may be greatest when expectations have been raised as a result of previous successes, and the medium does not want to disappoint the sitters or admit to waning powers. There may also be more complex issues, and perhaps we sometimes ask the wrong questions in our search for 'the truth.' As Edith Turner (1992) observed in relation to the removal of objects from patients in spirit healing, there are often two elements, the psychic and the material, that are not separated in the minds of peoples for whom the psychic level is a reality. When the shaman or healer sucks a harmful spirit, energy or object out a patient, and 'captures' it within a bone, sticks, leaves or some other substance, the material becomes the 'home' for the psychic energy. Edith Turner observed this with the Ndembu healer, Singleton, during the *ihamba*, when a hunter's tooth was removed from a female patient, and was then put in a pot and fed on red meat to prevent it from troubling her again. Turner saw something leaving the patient with her own eyes, and could only attest that her experience of the healing ritual did not align with an account based on assumption of trickery, even if the relationship between the gray blob that Turner observed and the tooth is not straightforward or clear.[14]

Jeffrey Kripal, discussing the physical trance medium Eusapia Palladino (1854-1918), who was known to 'cheat' on occasions, also points to the sometimes blurred lines between fact and fiction, stating that:

> it is almost as if the real needs the fake to appear at all, *as if the fact relies on the fiction to manifest itself, only to immediately hide itself again in the confusion of the fantastic hesitation that follows.* Put a bit differently, it is not as if the appearance of the sacred can be reduced to a simple trick, as if the shaman

is just a sham. It is as if the sacred is *itself* tricky. Even the well-documented medical placebo, after all, is a fake that has real effects [italics in the original] (2010, p. 52).

Kripal is reminded of a conversation with the physicist and psychical researcher Russell Targ, who as a young stage magician became aware that whilst performing a mentalist trick on stage, he began receiving genuine telepathic messages. 'The trick was a trick, but it was also, somehow, catalyzing the real deal' (ibid.). It might be simpler if there were always a clear dividing line between what is real and what is not, between fraud and trickery on the one hand and truth and honesty on the other. We do know, however, that there is a close connection between the physical, psychological and spiritual - if you smile when unhappy your body will produce the hormones that improve your mood, for instance (Wenner, 2009), so it is not too surprising that these boundaries can be blurred in the case of mediumship as well.[15]

Is There a Place for Scepticism in Ethnographic Enquiry?

When I undertook a study of Christian missions in Cameroon for my doctoral research the first question I was invariably asked upon my return from the field was, 'Well then, are they good or bad?' We are so used to polarised positions, or to avoidance of the question altogether. Instead of one black and white question one might ask, 'What does "good" mean in this context?' 'Good for whom'? 'What are the positive and negative effects of mission on different individuals and groups, both historically and today'? While these questions might yield more promising and nuanced answers, they were still the wrong questions from my perspective. I wanted to study relationships and dynamics, the intersection of belief, experience and practice. I sought to document the historical events and context in which missionaries were invited to work in rural Africa, and how different actors perceived their joint history. I have to admit, however, that I did start with the naïve assumption that the Bangwa and Mundani peoples would have a view on whether the missions were 'good' or 'bad.' After all I had been educated with the same dualistic mindset as my interlocutors back home. The question made no sense to my informants, not because they also wanted to discuss the sociological and ethnographic dimensions of their relationship with the missions, but because the answer was so obvious that it rendered the question meaningless. The universal response to such a question, accompanied by a look of bewilderment, was 'We have suffered,' followed by descriptions of long, often fruitless treks over mountainous forest tracks to the nearest health clinic, carrying the sick and dying, or while heavily pregnant. They talked of the lack of educational opportunities, of the absence of infrastructure and a cash economy, of feeling abandoned by the state and of a crushingly high infant mortality rate that threatened their development and survival as a people. Yes, life was better with the mission. It was on this foundation, and on their own terms, that the Bangwa built their future (Bowie, 2009).

There is a parallel with sceptical enquiry in ethnographic studies of the paranormal. We are culturally primed to ask, or at least think in terms of, true/false questions and then when, as good liberally-minded phenomenologists, we find them too difficult or threatening, to avoid them altogether. The tradition in the anthropology of religion is to ask not, 'Is it real?' 'Is it true?' but 'Who are these people and why do they think or imagine that this or that is true or real?' We resist passing judgment, often on the explicit or implicit assumption that the beliefs and interpretations of others are self-evidently ridiculous. We may remain unaware of the patronising neo-colonial message such an approach signals for our informants. It does matter to trance mediums and their sitters whether the phenomena they produce are the result of genuine mediumship or trickery. The stakes are high. Either there is an afterlife, and in certain circumstances those who have crossed over can continue to communicate with and influence the physical world, or there is not. If there is an afterlife do we have evidence for it, or does it remain in the field of pure speculation, imagination and faith?

Proving the continued existence of individual consciousness is generally an important stated aim of mediumship. People who have experienced evidential communication from someone who has died, or who have had a near death or out of body experience, usually claim to lose their fear of death. One of the patients studied by Peter and Elizabeth Fenwick typically reported that her near death experience,

> left a very positive view and comforting understanding of the whole process of death and dying, particularly the moment of death. I know now that there is nothing to fear, it is such a peaceful and graceful moment, and it has proved to me, beyond a doubt, that the spirit or soul does exist, outside of the body: I saw it! (Fenwick, 2008, p. 242).

Ethnographers walk a narrow line between empathising with and trying to see the world through the interpretive lens of another's culture, and keeping their critical faculties sharpened. The anthropological task of cultural translation involves being able to step back from a particular view of the world and set it alongside their own and that of others, particularly the academic other. Finding the balance between emic and etic views, and moving between them is what ethnography and anthropological interpretation is all about. What is sometimes lost in the process is an acknowledgement (despite the generally positive push in this direction of nearly half a century of feminist writing), of the culturally determined 'baggage' and strictly policed boundaries of academic discourse. Coming to judgment, honestly and self-consciously aware of one's own standpoint and perspective, is a crucial part of ethnographic engagement. Some people have a more naturally open accepting disposition, others a more critical and sceptical one, but in either case a sincere effort to chronicle what one sees, hears, experiences and thinks is a pre-requisite to the production of good ethnography. In answer to the question posed at the beginning of this section, 'Is there a place for scepticism in ethnographic enquiry?' we must answer affirmatively. But there is a caveat, it should be a scepticism that is open to the data, flexible enough to change its mind, and courageous enough to document honestly even seemingly impossible events.

This may all sound obvious, but as Jeffrey Kripal wrote in his summary of Dean Radin's first two books, *The Conscious Universe* (1997) and *Entangled Minds* (2006), there are three sociological facts when it comes to the relationship between science and parapsychology, namely:

(1) there is massive ethnographic, historical, cross-cultural, and now, scientific evidence that puts the existence of psi phenomena well beyond any reasonable doubt; (2) this data has been collected, analysed, meta-analysed and theorized, not by naïve enthusiasts, but by experimental psychologists, university-trained humanists, Nobel Prize-winning physicists, highly classified government military programmes, and elite corporate think tanks (some of which are already quietly proceeding to pursue new psi-based communications technology); and finally (3) despite all of this, parapsychology remains the favourite target of ideologically driven sceptics who insist on reverting to a predictable series of gross stereotypes and shaming techniques, mostly professional ridicule, to keep intellectuals interested in these matters sufficiently silent (Kripal, 2012, pp. xxxii-xxxiii).

These tactics are, as Kripal notes, effective, helped by a largely hostile media and the gate-keeping role of an extreme form of scepticism acting as gate-keeper to academic employment, advancement and publishing. In the final section of this chapter I therefore look in more detail at the nature of scepticism and its influence.

The Psychology of Scepticism

One of the great triumphs of the Enlightenment is arguably the expansion of knowledge made possible by the replacement of dogma and superstition with a rational, scientific view of the universe. All things were open to investigation by experiment and observation, and it seemed as if the human mind had replaced religious dictate as the source of true knowledge. Parapsychological research has, on the whole, regarded itself as a child of this Enlightenment tradition, and is often at odds with established religion as the men (and less often women) of mainstream science. To the surprise and frustration of many, the accumulated evidence of more than a century of serious effort, generally sufficient to convince those who undertook the studies, has failed to change the dominant materialist scientific paradigm. Many academics repeat and sincerely believe that there is no solid evidence of the survival of consciousness, or paranormal phenomena in general (such as mediumship, telepathy, clairvoyance or precognition). It follows that people who claim to have psychic powers must be fraudulent or mistaken. Such views are often held with vehemence and in ignorance of the research and practice of mediums and psychic researchers. An unsolicited email from someone who had read the short report I published on-line of the séance I attended with trance medium David Thompson surmised that I must either be gullible or out to make money from it. The correspondent described himself as 'open-minded' but the notion that such things could occur was evidently too far outside his view of the world to accept.[16]

This attitude represents what Robert Anton Wilson (1932-2007) referred to as a 'reality tunnel.' We all see the world through the lens of our subconscious mental filters and experience, and either fail to notice or rationalise away what does not fit with our view of reality (1983). Michael Polanyi (1891-1976), did more than most to bridge the gap between science, social science and philosophy. He was influenced by Lévy-Bruhl's writings on 'primitive rationality' and Evans-Pritchard's work on Azande witchcraft, oracles and magic (first published in 1937), in his insight that our language, social and conceptual frameworks influence the ways in which we interpret the world. If we think and reason within a particular 'idiom,' logical inconsistencies may go unchallenged and unnoticed – another version of Wilson's 'reality tunnel.'[17]

Cognitive dissonance

The white crow argument (that disproves the axiom that all crows are black) often put forward by those who study the paranormal is rather difficult to refute. If, however, you have a strong investment in all crows being black, and feel that your world will be dangerously threatened by the presence of a white crow, you are likely to react with irritation, hostility, fear or ridicule towards those who claim to have seen one. The observer might be mistaken or a liar. The bird might have been a seagull rather than a crow, or might have been tampered with – painted or perhaps genetically modified, a freak of nature. The basis of such reactions is summed up by the term *cognitive dissonance*, the idea that being faced with two contradictory situations causes discomfort. The more central the idea is to someone's core identity, the more painful the contradiction. The term 'cognitive dissonance' was coined by Leon Festinger, Henry Riecken and Stanley Schachter in their classic 1956 study of a UFO cult, *When Prophesy Fails*. The group in question had been told by means of channelled writing that the world would end on December 21st 1954, but that the faithful few would be rescued by a space ship at midnight on the December 20th. When no space ship arrived, and the expected cataclysm also failed to materialize, rather than decide they had been misled and abandon the cult, a channelled message was received to say that because of the faith of the few the end of the world had been delayed. Their reaction was to turn from secretive group to a proselytizing one. Festinger and his co-authors surmised that the cult members had invested too much in their beliefs, and they were too central to their daily lives, simply to abandon them. To relieve the dissonance felt when the prophesy was not fulfilled they took the measures of altering the prophesy to fit the circumstances, and trying to recruit more people to their beliefs in order to justify them.

A small UFO cult may be easy to dismiss, but the point is that we all experience cognitive dissonance when our core belief systems are challenged by conflicting data. Subsequent neurological studies designed to test for the presence of stress when cognitive dissonance is experienced have been linked to activation of particular areas of the brain. Van Veen *et al.* (2009, p. 1472), for example, concluded that 'our results are consistent with the action-based model of cognitive dissonance, which posits that conflict between cognitions evokes an aversive state because it potentially interferes with unconflicted, effective, goal-driven action.' They conclude their discussion with the claim that cognitive dissonance is an important concept in psychology because of its ability to explain and predict attitude change in a wide range of human behaviour, and that the dissonance caused can be mapped in the brain using an MRI scanner:

> Our results shed light on the cognitive and neurobiological basis of dissonance, and indicate that the magnitude of

conflict-related dACC [dorsal anterior cingulate cortex] and anterior insula activation predicts the subsequent attitude change. This result supports the core assumption of dissonance theory, that attitude change in cognitive dissonance is driven by conflict. It is the basis for a neural prediction of attitude change. Our findings have considerable implications for understanding attitude change in a wide range of contexts in which cognitive dissonance theory has found broad practical application, including politics, marketing, management and the evaluation of psychotherapeutic interventions (2009, p. 1473).

We might adapt an explanatory diagram to illustrate this process in the case of physical mediumship. If the Element represents material spirit manifestations, this will conflict with a view of the world that holds that such things are *de facto* impossible, and

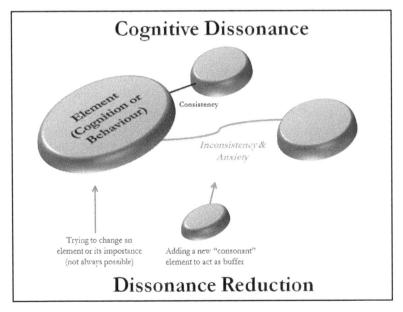

Figure 1. (Source: Wikimedia Commons)

cause anxiety. Consistency can be reconstituted by (1) changing one's beliefs and accepting that such manifestations do indeed occur, (2) by simply ignoring the phenomenon, (3) or by inserting new 'consonant buffer elements' (the manifestations were a hoax, a magic trick, an hallucination). The first option may be the most parsimonious but also requires the greatest change to the individual's view of the world and sense of self, and is therefore the one that demands the greatest psychological effort.

Mary Douglas, in her classic study *Purity and Danger* (1966) made similar observations, pointing out that anomalies may be treated in a variety of ways; redefined, eliminated, avoided, labelled as dangerous or elevated through ritual. The need to classify the world is basic to human social behaviour and affects every aspect of our lives. Anomalies are events or beliefs that cross categorical boundaries. Much humour depends on the shock or irony of something being in the wrong place. Often, however, it is no laughing matter. Many countries have laws or regulations intended to reinforce a wide range of category boundaries around sexual orientation or religious adherence, or lifestyle choices for example. To contravene these rules may result in discrimination, incarceration or even death. If you have a category rule that states that everything that exists is equal to the sum of its visible or measurable material parts, and that every part of a living being is subject to the laws of entropy, any evidence of communication from those who have died will be anomalous. It might not seem a very threatening idea, or even a rather encouraging and comforting one, but if you have invested large parts of who you are, and your understanding of the nature of the world in which you live in this rather simple materialist paradigm, it might appear dangerously destabilising.

The vehemence and determination with which a relatively small number of people attempt to persuade others, often with great success, that all apparent paranormal activity is an illusion, points to a particularly acute form of cognitive dissonance.

T.E. Lawrence described this attitude in himself before his death, describing it as, 'a kind of masochism, a stoic resolve to punish the wishful thinking one suspects is behind any belief in immortality.' He went onto explain that, 'It feels very stern, strong and noble to deny the thing one secretly longs for, and so to prove that one is quite able to do without it' (Sherwood, 1969, p. 49). The psychological effort of living in the shadow of death when death is seen as obliteration, finality, the end of all life, may be such that it can permit no distraction. Death denied, ignored or faced stoically takes energy, and the apparent weakness of those who hold out false hopes of an eternal future present a threat to this carefully erected edifice. Certainly there are honest seekers who simply claim that the evidence does not stack up, but then, to follow Albert Einstein's famous dictum, 'Not everything that counts can be measured. Not everything that can be measured counts'.

Pathologies of cognition

The pioneering psychologist and founder of transpersonal and humanistic psychology, Abraham Maslow (1908-1970), best known for his theory of a hierarchy of needs, identified twenty one 'pathologies of cognition,' both intellectual and emotional in his 1966 book *The Psychology of Science.* Charles Tart points out that while Maslow focuses on science as a system of knowledge his comments are also applicable to pathologies of knowing and learning more generally. It is not only hard-line sceptics who are subject to these pathologies. They are tendencies we all have to a greater or lesser extent. For instance, rationalisation can be an obstacle to knowledge. In Tart's paraphrase of Maslow, 'The brain's emotional circuits often react and form a judgment before the more intellectual parts have even gotten the message that something's happening, something's being perceived' (2009, p. 57). This would apply equally to both parapsychological investigators and hard-line sceptics. Other pathologies identified by Maslow apply more specifically to those who espouse reductionist materialism, such as 'Intolerance of ambiguity,' which Tart summarises as 'an inability to be comfortable with the vague and mysterious.' People who dislike ambiguity often 'generalize or rationalize too soon or too broadly, or oversimplify by ignoring parts of reality' (ibid., p. 58). Arguably people who like to deal with unambiguous data will be more attracted to the sciences than to the arts and humanities, or to social and cultural anthropology, a discipline that deals more in questions than answers. Scientists may therefore be overrepresented in this personality type. Academics in general will recognise in themselves the pathology of 'Intellectualization,' described by Tart in the following terms:

> Our ability to step back from the immediacy of experience, emotion, and bodily agitation to take a broader, more logical view of a situation is one of the greatest powers of the human mind. But considering it as always being the 'highest' ability, or using it compulsively…in all situations for all knowledge seeking, is maladaptive (ibid., p. 59).

Of the twenty one pathologies of cognition outlined by Maslow, academics in general and scientists in particular are guilty of, or susceptible to, a greater number than members of the general public as their (our) reputations and sense of self are so closely bound up with the life of the mind and professionalization of knowledge. Those who claim to be open to new data and interpretations, and in most cases probably sincerely believe this to be so, can be the most rigid when it comes to admitting new, contradictory evidence:

> Science then, can be a defence. It can be primarily a safety philosophy, a security system, a complicated way of avoiding anxiety and upsetting problems. In the extreme

instance it can be a way of avoiding life, a kind of self-cloistering. It can become in the hands of some people, at least, a social institution with primarily defensive, conserving functions, ordering and stabilizing rather than discovering and renewing (Maslow, 1933, p. 33, cited in Tart, 2009, p. 54).

Given these tendencies we should not be surprised that the boundaries between an ordered predictable world and one of seemingly impossible things is so keenly and emotionally defended.

Pseudo-scepticism

One of the frustrations for many of those who engage in serious parapsychological research or, in the case of anthropologists, tend to remain silent concerning their findings and interpretations when they fear that these might expose them to ridicule, is the studied ignorance of many of those who pose as sceptics. To ask questions, look for alternative explanations, and to re-examine material and conclusions is a healthy and productive form of scepticism. We need, however, to have a degree of competence in a field in order to evaluate the data coming out of it. Many academics are guilty of claiming the authority of 'science' to prognosticate on matters well beyond their area of expertise (and the media love it). This does a great disservice to science, which should be at the forefront of furthering knowledge - especially at the boundaries of the known and knowable – and to the general public, who are misled concerning the status of knowledge. Charles Tart is one of many investigators who has had experience of debunkers or pseudo-sceptics who 'are sometimes high-status scientists in other fields, but [who] don't bother to actually read the published reports of the experiments in parapsychology's refereed scientific journals, much less get their hands dirty by doing any experiments themselves' (2009, p. 67). In other cases the sceptic will admit that he or she is wrong when challenged, but go on to repeat their discredited point in the next interview or article.[18]

The weight of expectation

A final comment in this section concerns the relationship between experience and expectation. Some of those who attended David Thompson's séance with me in August 2011 had been to one or several of his séances before, or had sat in other similar circles. Some were developing their own physical mediumship. Even those like myself who were newcomers were well prepared through what we were given to read and through the pre-séance talk to know what to expect. How much weight should we give to these expectations in determining what people thought happened during the séance? It would have been quite difficult for anyone to raise doubts about the process, if there were any, during the evening without seeming disrespectful or hostile. This is not to say that David Thompson, or medium Christine Morgan, who acted as master of ceremonies, would not have been happy to deal with any specific issues - I had the impression that they would have, but there was no space for people to voice publicly any alternative interpretations of events. I found the very banality of much of the content of the séance (and this is a purely personal reaction) contrasted strangely with the extraordinary, seemingly 'impossible' notion, that a medium, tied and gagged in a chair, was being used by those who had died to form full or partial materialized bodies, and to sing and speak to us clearly and loudly as they moved around the room.

While I do not think that the séance I attended was simply a theatrical performance I cannot be sure. As the séance was conducted in complete darkness it would be difficult, despite all the precautions, to completely rule out the manipulation of objects and production of sounds by people within the room to give the impression of spirit activity. The medium Stewart Alexander is well aware of this problem when he writes that 'it cannot be denied that one of the greatest weaknesses of the physical séance room has always been that generally manifestations are inhibited by the presence of any form or degree of light,' and that 'quite understandably, such rooms have led many to suspect chicanery, although, irrespective of how it may appear, the total elimination of light is generally very necessary' (2010, p. 243). David Thompson had three helpers present, Christine, Sarah and Drew, who could potentially have moved quietly around the room on stocking-feet (as we had all removed our shoes). By placing chosen sitters who were part of a conspiracy next to them, so that it was not revealed that they were not holding hands, they would have been free to move around. The ectoplasmic hands felt by some of the sitters could have been those of the helpers, and the voices pre-recorded or produced by someone outside the room, relayed via a hidden speaker – possibly lowered from the ceiling. The uniformly loud volume of the spirit guides, as opposed to the rather softer voices of the deceased relatives, could have been a function of the volume setting on a speaker. I have no doubt that a gifted magician could introduce objects into a séance room, and perhaps even reverse the cardigan of a man strapped to a chair. I say *could*, as there was no evidence of hidden microphones or speakers, and the room was thoroughly searched. The way the sitters were invited to converse with the spirits would make a pre-recording almost impossible to manage with any degree of realism without assuming the connivance of all those involved. Objections concerning the conduct of séances in the dark, which is apparently a requirement for many mediums to produce ectoplasm, would not apply to Kai Muegge's séances, described above, which take place in red light. David Thompson's spirit team claim that they are working towards this, and there are photographs of Thompson producing ectoplasm taken in red light on his Circle of the Silver Cord website.[19]

I can well understand, judging from my own reaction, how easy it would be to simply ignore the events of the evening and get on with my life as if such things didn't and couldn't happen, to 'bracket them out,' as they had no reference point with the rest of my life. There is evidence that people often quickly forget even dramatic anomalous events that find no place in their conceptual schema. Another reaction I experienced was a sense of anti-climax that there were no great spiritual revelations. Those who came back from the dead to speak to us had little to say that they could or would not have said when alive. But that is the point, they had died and the medium (with the help of his ectoplasm) *was* their message. They were present in the room, able to talk to us, and to reassure us that death is the great lie. It was the very physicality of the occasion that gave it its supposed veracity. The challenge to each of those present at David Thompson's séance was that if death is not the end, what are the implications for the way we live our lives? Perhaps it is this challenge that often gives the sceptical response its messianic fervour.

Conclusion

William James struggled with the tension between his scientific training, with its measured, rational approach to religion, and the evidence before him of seemingly 'impossible' things. His conclusion after many years of investigation, published in his book *The Varieties of Religious Experience*, was that:

> The whole drift of my education goes to persuade me that the world of our present consciousness is only one out of many worlds of consciousness that exist, and that those other worlds must contain experiences which have a meaning for our life also; and that although in the main their experiences and those of this world keep discrete, yet

the two become continuous at certain points, and higher energies filter in (2008, p. 376).

It was not that James was no longer able to put himself 'into the sectarian scientist's attitude, and imagine vividly that the world of sensations and of scientific laws and objects may be all,' but that whenever he did so he would hear his 'inward monitor' whisper the word 'bosh.' Without claiming to have all the answers, or even to know the right questions to ask, the consistent experience of many of those who have observed, studied and been unsettled by 'impossible things' is to admit the reality of a world in which seemingly impossible things are in fact possible. It is not a world at odds with science, but certainly expands far beyond a narrow materialism. As James concluded:

> Humbug is humbug, even though it bear the scientific name, and the total expression of human experience, as I view it objectively, invincibly urges me beyond the narrow 'scientific' bounds. Assuredly, the real world is of a different temperament – more intricately built than physical science allows (James, ibid.).

The time lag in absorbing the extraordinary discoveries of modern science, both among many scientists, who admit they rarely read outside their narrow field of expertise, in the media and general public, is part of the issue. Theoretical physicist Henry Stapp notes that:

> The tremendous difficulty in reconciling consciousness, as we know it, with the older physics is dramatized by the fact that for many years the mere mention of 'consciousness' was considered evidence of backwardness and bad taste in most of academia, including, incredibly, even psychology and the philosophy of mind (2011, p. 139).

The scientific method with carefully replicated experimentation, and acceptance of new discoveries in theoretical physics, mathematics, cosmology and biology, should in theory shift Western conceptions of the possible away from a fixed Newtonian materialism. Some of the reasons why this is such a slow process have been explored in this essay. Anthropology as a discipline that has both scientific and humanistic pretensions ought to be well placed to bridge the gaps between religious and mystical beliefs, alternative cultural views of reality and empirical scientific research. These need not be at odds with each other and the denial of reason is not required in order for us to expand our understanding of the possible. As we live in a culture that accords the priority of truth to science I will give Stapp the last word:

> But where reason is honored, belief must be reconciled with empirical evidence. If you seek evidence for your beliefs about what you are, and how you fit into Nature, then science claims jurisdiction, or at least relevance. Physics presents itself as the basic science, and it is to physics that you are told to turn. Thus a radical shift in the physics-based conception of man from that of an isolated mechanical automaton to that of an integral participant in a non-local holistic process that gives form and meaning to the evolving universe is a seismic event of potentially momentous proportions (2011, p. 140).

If mediumship and the phenomena of the séance room are to find a more general acceptance it will be from the perspective of this non-local, holistic understanding of human consciousness and materiality. Ethnographers can readmit the extraordinary and impossible tales of others within this more expansive, shared understanding of reality.

Notes

1. There is an analogy here with the use of the term 'miracle', which assumes a certain natural order that is transgressed, an idea that similarly depends on a particular cultural view of the natural. I have discussed this at greater length in Bowie (2011).

2. Psychic investigator and writer, Lawrence LeShan states the problem thus: 'Impossible events do not occur. Therefore, if a scientist is faced with the fact that an impossible event has occurred – or daily fare as psychical researchers – the paradox must be resolved. This can be done only by redefining reality in such a way that what was previously impossible now becomes possible. If the theory must bow to the brute fact, we must be clear as to what is the theory and what is the fact. The paranormal event is the fact. Our definition of *reality*, which decides for us what is possible or impossible, is the theory' (2009, p. 63).

3. See, for instance, the discussions of paranormality and academic approaches to anomalous phenomena in Cardeña, Lynn & Krippner (2000), Kakar and Kripal (2012), Kelly & Kelly *et al.* (2010) and Escolar (2012), as well as the mediating work of writers such as Teilhard de Chardin (1881-1955) and Fritjof Capra (1975, 1982).

4. See, for instance, the detailed occult science of the Theosophist writers and mediums Anne Besant and Charles Leadbeater, whose 1908 volume *Occult Chemistry: Investigations by Clairvoyant Magnification into the Structure of the Atoms of the Periodic Table and Some Compounds,* influenced the work of Francis Aston, who was awarded the Nobel Prize for Chemistry in 1922 (Hughes, 2007), and a summary of scientific evidence for a conscious universe in Radin (1997). See also Hagelin (1987) on parallels between consciousness and unified field theories in physics.

5. One might cite, for instance, the work of Bohm (1980), Rosenblum and Kuttner (2011), and Stapp (2011) in the physics of consciousness; Tart (2009) on scientific evidence for parapsychological claims, Kelly and Kelly (2010) for a detailed analysis of the evidence from a primarily psychological and neurological perspective, and Davies (2013) and Beauregard and O'Leary (2007) on encounters between theology, spirituality, culture and neurobiology.

6. See, for instance, Sarangerel (2000), and Some (1994).

7. There are a number of accounts within the anthropological literature of anomalous experiences that cause the ethnographer enough disquiet to unsettle normative paradigmatic ways of thinking, at least for a time. See, for instance, several of the articles in De Vita (1992) and Young and Goulet (1994).

8. For a succinct account of contemporary physical mediumship see Hunter (2013).

9. There are many accounts of physical mediumship, and of some of the best known more recent trance mediums, able to produce ectoplasmic materialisations, e.g. Findlay (2010 [1931]), Brealy (2008), Halliwell (2008), Harrison (2008), Harris (2009), Alexander (2010). In addition to descriptions of the Scole Experiment (Solomon, 1999; Foy, 2007), there are transcripts and descriptions of trance mediums and physical phenomena on the websites of the Circle of the Silver Cord (http://circleofthesilvercord.net) and Felix Experimental Group (http://felixcircle.blogspot.co.uk).

10. Such precautions did not prevent the trance medium Helen Duncan (1895-1956) being tried as a fraud in 1933 and under the Witchcraft Act in 1944 – after unsettling the authorities as she appeared to possess details of top secret military operations, passed on through deceased members of the forces to their famlies (Brealey, 2008).

11. Stephen Braude is an experienced researcher and recorder of anomalous phenomena (Braude, 2003 and 2007).

12. Details of this séance are given on my Exploring the Afterlife blog, http://exploringtheafterlife.blogspot.co.uk/2011/08/materialisation-seance-with-david.html and Academia.edu website, http://www.academia.edu/2186310/Material_and_Immaterial_Bodies_Ethnographic_Reflections_on_a_Trance_Seance.

13. http://felixcircle.blogspot.co.uk/2013/05/physical-mediumship-under-strict.html Accessed 2.10.13.

14. Turner (1992, pp. 165-7) cites Lévi-Strauss' account of the Kwakiutl shaman Quesalid in Canada (1977, pp. 445-53) and Michael Harner's account of shamanic healing among the Jivaro in South America (1980, pp. 113-34) as examples of power objects, like the *ihamba* tooth of the Ndembu, that act as bridges or intermediaries between 'shamanic' and 'ordinary' states of consciousness.

15. A fascinating post-script to the notion of fraudulent mediums is the so-called 'Philip Experiment'. In the 1970s the Toronto Society for Psychical Research created a fictional character they called 'Philip' and sought to communicate with him in a traditional séance setting. After a year of regular sittings they were able to produce physical phenomena such as rappings and table levitation, and eventually direct communication with Philip. The experiment has been repeated several times with similar results elsewhere. There is a range of possible explanations for this, ruling out fraud, which seems improbable, including the notion that the collective energy and expectation of the group alone was able to produce measurable and observable phenomena, that they created a semi-material 'thought form' that had some

autonomy, or that they attracted and channelled another or other discarnate communicators who played along with the Philip deception. What is clear is that they were not communicating with an actual deceased individual who had lived the life described, as Philip was an intentionally anachronistic fiction (Owen, 1976). The experiment has been repeated many times with different fictional characters and equal success (http://www.youtube.com/watch?v=uZTNmB-UvFo).

16. Stewart Alexander (2010, pp. 248-9) divides sceptics of Spiritualism into three types, the most common being those whose views are based on ignorance of the subject. The second type he calls the 'informed sceptic' who, despite over 150 years of research, is not convinced. The third is the immovable 'fixed view sceptic' who is so sure that genuine mediumship does not exist that they lambast anyone who claims otherwise. This third type of sceptic is very vocal and active on the Internet. They often serve as the 'professional media sceptic', called in to give a 'balanced' view whenever programmes on the paranormal are broadcast on radio or television. This problem is hardly new. In the first decades of the Twentieth Century psychical researchers bemoaned the opposition of 'official science', particularly psychology, to the accumulation of evidence from well-trained, scientific researchers into paranormal phenomena (Coover, 1927).

17. A fuller discussion of Polanyi and Evans Pritchard can be found in Richard Werbner's 'Comment' in *JRAI* (2013).

18. A good example would be the debate between Rupert Sheldrake and Richard Wiseman over the dog, Jaytee, who could predict when his mistress would return home (described in Sheldrake, 1999). A detailed description of the differences between Sheldrake's and Wiseman and colleagues is set out on Sheldrake's blog (Accessed 4.10.2013): http://www.sheldrake.org/D&C/controversies/wiseman.html. An attempt to give voice to the strongest arguments for and against parapsychological phenomena is found in Krippner and Friedman 2010).

19. See David Thompson's website and blog, The Circle of the Silver Cord, http://circleofthesilvercord.net, for accounts of séances, recordings and photographs.

References

Alexander, S. (2010). *An extraordinary journey: The memoirs of a physical medium.* Beaconsfield: Saturday Night Press.

Beauregard, M. & O'Leary, D. (2007). *The spiritual brain: A neuroscientist's case for the existence of the soul.* New York: Harper Collins.

Bohm, D. (1980). *Wholeness and the implicate order*. London and New York: Routledge.

Bowie, F. (2003). Belief or experience? An anthropologists' dilemma. In C. Williams (Ed.), *Contemporary conceptions of God. Studies in Religion and Society 59* (pp. 135-60), Lewiston, Queenston, Lampeter: Edwin Mellen Press.

Bowie, F. (2009). The challenge of multi-sited ethnography. In I. Fowler and V. Fanso (Eds.), *Encounter, transformation and identity: Peoples of the western Cameroon borderlands 1891-2000* (pp. 184-198.). New York, Oxford: Berghahn.

Bowie, F. (2011). Miracles in traditional religions. In G.H. Twelftree (Ed.) *The Cambridge companion to miracles* (pp. 167-183.). New York, Cambridge, UK: Cambridge University Press.

Bowie, F. (2013). Building bridges, dissolving boundaries: Toward methodology for the ethnographic study of the afterlife, mediumship, and spiritual beings. *Journal of the American Academy of Religion, 81* (3), 698–733.

Braude, S.E. (2003). *Immortal remains: The evidence for life after death*. London, Boulder, New York, Oxford: Rowman & Littlefield.

Braude, S.E. (2007). *The gold leaf lady and other parapsychological investigations*. Chicago & London: University of Chicago Press.

Brealey, G., with K. Hunter (2008). *The two worlds of Helen Duncan*. York: Saturday Night Press.

Capra, F. (1975). *The tao of physics: An exploration of the parallels between modern physics and eastern mysticism*. London: HarperCollins.

Capra, F. (1982). *The turning point: Science, society, and the rising culture*. London: Simon & Schuster.

Cardeña, E., Lynn, S.J. & Krippner, S. (Eds.) (2000). *Varieties of anomalous experience: Examining the scientific evidence*. Washington DC: American Psychological Association.

Coover, J.E. (1927). Metaphysics and the incredulity of psychologists. In C. Murchison (Ed.) *The case for and against psychical belief* (pp. 229-264). Worcester, Mass.: Clark University. Reprinted by Kessinger Legacy Reprints.

Davies, O. (2013). *Theology of transformation: Faith, freedom and the Christian act*. Oxford: Oxford University Press.

DeVita, P.R. (Ed.) (1992). *The naked anthropologist: Tales from around the world*. Belmont, CA.: Wadsworth.

Di Nucci, C., & Hunter, J. (2009). *Charlie: Trance communication and spirit teachings*. Bristol, UK: The Bristol Spirit Lodge.

Douglas, M. (1966). *Purity and danger*. London: Routledge & Keegan Paul.

Escolar, D. (2012). Boundaries of anthropology: Empirics and ontological relativism in a field experience with anomalous luminous entities in Argentina. *Anthropology and Humanism, 37* (1), 27-44.

Evans-Pritchard, E.E. (1976 [1937]). *Witchcraft, oracles and magic among the Azande*. Abridged with an introduction by Eva Gilles. Oxford: Clarendon.

Fenwick, P. & Fenwick, E. (2008). *The art of dying*. London and New York: Continuum.

Festinger, L., Riecken, H., & Schachter, S. (1956). *When prophesy fails: A social and psychological study of a modern group that predicted the destruction of the world.* Minnesota: University of Minnesota Press.

Findlay, A. (2010 [1931]). *On the edge of the etheric: Survival after death scientifically explained.* San Diego, CA: The Book Tree.

Foy, R.P. (2007). *In pursuit of physical mediumship: A psychic autobiography.* London: Janus Publishing Company.

Friedlander, M.W. (Ed.) (1995). *At the fringes of science.* Boulder, CO.: Westview Press.

Hagelin, J.S. (1987). *Is consciousness the unified field? A field theorist's perspective.* Fairfield, IA: Maharishi International University of Management.

Halliwell, K. (2008). *Experiences of trance, physical mediumship and associated phenomena with the Stewart Alexander circle. Part one: Evidence of survival after death.* York: Saturday Night Press.

Hanegraaff, W.J. (2012). *Esotericism and the academy: Rejected knowledge in western culture.* Cambridge: Cambridge University Press.

Harner, M. (1980). *The way of the shaman: A guide to power and healing.* San Francisco: Harper and Row.

Harris, L. (2009). *Alec Harris: The full story of his remarkable physical mediumship.* York: Saturday Night Press.

Harrison, T. (2008). *Life After death: Living proof. A lifetime's experiences of physical phenomena and materialisations through the mediumship of Minnie Harrison.* Revised edition. York: Saturday Night Press.

Howard, A.J. (2013). Beyond belief: Ethnography, the supernatural and hegemonic discourse. *Practical Matters, 6,* 1-17. Published by Emory University, USA.

Hughes, J. (2007). Occultism and the atom: the curious story of isotopes. From *Physics World* September 2003, Bristol & Philadelphia: Institute of Physics Publishing 2007 (physicsworldarchive.iop.org). Downloaded from http://www.cwlworld.info/pw_article_sept03.pdf. Accessed 28 July 2013.

Hunter, J. (2011). Contemporary mediumship and séance groups in the UK: Speculating on the Bristol Spirit Lodge. *Journal of the Unitarian Society for Psychical Studies, 76,* 7-14.

Hunter, J. (2013). Contemporary physical mediumship: Is it part of a continuous tradition? *Paranthropology: Journal of Anthropological Approaches to the Paranormal, 3* (1), 35-43.

James, W. (2008 [1902]) *The varieties of religious experience: A study in human nature.* Rockville, MD: ARC Manor.

Kakar, S. & Kripal, J.J. (Eds.) (2012). *Seriously strange: Thinking anew about psychical experiences.* New Delhi: Viking Penguin.

Kelly, E.F., Kelly, E.W., Crabtree, A., Gauld, A., Grosso, M. & Greyson, B. (2010). *Irreducible mind: Toward a psychology for the 21st century.* Lanham, Boulder, New York, Toronto, Plymouth, UK: Rowman & Littlefield.

Kripal, J.J. (2010) *Authors of the impossible: The paranormal and the sacred.* London & Chicago: University of Chicago Press.

Krippner, S. and Friedman, H.L. (Eds.) (2010). *Debating psychic experience: Human potential or human illusion?* Santa Barbara, CA; Denver, CO & Oxford: Praeger.

LeShan, L. (2009). *A new science of the paranormal: The promise of psychical research.* Wheaton, Illinois & Chennai, India: Theosophical Publishing House.

Lévi-Strauss, C. (1977). The sorcerer and his magic. In D. Landy (Ed.) *Culture, disease and healing* (pp. 445-53). New York: Macmillan.

Lévy-Bruhl, L. (1985[1926]). *How natives think.* Princeton: Princeton University Press.

Owen, I.M. & Sparrow, M. (1976). *Conjuring up Philip: An adventure in psychokinesis.* New York: Harper & Row.

Polanyi, M. (1950). Scientific beliefs, *Ethics, 61,* 27-37.

Polanyi, M. (1952). The stability of beliefs. *British Journal for the Philosophy of Science, 3,* 217-32.

Radin, Dean (1997) *The conscious universe: The scientific truth of psychic phenomena.* New York: Harper Collins.

Radin, D. (2006). *Entangled minds: Extrasensory experiences in a quantum reality.* New York: Paraview.

Rosenblum, B., and Kuttner, F. (2011). *Quantum enigma: Physics encounters consciousness.* New York: Oxford University Press.

Sarangerel (2000) *Riding windhorses: A journey into the heart of Mongolian shamanism.* Rochester, Vermont: Destiny Books.

Some, M.P. (1994). *Of water and the spirit: Ritual, magic and initiation in the life of an African shaman.* New York: Penguin.

Sheldrake, R. (1999). *Dogs that know when their owners are coming home and other unexplained powers of animals.* London: Hutchinson.

Sheldrake, R. (2012). *The science delusion: Freeing the spirit of enquiry.* London: Coronet.

Sherwood, J. (1991 [1969]). *The country beyond: The doctrine of re-birth.* Saffron Waldon: C.W. Daniel.

Silvers, R.B. (Ed.) (2003). *Hidden histories of science.* New York: New York Review of Books.

Skultans, V. (1974). *Intimacy and ritual: A study of Spiritualism, mediums and groups.* London: Routledge & Kegan Paul.

Solomon, G. & Solomon, J. (1999). *The Scole experiment: Scientific evidence for life after death.* London: Piatkus.

Stapp, H.P. (2011). *Mindful universe: Quantum mechanics and the participating observer.* Second Edition. Heidlberg, Dordrecht, London, New York: Springer.

Stoller, P. & Olkes, C. (1987). *In sorcery's shadow.* Chicago and London: University of Chicago Press.

Tart, C.T. (2009). *The end of materialism: How evidence of the paranormal is bringing science and spirit together.* Oakland, CA.: New Harbinger Publications.

Turner, E. with W. Blodgett, S. Kahona, & F. Benwa (1992). *Experiencing ritual: A new interpretation of African healing.* Philadelphia: University of Pennsylvania Press.

Tymn, M.E. (2008). *The articulate dead: They brought the spirit world alive.* Lakeville, Minnesota: Galde Press.

Tymn, M.E. (2013). *Resurrecting Leonora Piper: How science discovered the afterlife.* Guildford: White Crow Books.

Van Veen, V., Krug, M.K., Schooler, J.W., & Carter, C.S., (2009) Neural activity predicts attitude change in cognitive dissonance. *Nature Neuroscience, 12* (11), 1469–1474.

Wenner, M. (2009). Smile! It could make you happier. *Scientific American*, October 14th, http://www.scientificamerican.com/article.cfm?id=smile-it-could-make-you-happier (Accessed 3.10.13).

Werbner, R. (2013). Comment: The opposite of Evans-Pritchard'. *Journal of the Royal Anthropological Institute (N.S.), 19*, 650-655.

Wilson, R.A. (1983). *Prometheus rising.* Las Vegas, NV: New Falcon Publications.

Wilson, D.G. (2013). *Redefining shamanisms: Spiritualist mediums and other traditional shamans as apprenticeship outcomes.* London: Bloomsbury.

Young, D.E. & Goulet, J-G. (Eds.) (1994). *Being changed by cross-cultural encounters: The anthropology of extraordinary experience.* NY: Broadview Press.

Gordon Higginson's medium's cabinet at the Arthur Findlay College, Stansted, England.
Photograph by Shannon Taggart.

AN AGNOSTIC SOCIAL SCIENTIFIC PERSPECTIVE ON SPIRIT MEDIUM EXPERIENCE IN GREAT BRITAIN

HANNAH GILBERT

Psychical research and parapsychology have accumulated an impressive body of research into Western spirit mediums. In 1848, the Fox sisters' rudimentary methods of communicating with spirits[1] became public, which in turn provided the catalyst for a new wave of spirit mediumship. Members of the scientific community were quick to direct their attentions to this new phenomenon, seeking to use the latest scientific techniques in order to evaluate whether mediumship provided evidence for life after death. There was, from the offset, a recognisable split between supporters and debunkers, a dichotomy that still occurs in the contemporary field of mediumship research. For some, experiments seemed unable to prove how mediums were able to provide such phenomena unless they were what they claimed to be. For others fraud was prevalent, and numerous reports detail the various mundane methods employed in public demonstrations and smaller sized séances. In the pursuit of what is considered acceptable or authentic *scientifically credible* proof, mediums have been tried and tested time and time again; in the field, as well as in the controlled settings of a laboratory (see Cerullo, 1982; Gauld,

1982; Oppenheim, 1988). In some areas of psychology, and in other disciplines of science, some researchers and academics would argue that the debunkers have effectively done their work. Certainly, this is a position frequently demonstrated and argued by representatives of the skeptical community, who often align with the atheistic materialist scientific-rationalism led by popular scientists like Richard Dawkins (who has himself been publically critical of spirit mediums).

But spirit mediumship persists. If anything, recent times have seen a notable rise in both the frequency and consumption of spirit communication. Spirit mediumship is, after all, a highly attractive enterprise, offering the chance to reconnect with those we have loved and lost, proposing promises for evidence of post-mortem survival. Recent studies concerned with bereavement and grieving have identified the therapeutic benefits of 'continuing bonds,' - arguing that maintaining a connection with the dead can offer enrichment for the living (Klass, Silverman & Nickman, 1996), a concept that adds weight to the kinds of post-mortem relationships negotiated and supported through spirit communication. Certainly, spirit mediumship is concerned with continuing bonds, the aim of which lies at the heart of its practise. For outsiders, it is easier to explore the outer signs of mediumistic experience: how spirits are embodied and negotiated by mediums during their demonstrations, for example. Equally, the use of experiments designed to test specific hypotheses can generate particular data sets using the performances and experiences of mediums. But how is spirit communication *experienced by the medium*? How do individuals become mediums? It is important to note that - as embedded as spirit mediumship is as a public practise that incorporates the involvement of others - the spirit medium is an individual with a biography of private spiritual encounters.

Agnostic Social Science

The on-going prevalence of spirit mediumship surely begs its consideration as an important and necessary topic of research. Furthermore, it is clear that there is something missing from research approaches that focus *exclusively* on whether or not mediumship is scientifically measurable. As Hess (1993), Northcote (2007) and Wooffitt (2006) have demonstrated, there are distinctive discursive factors that surround the ways in which individuals make claims about extraordinary experiences and their authenticity, and the language and means with which debunkers or skeptics strive to undermine their validity whilst maintaining their own. These authors are less concerned with the ontological debate, and more focused on how facts are constructed in discourse. This is in line with a new crop of researchers who adopt a distinctive perspective on the kinds of experiences and phenomena of which spirit mediumship is often associated: *agnostic social science.* The use of agnostic here emphasises an approach to research topics that aims to avoid starting out with predisposed conclusions regarding the validity of certain phenomena or experience. Such is particularly important for topics concerning belief systems that may differ from the widely accepted Western materialist-rationalist framework dominant in much of contemporary academia. Agnostic social scientific studies are not generally concerned with proving or disproving particular world views; rather, they acknowledge that some areas may be ultimately unknowable to them. This may be particularly important for those who are not able to assess or examine the realities of their research participants or communities.

For an agnostic social scientific study of mediumship, the research agenda is less concerned with whether or not mediumship is something we can *objectively validate,* but rather seeks to explore its social richness. This includes the analysis of individual spiritual experiences; as social performances that are meaningful to their public consumers; and the dynamics of the community/ group within which it operates more generally. Such an approach may be interested in the social significance of mediumistic experience, and seek to situate such phenomena within the environments and settings in which they occur and are practised. A similar approach has already found a firm foothold in the historical literature, with detailed discussions concerning the relationship between spirit mediumship and society, focusing on areas such as bereavement, class, gender and politics (see, for example, Barrow, 1986; Bourke, 2007; Carroll, 2000; Hazelgrove, 2000; McMullin, 2004; and Owen, 1990).

There are important ethical issues that may also arise from such an approach; namely, how we treat, make sense of, and represent those we are studying. Agnosticism should not mean indifference, and in some cases researchers may be changed by their research. Rather, the importance of starting research from an agnostic position is to try and encourage reflexivity of one's own potential biases, and to be prepared to take people seriously. My own approach has been influenced by grounded theory, ethnomethodology and feminist perspectives, which encourage the use of data as the grounding for theory (rather than using data to test an existing theory), and which prompts the researcher to be conscious and reflective of their own *process* of research. Such interests are reflected increasingly in anthropology, with more anthropologists discussing the significance of their field experiences, and the impact that such has had upon their research. Anthropology is perhaps ideally suited to such considerations, as the method of ethnography is intensive, often situating individuals in an environment very different to their own, for long periods of time away from family and friends: a unique opportunity for immersion in another culture. Edited collections such as those offered by Goulet & Miller (2007) and Young & Goulet (1994) have brought together a collection of papers by researchers who have acknowledged their own extraordinary experiences, and considered the repercussions of such in regards to their own meaning making, how they relate to and understand their informants, and wider issues regarding the nature of experiences. Their work complements a shift in ethnographic theory that acknowledges the researcher as an individual who brings their own humanity into the field. Bowie (2012) has recently argued for cognitive, empathic engagement in research, which she describes as:

> ...cognitive, in that it demands the ethnographer adopts the categories of his or her informants, and uses this knowledge to interpret the world by means of those categories... It requires a certain empathy with the views of the other and an effort to enter their social, emotional, and mental world, however partial this attempt might be, or however different such categories are from one's own... [it also] requires an active engagement with another way of thinking, seeing and living. (Bowie, 2012, pp. 105-106)

In Bowie's approach, the researcher does not necessarily need to adopt the worldviews offered by their informants, but they do need to *really* look at what their informants believe and the worlds in which they live. Furthermore, it seeks to elevate the representation of informants from mere lynchpins of an academic enquiry into real, living, experiencing and sensuous human beings whose ways of life should be respected.

Studying Mediums

In 2003, I started a PhD at the University of York in order to explore the ways in which contemporary British spirit mediums represent and experience spirit contact. I used three specific data sets: participant observations of public demonstrations; semi-structured interviews with mediums; and discursive analysis of medium autobiographies. These data sets were thought to complement the social reality of spirit mediumship in everyday life: in the ways in which mediums present spirit contacts to their audiences, as well as how they themselves reflect upon their experiences in interview, or an autobiography (Gilbert, 2008).

The main focus of this research was to explore spirit mediumship as something lived and embedded within the world, something that is both a set of private spiritual experiences, and the demonstration of non-corporeal spirits in public performances. I had no way of assessing the authenticity of their claims, and such would have been far beyond the scope of my thesis. Because of this, my interests were not concerned with whether or not mediums could scientifically prove that they were in contact with a real, interactive spirit world, but rather treated the spirit world as something *socially* real and meaningful. As McClenon (1994) has argued:

> Sociologists and anthropologists are often unable to determine if their informants are lying or have reconstructed their memories of events... If observers *believe* that a particular event occurred, then that event is sociologically real. It affects those who believe in it. (McClenon, 1994, p. xi)

The move away from issues concerning scientific validity may seem to ignore what many researchers would argue is of crucial concern to mediumship research, but there are weaknesses to an approach that focuses primarily on this kind of ontological question. In one respect, it provides an opportunity to avoid becoming entangled in issues that researchers may be unable to adequately examine, and which complicate and confuse the aims of their research agenda. Hunter (2010) has raised important issues about the problems inherent in treating experiences as 'social facts'- arguing that to treat experiences as such risks undermining individuals and their experiences, whilst enabling the researcher to adopt a safe position within the wider academic arena. I would stress, however, that to treat experiences as social facts does not suggest that the researcher implies that the ontological realities in question are unimportant. Rather, it acknowledges that there are limits to what researchers can and cannot do, and that the emphasis is on recognising, as McClenon (1994) states, that these experiences *are real* for the people who report them, and that the researcher subsequently positions them as such.

As mentioned earlier, information about spirit mediums themselves has, for a long time, been under-examined,[2] and deserves higher prominence in the research literature. While researchers such as Fontana (2003) argue that accounts from such individuals – that is individuals who ascribe to particular religious frameworks – are likely to be heavily biased and potentially unreliable, this is not reason enough to dismiss them. Rather, these accounts are valuable in their own right. To treat accounts as 'sociologically real' does not infer that we must consider them uncritically, but it does encourage us to give attention to how people make sense and communicate their experiences. It is precisely in people's accounts that we can start to gain access into their worlds. Also, we should be wary of assuming that those who ascribe to particular world views are *automatically* 'heavily biased' and 'potentially unreliable'.

Particularly for mediums, an affiliation with specific religious or spiritual frameworks reflects a distinct process of meaning making and experience: rarely, it seems, do mediums enter in to such affiliations without a succession of meaningful experiences that encourage them to question, and perhaps adjust their own notions of reality. There are a number of social processes and experiences that influence those who become mediums. Looking into individuals' backgrounds and gathering data about their life experiences, is an important part of understanding spirit mediumship sociologically. If we consider the experiences surrounding spirit mediumship as sociologically real, then we may be able to gain insight into this phenomenon as something that 'affects those who believe in it'- who do not necessarily operate in accordance with scientific experiments, but do so in a number of specific social and private situations.

While my doctoral project (Gilbert, 2008) was rather modest in its sample size (I attended ten demonstrations, interviewed seventeen mediums, and analysed five autobiographies), there emerged a number of interesting features about the biographical experiences of contemporary spirit mediums, the ways in which they account for their spiritual experiences, and the dynamics of their performances of spirit communication. In this chapter, I have chosen to focus on some of the biographical features of medium accounts, and will aim to highlight some of the processes relevant to understanding how individuals become practising spirit mediums. It is difficult – perhaps even impossible – to provide a categorisation of mediumistic characteristics that would be applicable and representative of all practising mediums. Spirit mediumship is experienced and practised by a variety of different people, from a variety of different backgrounds. Experiences of spirit can also be highly individualistic, and the ways in which mediums actually experience their spirit contacts differs from medium to medium, although the most common means are seeing, hearing and/ or sensing spirit, and via thought transmission (for instance, receiving random images from spirit that they must make sense of for their recipients). It is important to note that some of the findings discussed here were not applicable to all the mediums I interviewed. However, they were significant for the majority, and so I would argue constitute a valid insight into the social lives of some contemporary spirit mediums.

Childhood

It has been suggested elsewhere that a number of psychic or spiritual practitioners have had spiritual experiences since early childhood (Emmons, 2000; Emmons & Emmons, 2003; McClenon, 1994). While some of my informants stated that their mediumship had been facilitated by a spontaneous spiritual experience later in life, the majority told me that they had first experienced spirit at an early age, often as young as four or five. These experiences generally occurred unexpectedly, for example, one of my informants' first apparitional encounters involved seeing a figure appear and walk through a wall while he was alone in his bedroom. Early spiritual experiences often occur when the experient is alone, a feature that remains consistent throughout their lives. Experiences of spirit did not usually involve communication, rather, the experient was simply aware that they had seen, heard or sensed something unusual.

What was also typical about these early spiritual experiences is that they often became a source of concern for the experient. Many of the mediums I spoke to stated that they were well aware of social prejudices about such experiences, and understood that what they had experienced was not something typical of everyday life for most people. In some cases, informants would state that they distanced themselves from their experiences, as it made them question their mental health, or thought that it might jeopardise their respectability. In instances where they had reported their experiences to others, it was typical that their accounts were met with a degree of discomfort, and that they were advised to keep such things to themselves (see also Emmons, 2000). In instances, however, where their reports were met with a more sympathetic response, it was still common for mediums to be unsure of what they had experienced. In all cases, the mediums I spoke to did not consider themselves to have genuine mediumistic abilities until later in life.

Acceptance and Development

Most of the accounts I collected suggested that there is a significant gap between these early spirit experiences and the period during which individuals come to accept that they have mediumistic abilities. This seems influenced primarily by their own acceptance, the active acceptance of others, and a developmental period – usually facilitated within a development class or group – where they learn how to harness communicative abilities with spirit contacts. Such development periods orientate towards a socialisation of mediumship as performance, where fledgling mediums learn how to perform mediumship publically, and gain social approval and acceptance as to the authenticity of their abilities. This is not to imply that mediumship performance is explicitly a performance as one might associate with acting, rather it refers to the social norms and the accepted discursive process of engaging in spirit communication in a public arena. The influence of message recipients during mediumship demonstrations is hugely important, and it is essential that the spirit contact is identified as connected to the message recipient, and that the messages themselves are meaningful. Wooffitt (2006) has demonstrated that the conversation between medium and message recipient needs a 'yes' at certain moments in the exchange in order for the message delivery to proceed successfully. Mediums are sensitive to the responses of their message recipients, as they are sensitive to the responses of their peers during development, and it is particularly crucial during large scale demonstrations that they select the right recipient for their spirit contact from the numerous possibilities in the audience.

The majority of mediums that I spoke to cited the relevance of an already established medium who recognised their as yet untapped potential. Often, they cited that this acknowledgement came unexpectedly. Typically, this acknowledgement came during Spiritualist meetings or public demonstrations of mediumship, during which time an established medium would tell them that they had mediumistic abilities that they should develop. It was not clear from the accounts what – if anything – facilitated this interaction, but their accounts stressed that this was important for them as they had not previously considered themselves to have mediumistic potential. Also, many mediums explained that their attendance at such Spiritualist activities was not motivated by their own curiosity about potentially having mediumistic abilities: they were not actively seeking to become a spirit medium. Most of the mediums I interviewed displayed an awareness of potential negative inferences that could be made about their identity as mediums – that is - that they were predisposed to favouring paranormal explanations, were easily suggestible, and so on. On the contrary, their accounts stressed that they maintained a distinct level of criticism about mediumship and their paranormal experiences, and that it was the persistence of experiences that could not be explained as anything other than evidence of spirit that led them to accept they had mediumistic abilities (for a similar discussion regarding individuals reporting paranormal experiences see Wooffitt, 1992). A number of reasons were given as to why they had become involved in Spiritualist activities, and it was typical for mediums to cite that they were motivated by the concerns of others, for example, a family member had been recently bereaved who they were looking to support.

The significance of legitimating others seems extremely important for contemporary mediums. Their accounts suggest an initial reluctance to accept their experiences at face value, though they prioritise experience as a key to knowledge. They are critical about accepting a belief in spirits until they feel they have exhausted all other potential explanations. Undergoing a developmental period seems important for mediums not simply because it enables them to hone their skills and learn how to perform spirit communication, but because it provides a social arena whereby others are able to provide their own experiential proof for the mediums' claims. My findings suggest that becoming a medium is as much about being recognised and legitimised by others as an authentic spirit communicator, being accepted as part of a group, as it is in finding a role for their abilities. This is emphasised by the significance they give to others' experiences: the experience of others is just as importance as the mediums' own, particularly during the developmental period (see also Emmons, 2000). While the pursuit of authenticity from recipients is an ongoing concern, it is also crucial that they find support and validation from others who constitute 'their' community. Mediumship performances, furthermore, operate in conjunction with others. This relates to the significance of mediumship as a social action, as something that can be identified as a process involving numerous agents. As Meintel (2007) states "clairvoyance is a *social* experience. Apart from the fact that several people may perceive the same invisible phenomenon at the same time, there is the unspoken communion that is necessary in order to give clairvoyance to another" (Meintel, 2007, p.155).

Conclusion

What the interview data seem to stress is that individuals do not believe that they are mediums, or begin to practise as such, based on an innate sense of mediumistic identity from birth. While many may believe that some people are born with an innate potential, this is different to *becoming* a medium. Individuals may have mediumistic potential and yet do not develop into mediums. The developmental period is important as a rite of initiation, both for the mediums' acceptance of their identity, and for their acceptance by others. Those who have early spiritual experiences seem to regard them as a source of uncertainty. This does not necessarily mean that they denied the existence of spirits during those early years, but rather suggests that they do not come to the conclusion that these experiences mean that they have mediumistic abilities. Becoming a medium relates to being accepted and legitimised. This involves being recognised by someone who is already established as a spiritual practitioner, and from ongoing experiential proof from others who are involved in the development of their mediumistic abilities. It is only after they have been recognised, and others have affirmed the authenticity of their messages from spirit, that mediums start to accept their identity as a spirit medium.

These issues are only a very small example of the kinds of findings an agnostic social scientific approach to the study of spirit mediumship may yield. Such approaches raise a number of important questions, and I sincerely hope that more researchers will adopt and support this approach. Spirit mediumship, among other such phenomena and experiences, is still an area ripe for research. Contemporary mediums have fascinating accounts, and should be sought more keenly as gatekeepers to the social world in which they operate. Research adopting an agnostic social scientific approach demonstrates that using such methods can provide new, perhaps unexpected, insights that may encourage a more holistic and detailed understanding of the phenomenon of spirit mediumship (e.g. Emmons & Emmons, 2003; Hunter, 2009; McMullin, 2004; Meintel, 2007). This is not to deny the importance of other approaches, for example, enquiries regarding the ontological authenticity of mediumistic claims. However, I would argue that, particularly in the field of Western spirit mediumship research, the literature on this subject is largely saturated by such debates, which distinctly over-shadow an appreciation of the complexity of mediumship as a public practise and private experience. For example, when I started my PhD in 2003, there was very little material that was not concerned with testing mediums, or recounting the historical development of Spiritualism and the Victorian fascination with the supernatural. Thankfully this has changed, with an increase in researchers taking mediums' and mediumship seriously, and recognising that it is a valid subject of study with much to yield in our understanding not only of mediumship itself, but of spiritual experience, our ways of dealing with bereavement, community dynamics, contemporary Spiritualism, and more. Taking an open minded stance that regards such subjects seriously, in turn, has implications for much wider areas of research and our understanding of private and public life, as well as how we, as researchers, conduct our investigations

Acknowledgements

Thanks to Mark Schroll for inviting an earlier version of this paper for the *Rhine Online* newsletter, and to Jack Hunter and David Luke for including it here, and for their editorial guidance which has certainly improved it. Thanks to Andy Sharp for proofreading.

Notes

1. The 'knocks in response to questions' style of mediumship practised by Kate and Margaret Fox was not overly practiced by other mediums, whose methods of spirit communication would embrace a range of physical phenomena as well as distinct messages from, and contact with, spirit entities.

2. There is, I must add, a good deal of literature concerning certain mediums, although much of this is restricted to mediums who practised in the early days of the Spiritualist movement.

References

Barrow, L. (1986). *Independent spirits: Spiritualism and English plebeians, 1850-1910*. London: Routledge.

Bourke, J (2007). "Rachel comforted": Spiritualism and the reconstruction of the body after death. In M. Mitchell (Ed.). *Remember me: Constructing immortality. Beliefs on immortality, life, and death* (pp. 51-63). New York and London: Routledge.

Bowie, F. (2012). Devising methods for the ethnographic study of the afterlife: Cognition, empathy and engagement. In J. Hunter (Ed.) *Paranthropology: Anthropological approaches to the paranormal* (pp. 99-106). Bristol: Paranthropology.

Carroll, B.E. (2000). "A higher power to feel": Spiritualism, grief, and Victorian manhood. *Men and Masculinities, 3* (1), 3-29

Cerullo, J.J. (1982). *The secularization of the soul: Psychical research in modern Britain.* Philadelphia: Institute for the Study of Human Issues.

Emmons, C.F. (2000). On becoming a spirit medium in a "rational society." *Anthropology of Consciousness, 12* (1-2), 71-82

Emmons, C.F. & Emmons, P. (2003). *Guided by spirit: A journey into the mind of the medium.* New York, Lincoln and Shanghai: Writers Club Press.

Fontana, D. (2003). *Psychology, religion, and spirituality.* Oxford: Blackwell.

Gauld, A. (1982). *Mediumship and survival: A century of investigations.* London: Paladin.

Gilbert, H. (2008). *Speaking of spirits: Representations and experiences of the spirit world in British spirit mediumship,* unpublished doctoral thesis, University of York.

Goulet, J.-G. & Miller, B.G. (Eds.) (2007). *Extraordinary anthropology: Transformations in the field.* Lincoln & London: University of Nebraska Press.

Hazelgrove, J. (2000). *Spiritualism and British society between the wars.* Manchester: Manchester University Press

Hess, D. (1993). *Science in the New Age: The paranormal, its defenders and debunkers, and American culture.* University of Wisconsin Ptess

Hunter, J. (2009). *Talking with the spirits: An experiential exploration of contemporary trance and physical mediumship,* unpublished undergraduate dissertation, University of Bristol.

Hunter, J. (2010). Talking with the spirits: More than a social reality? *Paranormal Review, 54,* 9-13.

Klass, D., Silverman, P.R. & Nickman, S. (Eds.) (1996). *Continuing bonds: New understandings of grief.* Philadelphia: Taylor and Francis

McClenon, J. (1994). *Wondrous events: Foundations of religious belief.* Philadelphia: University of Pennsylvania Press.

McMullin, S. (2004). *Anatomy of a séance: A history of spirit communication in Canada.* McGill-Queen's University Press

Meintel, D. (2007). When the extraordinary hits home: Experiencing Spiritualism. In J.-G. Goulet & B. G. Miller (Eds.), *Extraordinary anthropology: Transformations in the field* (pp. 124-157). Lincoln & London: University of Nebraska Press.

Northcote, J. (2004). *The paranormal and the politics of truth: A sociological account.* Exeter: Imprint Academic

Oppenheim, J. (1988). *The other world: Spiritualism and psychical research in England, 1850-1914.* Cambridge: Cambridge University Press.

Owen, A. (1990). *The darkened room: Women, power and Spiritualism in late Victorian England.* Philadelphia: University of Pennsylvania Press.

Wooffitt, R. (1992). *Telling tales of the unexpected: The organisation of factual discourse.* Hemel Hempstead: Harvester Wheatsheaf.

Wooffitt, R. (2006). *The language of mediums and psychics: The social organization of everyday miracles.* Aldershot & Burlington: Ashgate

Young, D.E. & Goulet, J.-G. (Eds.) (1994). *Being changed by cross-cultural encounters: The anthropology of extraordinary experience.* Broadview Press

Spiritual healing at Lily Dale, NY. Photograph by Shannon Taggart.

SPIRITS IN THE CITY: EXAMPLES FROM MONTREAL

DEIRDRE MEINTEL

In this chapter, I try to show that direct spirit contact is part of normal everyday reality for many people in the city of Montreal, situated in the province of Quebec, Canada. Most of the cases of spirit contact I will present here concern a Spiritualist congregation that I have followed for many years. Most of this chapter will focus on Spiritualist beliefs and practices surrounding spirit contact as I have had occasion to observe them. Spiritualists describe contact with a plethora of spirit entities that come about by various means. Even those who do not experience such spirits themselves often believe that others around them do; for example, members of the same spiritual development group, mediums they know, and so on. Many consider urban spaces – homes, in particular – as the habitat of spirit entities with whom it is possible to interact. Such entities may be evil spirits, benevolent ones or "lost souls" trapped on the earth plane, unable to move on to the world of spirit without help.

After discussing Spiritualist beliefs and practices, I will look at some of the other religious movements active in Montreal where spirit contact is central and that, in some cases, overlap with Spiritualist networks and inspire Spiritualist ritual practice.

Finally, I will consider the ways in which Montreal's religious landscape has been shaped by factors that affect many other large cities in North America and Europe. At the same time, I will argue that, somewhat paradoxically, Quebec's rapid secularization, beginning in the 1960s, may have contributed to shaping a religious landscape in which many are attracted to groups that encourage members to call upon and interact with spirits. First, though, let us take a brief look at the Quebec social and historical context as regards religion.

The Quebec Context

Spiritualism, like the other religious currents mentioned herein, took root in Quebec following the 'Quiet Revolution' (*la Révolution tranquille*), a time of dramatic social change in the province (1960-1966) (Linteau *et al.*, 1989). During this period, the State took over the social welfare, educational and health systems that had long been the fief of the Catholic Church. Meanwhile the religious practice of the Catholic faithful was declining rapidly (Linteau *et al.*, p. 336; Bibby, 1990), and the ranks of the clergy and other religious devotees were depleted. As the political system became liberalized in the 1960s, Quebec society became thoroughly secularized and far more open to religious diversity (Linteau *et al.*, 1989). The new climate of religious freedom has made for an ever more diversified religious landscape.

Recent years have seen an ever-increasing number of places of worship in the province, especially in cities (Germain & Gagnon, 2003). In part, this is due to immigration. The relative demographic weight of immigrants in the population has been growing steadily: in 1996 immigrants accounted for 9.4 per cent of the province's population, whereas in 1951 they represented only 5.6 per cent (Immigration et Communautés Culturelles Québec, 2004). By 2001, according to census data, this figure had risen to almost 10 per cent. The number of Muslims grew 140 per cent over the 1990s (MRCI, 2002), mostly due to immigration from Lebanon, Morocco and Algeria, as well as West Africa and Pakistan. Concerns about the integration of this culturally diverse religious group have recently stirred debate over the adjustments to be made by the receiving society to new religious groups.

Religious diversity among native-born Québécois has also grown a great deal in recent years. While some have converted to Islam, Buddhism, or to Evangelical religions, others have discovered forms of spirituality that have either developed in situ from various sources, or that present themselves as contemporary versions of ancient traditions such as Druidism, Native inspired shamanism, Wicca and so on. Note that none of these require conversion, such that those brought up Catholic sometimes retain certain elements of Catholic identity and religious observance (Meintel, 2011). Many of these spiritual currents involve beliefs in spirits and spirit contact. One of the findings from the broad study I am carrying out with a number of other researchers, as well as in my work on Spiritualists, is that that the mainstream Québécois (French-speaking, born in Quebec and baptized in the Catholic faith), who frequent such groups are unlikely to discuss this openly with others. Groups that encourage spirit contact thus tend to remain under the radar, so to speak.

Spiritualism in Quebec

Montreal Spiritualists are part of a movement that began in 1848 in the New York State (U.S.A.) in a religious climate already stirred up by Transcendentalism and Swedenborgianism (Aubrée & Laplantine, 1990; Nelson, 1969). Over the latter part of the nineteenth century, the movement spread across the United States and across the Atlantic to England and points beyond, influencing French Kardecism as well as other European religious currents. Eventually, the movement was to come back across the Atlantic to Montreal. In 1967 a married couple of ministers from England founded the Spiritualist Church of Healing (SCH),[1] where my research is focused. The founders departed in 1975, leaving a young francophone minister, Michel, as pastor. Frenchspeaking Québécois, mostly disaffected Catholics, soon composed the great majority of the membership. At present its ministers, including Michel, are of Catholic background. Most in the congregation grew up in working-class Francophone neighbourhoods in Montreal and nearby suburbs; many have resided in the same general area all their lives.

At present, those who attend services at the church (many more than its official membership of 275), are mostly natives of Montreal and the surrounding area whose first language is French. The congregation has become noticeably younger over the last few years; most attending services are adults from about thirty to late sixties, with a smattering of older and younger individuals. Usually women well outnumber men at services, though there are as many men as women among the ministers, mediums and healers who practice in the SCH. Unlike most Spiritualist groups in Montreal, the SCH has legal status as a church, such that its ministers perform marriages, including gay marriages, and officiate at funerals. Requests for such rituals often come from non-members who seek to mark these rites of passage in a religious fashion but without constraints as to their religious belonging or practice.

Like Spiritualist groups in the US (Zaretsky, 1974, p.77) the SCH's financial means are limited. Donations and the collections that mark every service barely cover rent, heating and the air conditioning installed a few years ago. None of the five ministers, who include two women, are salaried, nor are the mediums and healers who contribute their efforts at church services. The SCH occupies a rented space on two floors on a slightly seedy strip of a central artery located near a metro station in downtown Montreal.

Marked only by a cardboard sign in its narrow doorway, the church is easy to miss among the many small businesses on the block. Inside, the decor is simple, adorned with symbols from the Catholic tradition, and others. A Bible (King James version) is on prominent display. The walls are hung with paintings, in a 'New Age' style, of angels and other spirit entities, including several that depict Natives, as well as one of Jesus.

Upstairs, one finds a meeting room lined with bookshelves (the SCH library), a kitchenette and a small office. On this floor, more traditional sacred images are displayed, including one of the Sacred Heart. Decorations adorn the church for holidays, including Valentine's Day, Mother's Day and St. Patrick's Day as well as Christmas and Easter.

The regular activities of this church are described in greater detail elsewhere (see Meintel, 2003, 2007a, 2007b), so I will only summarize them here. Services include prayers, hymns (mostly Protestant classics translated into French), and clairvoyant messages given by mediums. Occasionally services feature a medium going into 'deep trance'; i.e. channelling, about which more at a later point. A healing service held on Sundays features the 'laying on of hands.' Apart from services, closed groups ('circles' in classical Spiritualist terminology), meet biweekly or on a weekly basis under the supervision of a minister-medium. The object of these groups is to develop the members' spiritual gifts, especially their clairvoyant capacities, under the supervision of an experienced Spiritualist minister/medium. After a guided meditation, members practice one or another form of clairvoyance. For example, they might be asked to 'see' what several others in the group need on a spiritual or material level. Alternatively, they might be asked to place a personal object on a tray and then (in the dark), choose an object and sense what they can from holding it. Often Michel, the pastor, gives a number of messages at the end of the session and occasionally channels one of his guides, or several in turn.

Like the other six Spiritualist groups in Montreal I have observed (I have had limited contact with a seventh), the SCH shares the basic principles of Spiritualism, though the vocabulary is variable. These include the existence of God, sometimes termed 'Universal Intelligence,' individuals' responsibility for their actions, the consequences of their actions in the afterlife, the continued existence of the human soul and the eternal progress available to it, and the possibility of communion with spirits, and so on. Of the seven groups in Montreal, the SCH is the most Francophone – which means that its members are likely to have grown up Catholic.

The Research

The research on Spiritualists is based principally on participant observation at SCH activities, with occasional interviews with the pastor, Michel, and interviews with about 20 key informants (evenly divided by gender). Key informants are mostly in their forties and fifties, with several who are a bit older, and have been going to a closed group for at least three years. Most of the study participants work full-time, some in the lower echelons of the health care system (for example as home caregivers and massage therapists), some in service jobs (sales clerk, for example), and others in skilled occupations (as mechanics and so on). Some older individuals finished high school as adults, or not at all, and few have post-secondary education, (though this seems to be changing among younger members of the congregation). Most have been divorced at least once and are in a stable couple relationship, as is the case for Michel.

The other religious currents mentioned herein have been studied in a broader project conducted over the past three years by a team of researchers[2] on religious currents established in Quebec since the 1960s, whether in long-established religions or those new to the province (Meintel, 2011; Mossière & Meintel, 2010)

Contacting the Spirits

Central to Spiritualist beliefs is the notion that direct contact with the spirits of deceased persons is possible. Apart from the basic principles mentioned earlier, my informants, like other Spiritualists (Meintel, 2005),[3] believe that we all have spirit guides who help us in daily life and that we all (including non-religious persons), have received spiritual gifts, be they for different types of healing (by the laying on of hands, at a distance...) or clairvoyance. The latter takes various forms: via objects in psychometry, through 'feeling' (*le sentir*), visions, and clairaudience (hearing sounds and words from the spirit world). Other gifts include astral projection (being in several places at once), spirit-inspired speech and art, automatic writing (little practiced in the SCH), and so on. These gifts can be developed and employed to do harm or good.

Spiritualist tradition holds that everyone has a number of spirit guides. The most important of the Spirit guides is the 'Gatekeeper,' one who allows other spirits to come through or prevents them from doing so in cases where mediums go into 'deep trance,' also known as channelling. Typically, in the SCH, the Gatekeeper is the spirit of a Native. It is interesting to note that British Spiritualist authors of earlier generations often make mention of 'Red Indian spirit guides' (for example, Marryat, 1920), something that Nelson (1969, pp. 55-58; 75-76) notes as well. A number of those who are very involved in the SCH as healers and mediums, mostly men, also pursue neo-shamanistic practices (sweat lodges, vision quests); some have Native spiritual teachers, but not necessarily from Quebec. The influence of neo-shamanism (often termed 'Native Spirituality' by those concerned), is often felt at the SCH. Besides representations of Natives and Native spirits on the walls of the main hall of the church, one notes the shamanistic drumming that has accompanied the healing service on a few occasions. Individuals bring dreamcatchers, stones they consider sacred, and other shamanistic artefacts (along with those of other religious traditions) to Michel, who prays over them for the union between the owner of the object and the spirits that govern it.

Spirit guides, especially Native guides, are often mentioned in Spiritualist services and other religious activities. Michel occasionally channels his Native 'gatekeeper' guide (termed 'spirit control in older Spiritualist writings, see, for example, Barbanell, 1942, p. 85), in meetings of the closed groups and, more rarely, at church services. He may also channel other spirits including a Catholic nun, a male Chinese guide, a young Inuit boy (considered a 'Joy Guide' since he brings playfulness, humour and laughter), a rabbi who lived centuries ago, and a man who was a natural scientist in his earthly life. One of the female ministers (all the ministers are mediums), occasionally channels her male Native guide. Michel holds that Native guides are so often gatekeepers because 'they were a spiritual people and we are on their land.' It is possible that the proximity to Native Americans affected Spiritualism in its beginnings in upstate New York (home to the Iroquois nation), because 'Red Indian' guides are often mentioned in British Spiritualist works (for example Barbanell, 1942; Marryat, 1920).

On the negative side, the Spiritualists I have interviewed all believe in 'evil entities' ('*mauvaises entités*'). While they may or may not believe in Satan, they hold that there are spirits of deceased individuals who do harm by attacking people or seducing them away from their spiritual development, sometimes in a literal sense, as we shall see. Virtually all those I have interviewed had some such experience to recount. For several, their first contact with Michel, and thus with the SCH, was when they sought help for dealing with attacks by harmful spirits; sometimes at the instigation of persons who wished them ill.

All the foregoing beliefs form part of the lived experience of my informants, or those close to them. Many have seen angels, spirit guides and other spirit entities, and on rare occasions, negative ones. In fact, belief in guides and healing is integral to the ritual activities of the SCH, as well as the belief in mediumship, or communication with spirits. Many exercises that are done in the closed groups are oriented toward helping participants develop contact with their spirit guides. Angels are mentioned in the seven principles, and several of my informants report seeing them. Animals are believed to have spirits and a life after death, and at church services mediums often give messages to those present concerning their pets, living and deceased.[4] Also, thoughts are believed to take perceptible form; a medium can see, for example, 'negative thought forms' around an individual who is afflicted by the jealousy of others.

Another category of beliefs includes notions that are widely subscribed to by Spiritualists but are not considered integral to Spiritualism. Many are taken from other traditions; for instance beliefs about reincarnation and chakras. Unlike many who frequent the SCH, Michel is sceptical about reincarnation. On the other hand, he holds, as do many Spiritualists, that a pre-birth phase of life begins about a year and a half before conception; thus he often sees children in clairvoyance long before they are conceived. In the same category of beliefs we also find what I call the 'Catholic substratum' of religious belief and devotion. While not essential to Spiritualism, Catholic beliefs and practices are often mentioned by ministers and mediums at the SCH. Such references flavour the atmosphere of this group and permit many who still maintain ties with Catholicism, to feel at home there.

Finally, there is a kind of Spiritualist 'lore'; that is, notions current among Spiritualists that some believe (for example, the idea that a candle suddenly going out is the act of a lower spirit entity). Most of my informants have occasional recourse to astrology, tarot, crystals and so on, but clearly separate such practices from Spiritualism itself.

Belief in spirit contact is central to all SCH activities, including the meetings of the closed group. This belief is reaffirmed when the basic principles of Spiritualism are read aloud at the beginning of church services, as happens often. Moreover, spirit guides are often invoked in the guided meditations that mark many services as well as the meetings of the closed group. Here, when members exchange information after the clairvoyance exercise, they often say that they do not know how to interpret what they saw. Typically Michel will tell them to 'ask your guides.' During church services when mediums address messages to individuals in the congregation, they often mention 'your Native guide,' an ancestor or some other spirit entity. As mentioned, channelling by Michel or another minister is occasionally featured in SCH services. One of the mediums sometimes does portraits of the guides she sees around individuals.

For Spiritualists (and this is true of the other groups mentioned later in the chapter), belief in the existence of spirits, and the possibility of direct contact with them, is in no way an abstraction; rather, it is part of lived experience, be it their own or that of others whom they trust. All my informants have received healing and clairvoyant messages. Most also act as healers themselves in the weekly healing service; some have given messages to others at church services in the role of apprentice mediums, and all have done so in the context of the closed group. For these activities, participants invoke their spirit guides, or often 'my guides and angels,' as a matter of course; guides are seen as partners in the process of transmitting healing or clairvoyance, and angels as protectors.

Experiential Narratives

Marie, not quite 50 when I interviewed her, has a university degree. Like most in the SCH she is of Catholic background. She has known Michel for over 25 years, and after a long battle with serious illness began to work as a medium and healer at the SCH.

> When my guides of Light and angels work with me, I get things just like I'm seeing you now, it's like a screen that's in front of me…I hear, I feel, there are images, there are symbols…

Elisabeth, in her late 50s at the time of the interview, highlights the role of her guides in her healing work at the SCH:

> I see colours. The first time, for the whole healing service, I saw colours for each person (I worked on)…I didn't know why this person had one colour and that person another. But I told myself, the important thing is transmitting, to see the colour and work with it … I'll understand later on; the guides will inspire me and…in fact, they did and they gave me other tools to work with, too.

As regards clairvoyance, she says that over time, 'I've learned to work more with my guides for giving clairvoyance and to trust them.' Now that she is speaking from the pulpit on occasion, Elisabeth has found that instead of writing her presentation in advance, as she did at first, 'I feel more and more that I should do them direct. I have a guide who is pushing me to go direct, "cold," so to speak, without paper or anything.'

Contact with spirits goes well beyond ritual contexts. Indeed, calling upon their spirit guides is a normal part of life for all my key informants, whether or not they work as mediums or healers at the SCH. All have developed (without direction from Michel), a personal, often eclectic, routine of spiritual practices; including meditation, prayer, and spiritual reading, amongst others. A number incorporate neo-shamanistic practices as well (sweat lodges, for example). All pray for 'protection' (from negative energies) on a daily basis. Most have felt the physical presence of the spirit of a deceased loved one or pet, and most have felt the presence of spirit guides.

In some cases, saints from the Catholic pantheon are invoked.

> I pray all day long, no special time…driving my truck, I don't even listen to music…Sometimes, going from Montreal to where I live – it's an hour – I repeat for the hour "Merci Jésus, for being with me," like a mantra, or "Saint Joseph, pray for me, hear my prayer." It's always working…

Nancy, a massage therapist, finds that

> When I'm giving massages, I feel presences…Sometimes I have the impression that they've taken my hands and are guiding me. Sometimes they are behind the person. Sometimes in front of them…I'll get colours, I ask, "What's up with that?" Sometimes I give the information to the person, sometimes I just send it to the person and it works by itself.

Daniel, a former machinist, divorced and now remarried, suffered serious injury in a work-related accident and now holds a desk job in hospital. He speaks of his experiences meditating at home after his accident:

> I do astral travelling in meditation. It's conscious, very much so. I've seen myself go out of my body…and my gatekeeper, he's a chief from Arizona…When I started seeing him, he told me his name. Michel said I got it right…One time I

saw the gatekeeper guide and he took me away, I walked up a pyramid, there was a sort of goddess figure sitting in the lotus position…and then it was cut off because the phone rang. It was the hospital phoning me to say I'd be operated on such and such a date.

Love, Sex and Spirits

Matters of romantic love are often marked by encounters with spirit, as was the case for Daniel. At a time when his relationship with Annie, now his wife, was beginning to deepen, he recounts seeing an angel over their bed.

> He went up to the ceiling; he was all over the wall…huge. His wings went from one wall to the other. I wasn't in meditation or anything. Annie was sleeping, then she really freaked out (when I told her).

For several Spiritualists, problems of love and sexuality have involved experiences of unwanted 'astral projection'; that is, the spirit presence of a living person. Interestingly, the latter is usually presumed to be another Spiritualist, someone with mediumistic capacities. Roger, 62 and long divorced, recounts:

> (When) I was still with my ex-wife, I was in bed one night, and I felt someone pulling me out of the bed…I felt so bad and my heart started shaking…Because I felt someone was pulling me out of there to go somewhere else…Not long after that, I separated (from my wife)…Like it threw me out of the bed, you know?…There was someone pulling me. I know there was someone…At the church back then, we had some people that were doing this, you know, going into someone's house (in spirit form)…

For Nancy, the astral presence was that of Etienne, a healer she had met at the SCH:

> He seems nice, but he projected himself into my place. He came physically, but then he comes in another form, and he would wake me up in a sexual way, and it wasn't a good feeling. It was, like, his astral travel…Then he came several times and did things to make my friends go away… My friend, she said, "Nancy, I have the impression that he wants me to go. I can't believe how much I just want to leave."

In language reminiscent of Favret-Saada (1977), Nancy concludes: "So I asked Michel for help because I wasn't strong enough. Etienne, he's strong, he's really, really strong."

Spirits considered malevolent may also approach the living in a sexual way. When a young woman mentioned such an experience in the closed group, Michel was quite concerned. In his view, this is the work of a 'lower entity,' the spirit of a deceased person who wants to control the person he or she has targeted. Daniel, for example, relates how a female spirit 'attacked' (his term) him.

> I've always had a weakness for beautiful women. Once, in the beginning (of his contact with Michel and the SCH) I was sleeping, it was as if I was dreaming but it wasn't a dream. I was there, really conscious of everything going on. And this energy comes out on me. It was like an extremely beautiful woman, a naked woman, and she got on me and she started making love to me. And I couldn't stop and I didn't want to stop. That's the worst part. I didn't want to stop…and it went all the way.

From a Spiritualist point of view, Daniel's encounter with a seductive spirit was an attempt to derail his new spiritual practice. Michel often reminds his students of the importance of praying regularly for spiritual protection and counsels them to avoid 'esoteric' environments and individuals; that is, those who contact spirits outside of a religious framework for personal power or gain.

Lower Entities

Virtually all of my informants have experienced attacks by 'evil entities,' or at least their unwanted presence. Evil entities are the spirits of the dead who are at a low point in their spiritual development and seek to control living persons, do them harm, pull them away from their spiritual development and sometimes, seduce them into sexual dependency. The more general category of 'lower entities' also includes wandering or 'vagabond' spirits, those who are dead but cannot grasp the fact and who haunt spaces inhabited by the living, either because of sudden death, or because they did not believe in an afterlife. Very occasionally, experienced mediums might form a 'rescue circle' where one goes into deep trance and incorporates the lost spirit and another helps the spirit to move away from the earth plane and into the next life.

> After the clairvoyance exercise, it's Nancy's turn and she doesn't talk. She starts sobbing, eyes closed. Michel goes to hear and does what looks like healing, except that this time he took both her hands. (Usually healers don't touch the other person.) Eventually she comes to, smiles, has no memory of crying. Michel explains that it was someone caught in a transatlantic plane crash that was all over the news last week. Nancy had told us of a premonitory dream she had several weeks before the crash that she found very frightening. Then it was confirmed. On this occasion,

Michel tells us it was the spirit of a person on that plane.
(Field notes, closed group, November 11, 1999)

Later Michel explains that what looked like healing was an effort
to help the lost spirit move on his way, and secondarily, to help
Nancy not to suffer further effects of his presence. Several of
my informants believe their young daughters have been beset
by unwanted spirit presences. Some report that they have been
personally attacked themselves by evil entities and that their
homes have been the site of nefarious spirit activity in the past.
In some cases, those so attacked believe this to be the result of
'black magic' (*la magie noire*) of individuals who sought to do
them harm.

Free will has an important place in Spiritualist thinking, such
that each is responsible for his own actions. At the same time,
belief in spirit shapes everyday life practices. Spirit guides are
called upon for help and protection, while negative spirits are seen
as aiding and abetting negative tendencies and behaviours, such
as drifting away from spiritual practice. Conducting mediumistic
activities, and even meditation, can leave one vulnerable to evil
spirits; thus the importance given to the 'Our Father' at the
beginning and the end of closed group meetings. Feeling the
presence of guides and angels, and sometimes actually seeing
them is part of the experience of the Spiritualists I have met.
Moreover, the spirit existence of the living enters into ordinary
lived experience through astral projection.

Spirit Contact in the Montreal Context

Direct contact with spirits is a feature of a number of other groups
that are part of Montreal's religious landscape as it has developed
in recent decades. We find, for example, an Umbanda group that
functions as an integral part of a 'temple' in Brazil. While most

of its members are of European or Québécois background, its rituals (in Brazilian Portuguese), centre on incorporation of the same types of spirits as in Brazil (Hernandez, 2009). We also find a number of Neo-Shamanic groups, including Reclaiming Witchcraft, Core Shamanism,[5] and a Native spirituality group. These groups do not have the same working class flavour as most Spiritualist congregations in the city; rather, they attract mostly students and members of the liberal professions. Moreover, they rely on the Internet, more than do the Spiritualists, for organizing ritual activities. However, because a number of Spiritualists are engaged with Native Spirituality, there is a certain overlap between the SCH membership and the Neo-Shamanic groups. For example, a long-time member of the SCH holds sweat lodges that attract individuals from various Neo-Shamanic groups.

In Neo-Shamanic groups, regular participants learn to do shamanic travel in order to contact their personal spirits, be they ancestors, power animal spirits, or spirit guides (Normandin, 2010; Corneiller, forthcoming). Drumming (live or recorded) and dancing may help induce shamanic travel. SCH activities show evidence of Neo-Shamanic influences; for example, Native style drumming at the healing service; a clairvoyance exercise in the closed group, focusing on contact with a spirit guide in animal form; the dream-catchers, sage and stones brought by members to closed group meetings.

Spiritualist groups, which occupy private homes or rented spaces, are almost invisible in the city landscape. Likewise, the other groups that give importance to spirit contact are mostly invisible socially. When Neo-Shamanic groups meet indoors, it is normally in private homes, as does the Umbanda group. More rarely, a number of Wiccan groups may gather together in a rented public space, as did many from druidic and Neo-Shamanic groups throughout Quebec for an event designed to bring English and French-speaking practitioners together. Neo-Shamanic rituals are often held in public green space, but in

such a way as to attract little attention (Mount Royal Park, in
the central part of the city is a popular site).[6] To some extent, this
discretion is a consequence of the limited resources available to
such groups, who do not have the means to purchase buildings
or land of their own. However, as I will argue in the following
section, the reasons for the limited visibility of groups that
engage in spirit contact go beyond the economic.

The Private, the Public and the Secret

Many scholars write of the 'privatization' of religion in modern,
secular societies (For example Hervieu-Léger, 2003; Luckmann,
2003). We find that religion (or 'spiritual practice' as many of
those concerned call it), is not only part of the private sphere, but
also a matter of great discretion among members of the social
majority (French-speaking, native-born Québécois). Montreal,
and more generally Quebec, presents a very interesting case of
unequal visibility and invisibility of religious (spiritual) groups.
The Catholic history of Montreal is omnipresent in the great
number of Catholic churches, presbyteries, convents and schools,
some of which now have other functions. Catholic church bells
can often be heard in most central city neighbourhoods. However,
this visibility does not necessarily extend to the actual religious
practice, often hybrid, of those who identify as Catholic.

Most of those in the groups mentioned herein, including the
Spiritualists, do not discuss their religious beliefs with colleagues,
friends or family members, unless they sense receptiveness. Older
practitioners of Wicca and Druidry are often secretive, sometimes
out of religious conviction that rituals and magical practices must
be kept secret to retain their power, but also due to the fact that
some have suffered harassment or even been fired from jobs for
religious reasons in decades past. According to Roberts (2010),
French-speaking covens are especially secretive, no doubt in part

due to the hegemony of Catholicism in their social milieu. In today's context, religious actors use discretion as a way to avoid ridicule and conflict and, for professionals, to avoid scandalizing their clients.

Thus, activities oriented towards making contact with spirits tend to take place either outdoors in secluded locations, or in the initiator's home or that of another group member. At the same time, private homes seem to be focal points for negative spirit influences. Many Spiritualists I have met have experienced these in the past; at the same time the notion that homes are vulnerable to 'invasion' by evil forces seems to go far beyond the Spiritualist milieu.[7] Interestingly, I find no mention of such attacks on homes in the older Spiritualist writings I have consulted.

Michel is the only medium at the SCH who performs exorcisms; these are done in private, and never during church services. He receives hundreds of calls every year for help in exorcizing homes of troublesome spirits. More rarely he exorcizes individuals, often those who have frequented esoteric milieus or who have a history of drug addiction. Quite a number of such requests come from persons of Mediterranean background (Italian, Greek, Portuguese), but many others come from mainstream Québécois.

What is most interesting here is the fact that requests for exorcism concern the private spaces inhabited by those who are afflicted by troublesome spirits; moreover, those who feel afflicted are not usually Spiritualists, but rather come from a variety of religious backgrounds, probably Catholic for the most part. In hunting and gathering societies, including Native North Americans, Nature is sacred, and certain natural sites may be surrounded by taboos. In present-day Montreal, it seems that, along with those actively involved in contact with spirits for positive ends, there are many more who believe that spirits can harm them in their domestic environment.

It is as though not only religion, but also spirit presence – positive or negative – has been 'privatized' and thus remains largely invisible. Though this invisibility extends to many other types of religions in the Montreal context, it is all the more pronounced in the case of religions and spiritualities where spirit contact is normalized. However, there is reason to believe that this may change, given that many younger Pagans are less secretive than older ones about their practices and sometimes hold rituals open to the public. They are also likely to be visible in certain settings (such as at the Pagan Society at Concordia University in Montreal, for example), as well as on the Internet. This openness does not extend to those of older age groups, especially those who feel that their professional or community status would be compromised if their activities involving spirit contact were known. Whereas academic researchers in Brazil are sometimes known to conduct Umbanda rituals when sending out grant proposals, most spirit contact by liberal professionals in Quebec is likely to be conducted in private – at least for the time being.

Conclusion

One might well ask, how typical is Montreal's religious scene, or at least the part we have described here, as compared with those to be found in other large urban centres in North America and Europe? As I have discussed elsewhere (Meintel and Le Blanc, 2003), factors related to globalization are at work in all these contexts, including: 1) immigration from different and more varied regions, bringing new religious influences; 2) greater mobility of the population as a whole, such that travellers returning home may bring new religious perspectives with them; 3) the role of the Internet in religious networks and in the diffusion of religious symbols, ideologies and socialization. More specifically, as regards religious currents where spirit contact is central, one might also note the emergence of Native spiritual leaders who develop non-Native clienteles and whose sphere of influence goes beyond Native milieus, and in some cases extends beyond North America.

However, the particularly effervescent character of contemporary religious diversity in Quebec owes itself not only to an ever-growing supply of new religious resources, but also to what seems to be a widespread 'demand' for a certain kind of religious resource. It was only in the 1960s that Catholicism lost its political and social hegemony in the province. In but a few years, the normative frameworks of the past were overturned, with dramatic effects on family structures (access to divorce, birth control and abortion, widespread cohabitation without marriage, and so on). Old-stock Francophones who comprise the social majority, as well as many more recent arrivals, remain at least nominally Catholic; moreover, the sociologists Lemieux and Millot (1992) find that most Québécois are believers in a transcendent reality. At the same time, affirming religious convictions is somehow associated with the 'great darkness' (*la Grande noirceur*) of the years of clerical domination.

Over years of research in Quebec, I have found almost no self-declared atheists, though many claim to have 'no religion' (i.e., no particular denominational affiliation). While conventional Catholic practice has declined greatly, there seems to be widespread searching for what I call 'tools for transcendence'; that is a shared connection with the sacred and frameworks of meaning for dealing with the problems of modern life. This seems to be more so the case in Montreal than elsewhere, though this is difficult to demonstrate in quantitative terms. The very rapid secularization of Quebec has not only opened the province to new religious influences, but has also generated new needs for meaning, thus creating clienteles for religious groups, such as SCH. Although a few Catholics convert to Islam, or Evangelical churches, many more seek spiritual sustenance in other types of religious groups, sometimes in combination with Catholic practice. These are movements defined by subjective experience rather than doctrines and dogmas, where boundaries are fluid and conversion a non-issue. In such religious currents, spirit contact is often an important means of bringing the sacred into deeply felt, embodied experience.

Notes

1. Pseudonyms are used for the church and for individuals mentioned in the text.

2. Supported by the Fonds Québécois pour la Recherche Sur la Société et la Culture (Quebec) and the Social Sciences and Humanities Research Council (Canada).

3. I refer to my informants at the SCH as "Spiritualists"; however, few of them think of Spiritualism in terms of denominational affiliation.

4. The belief that pets share in the afterlife seems to have long been widespread in Spiritualism (e.g., Barbanell, 1940).

5. Core Shamanism was developed by the anthropologist Michael Harner. For further information, see http://www.shamanism.org/ (consulted on August 18, 2009).

6. Some Montreal Wiccans hold that only outdoor green spaces should be used, while others; e.g.,'Urban Pagans', use spaces such as the subway, abandoned warehouses and so on (Roberts, 2009)

7. It is well known that Catholic dioceses in Europe as in North America have experienced an increase in requests for exorcisms in recent years (see Chossonery, 1999).

References

Aubrée, M., & Laplantine, F. (1990). *La table, le livre et les esprits: Naissance, évolution et actualité du mouvement social spirite entre France et Brésil*. Paris: Éditions J. C. Lattès.

Barbanell, S. (1940). *When your animal dies*. London: Psychic Press.

Barbanell, S. (1942). *When a child dies*. London: Psychic Book Club.

Bibby, R. (1990). La religion à la carte au Québec: Une analyse de tendances. *Sociologie et Societies*, 22, 133.

Chossonery, C. (1999). Le renouveau de l'exorcisme. In P. Wallon (Ed.), *Guérir l'âme et le corps* (pp.126-126). Paris: Albin Michel.

Corneillier, F. (Forthcoming). *Le groupe spirituel Shamanika*. Working Paper. Groupe de Recherche Diversité Urbaine, Montréal. Digital version: http://www.grdu. umontreal.ca/en/publications-workingpapers.html

Favret-Saada, J. (1977). *Les mots, la mort, les sorts*. Paris: Gallimard.

Germain, A., & Gagnon, J. -E. (2003). L'autre, là où on ne l'attendait pas ... Les lieux de culte des minorités ethno-religieuses. In M. Venne (Ed.), *L'annuaire du Québec* 2004 (pp.294-301). Saint-Laurent, Québec: Fides.

Hernandez, A. (2009). *Un groupe umbanda à Montréal*. Working Paper. Groupe de recherche Diversité Urbaine, Montréal. Digital version: http:// www.grdu.umontreal.ca/en/publications-workingpapers.html

Hervieu-Léger, D. (2003). Pour une sociologie des "modernites religieuses multiples": Une autre approche de la "religion invisible" des sociétés européennes. *Social Compass*, 50, 287-295.

Immigration et Communautés Culturelles Québec (2004). *Population immigrée recensée au Québec et dans les régions en 2001: caractéristiques générales*. Quebec: Gouvernement du Québec.

Lemieux, R., & Milot, M. (Eds.) (1992). *Les croyances des Québécois: Esquisses pour une approche empirique. Les Cahiers de recherches en sciences de la religion* 11. Quebec: Université Laval.

Linteau, P.-A., Durocher, R., Robert, J.-C., & Ricard, F. (1989). *Histoire du Québec contemporain, Tome II: Le Québec depuis 1930*. Montréal: Éditions Boréal.

Luckmann, T. (2003). Transformations of religion and morality in modern Europe. *Social Compass*, 50, 275-285.

Marryat, F. (1920). *There is no death*. London: William Rider and Son, Ltd.

Meintel, D. (2011). Catholicism as living memory in a Montreal Spiritualist congregation. *Quebec Studies, 52*, 69-86.

Meintel, D. (2007a). When there is no conversion: Spiritualists and personal religious change. *Anthropologica*, 49, 149-162.

Meintel, D. (2007b). When the extraordinary hits home: Experiencing Spiritualism. In J.-G. Goulet and B. G. Miller (Eds.), *Extraordinary anthropology: Transformations in the field* (pp.124-157). Lincoln, NE: University of Nebraska.

Meintel, D. (2003) La stabilité dans le flou: Parcours religieux et identités de Spiritualistes. *Anthropologie et Sociétés, 27*, 35-64.

Meintel, D., & LeBlanc, M. N. (2003). La mobilité du religieux à l'ère de la globalisation. *Anthropologie et Sociétés, 27*, 5-11.

Mossière, G., & Meintel, D., (2010). Tradition and transition: Immigrant religious communities in urban contexts (Quebec). In R.D. Hecht and V.F. Biondo (Eds.), *Religion in the practice of daily life*. Santa Barbara, CA: Praeger.

Nelson, G. K. (1969). *Spiritualism and society*. London: Routledge and Kegan Paul.

Normandin, A. (2010). *Le cercle de tambours montréalais de la fondation des etudes chamaniques: Une étude ethnographique*. Working Paper. Groupe de Recherche Diversité Urbaine, Montréal. Digital version: http://www. grdu.umontreal.ca/en/publications-workingpapers.html

Roberts, R. (2010). *La communauté "Reclaiming" de Montréal.* Working Paper. Groupe de Recherche Diversité Urbaine, Montréal. Digital version: http://www.grdu.umontreal.ca/en/publications-workingpapers.html

Roberts, R. (2009). *"It's all a giant web": Syncretism, agency and (re)connection in a contemporary pagan community.* Unpublished Masters thesis, Départment d'Anthropologie, Université de Montréal.

Zaretsky, I. I. (1974). In the beginning was the word: The relationship of language to social organization in Spiritualist churches. In I. I. Zaretsky and M. P. Leone (Eds.), *Religious movements in contemporary America* (pp.166-222). Princeton, NJ: Princeton University Press.

Brian in the medium's cabinet, Arthur Findlay College, Stansted, England. Photograph by Shannon Taggart.

MEDIUMSHIP AND FOLK MODELS OF MIND AND MATTER

JACK HUNTER

This chapter explores the role of experiences with trance and physical mediumship in the development of folk models of mind and matter, at a non-denominational spiritualist home-circle called the *Bristol Spirit Lodge*. Mediums and sitters often claim that mediumship has led them to understand the world differently, and to appreciate that the standard materialistic view of science is inadequate as an all encompassing model of reality. Certain key themes and concepts have emerged from my informants' experiences with mediumship that hint at alternative models of understanding the relationship between mind and matter, including the idea that bodies are permeable, that matter is essentially non-physical, that consciousness is far more expansive than our normal waking state would lead us to believe, and that persons are multiple, can survive death, and may be influenced by external spiritual entities.

To begin, we will briefly examine the anthropological debate over spirit possession, taking a quick tour through the various theoretical models developed to account for the existence of this human phenomenon. This will be followed by an introduction to the history of Spiritualism, and in particular to physical mediumship, in order to give an idea of the kind of spirit mediumship that forms the basis for discussion in this chapter. The chapter will conclude with an analysis of extracts from ethnographic interviews with members of the Bristol Spirit Lodge.

Ethnographic Parallels

Ethnographic parallels of spiritualist mediumship can be found in the many varieties of what are loosely labelled 'spirit possession' traditions (Schmidt & Huskinson, 2010; Dawson, 2011), and what I.M. Lewis refers to as 'ecstatic religions' (Lewis, 1971), which occur, in one form or another, in almost all human societies. Spirit possession can be broadly defined in Janice Boddy's terms as:

> ...the hold over a human being by external forces or entities more powerful than she. These forces may be ancestors or divinities, ghosts of foreign origin, or entities both ontologically and ethnically alien... (Boddy, 1994, p. 407)

The term 'spirit possession' is used quite broadly to refer to a set of related, though not necessarily identical, phenomena (Lewis, 1988, p. 24), including both the belief that spirits can involuntarily occupy the body of an individual, causing illness, and the voluntary incorporation of spirits, ancestors and deities for social and ritual reasons. This voluntary incorporation is usually referred to as 'mediumship.' The discussions that follow in this chapter are primarily concerned with the voluntary incorporation of spirits.

The belief that the body can be temporarily inhabited by non-physical beings is particularly widespread. Erika Bourguignon (1973), in a cross-cultural study of 488 widely distributed societies selected from a compendium of 'adequately described cultures' (1973, p. 11), determined that ninety percent of her sample societies utilised some form of institutionalised altered state of consciousness, and that seventy percent of the sampled societies associated such states with the notion of spirit possession (Bourguignon, 1973, pp. 9-11; 2007, p. 375). Of course, there are important differences between the world's various spirit possession traditions, which, like all human practices, differ in their cultural expression, but all share the common theme of utilising altered states of consciousness, of one form or another, as a means to interact with the 'spirit world' and the divine (Dawson, 2011, p. 9).

The Euro-American Spiritualist movement was, and is, therefore, part of a much wider human phenomenon, but while anthropology has been predominantly concerned with investigating spirit possession practices in Non-Western societies, there has been a distinct lack of research into contemporary Euro-American spirit mediumship (see Gilbert and Meintel in this volume, Nelson, 1969; Skultans, 1974 and Emmons, 2008 for notable exceptions), and even less on contemporary trance and physical mediumship. The research presented here, and elsewhere (Hunter, 2011; 2012a; 2012b; 2013) is intended to help fill this gap in the ethnographic record.

Theories of Spirit Possession

Anthropological investigations of spirit possession practices have usually tended towards the dominant explanatory frameworks of functionalism, pathology (psychological and medical), performance studies, and, more recently, cognitive science and neurophysiology. (Stoller, 1994, p. 637; Dawson 2011). We will now briefly examine some of these approaches, before outlining the methodological approach employed in this chapter.

Functionalist interpretations generally hold that spirit possession performs an essential function for the social group within which it is practiced. Lewis (1971), for example, has argued that spirit possession rituals often serve as 'thinly disguised protest movements directed against the dominant sex' (or, indeed, any other dominant group), because during the period of possession the possessed is 'totally blameless' for their actions; 'responsibility lies not with them, but with the spirits' (1971, pp. 31-32), allowing the socially repressed to vent their frustrations publicly. Functionalist analyses of spirit possession in this vein have been very popular amongst anthropologists and have been applied to numerous societies worldwide (Giles, 1987, p. 235). These include accounts of the Zar possession cult of Northern Sudan (Boddy, 1988), spirit possession amongst the Digo in Southern Kenya (Gomm, 1975), amongst Brazilian mediums (Fry, 1986), in the case of spontaneous epidemics of spirit possession in Malaysian factories (Ong, 1988), and even in a Spiritualist home-circle in 1960s Wales (Skultans, 1974).

Psychoanalytic approaches to spirit possession are less widespread, but are perhaps best represented by Gannanath Obeyesekere's (1984) seminal study of spirit possession in Sri Lanka. Obeyesekere interpreted possession as a symptom, along with other symbolic bodily expressions (for example the matted hair of priestesses), as outward symbols of repressed negative life experiences. Psychoanalytic interpretations of spirit possession emphasize 'past traumatic and distressful experiences' in the lives of the possessed (Budden, 2003, p. 28), and suggest that the behaviours and psychological sensations associated with the possession state are symbolic symptoms of the unconscious repression of such negative life experiences.

The association of spirit possession with pathology has been a persistent and widespread theme in anthropological and other social-scientific analyses (Csordas 1987; Zingrone, 1994, pp. 102-103; Emmons, 2008, p. 72). Specifically, spirit possession has been associated with epilepsy (Carrazana *et al.*, 1999; Jilek-Aall, 1999), nutrient deficiency (Kehoe & Giletti, 1981; Bourguignon *et al.*, 1983, p. 414), psychosis (Goff *et al.*, 1991), and dissociative identity disorder (Braude, 1988; Taves, 2006, p. 123). From this perspective, then, spirit possession is understood as a symptom of underlying pathology, indeed spirit possession has even been controversially classified as a culture-bound syndrome in the DSM-IV (Lewis-Fernandez, 1992; Cardeña *et al.*, 2009).

Cognitive approaches to spirit possession have been gaining increasing traction within anthropology, primarily following the lead of pioneering work by Stewart Guthrie (1980; 1993) and Pascal Boyer (2001) on cognitive approaches to supernatural belief. Specifically, the work of Emma Cohen (2008) has been particularly influential. Cohen discerns two primary forms of spirit possession: pathogenic possession, in which possession by spiritual beings is understood to be the underlying cause of illness, and executive possession, being the deliberate, and desired, incorporation of spirits, often called spirit mediumship. Cohen suggests that the cognitive processes underlying pathogenic possession are the same as those normally involved with the 'representation of contamination,' while the cognitive faculties involved in executive possession usually deal with 'the world of intentional agents.' From this perspective, then, spirit possession is nothing more than the misinterpretation of otherwise normal cognitive schema.

While it is undoubtedly true that each of the approaches outlined above provides insight into the sociological functions and psychological underpinnings of spirit possession experiences and practices, it is also fair to say that none of them is able to provide a complete explanatory model of spirit possession. Functionalist models frequently fail to take into account the experiences and understandings of the possessed themselves (Bowker, 1973; Boddy, 1988, p. 4), and do not always correspond with the ethnographic facts (Wilson, 1967; Rasmussen, 1994,

p. 76). Similarly, cognitive approaches have been criticised for their reduction of particularly complex social and experiential phenomena to highly specific, not to mention speculative, cognitive processes (Halloy, 2010). Pathological interpretations also fall short of the ethnographic reality, with mediums often displaying fewer signs of mental illness than non-mediums in a variety of different cultural contexts (Moreira-Almeida *et al.*, 2008, p. 420; Roxburgh & Roe, 2011, p. 294), and preliminary neurophysiological research suggests that there are significant neurophysiological differences between possession states and pathological states, such as epilepsy (Oohashi *et al.*, 2002; Hageman *et al.*, 2010). Indeed, recent research suggests that mediumship represents a distinct state of consciousness correlated with quite distinct neurophysiological activity (Peres, *et al.*, 2012; Delorme, *et al.*, 2013)

Methodological Orientation: An Experiential Approach

The approach employed here, then, will not begin from the assumption that spirit possession is a pathological condition, and nor will it assume that mediumship is a purely social-functional phenomenon (though it undoubtedly does perform social functions). Furthermore, rather than attempting to reduce the complexity of spirit possession to specific cognitive and neurophysiological processes, the research presented here seeks to take the first-hand experiences of fieldwork informants seriously, at face-value, in order to explore what such experiences might tell us about their world-view, and the development of specific folk models of mind and matter. I use the term 'folk' here to refer to models of understanding the mind and matter built upon personal experience, inference and intuition, that is how models of mind are formed from personal experience (Berlotti & Magnani, 2010, p. 252). This emphasis on experience falls neatly in line with what folklorist David J. Hufford has called the experience-centred approach. Hufford argues in favour of the 'experiential source hypothesis' (ESH) as a tool for investigating 'supernatural' beliefs and experiences. The ESH breaks away from the more widely accepted cultural source hypothesis, which holds that paranormal experiences and beliefs arise from the diffusion of specific cultural ideas, in favour of the notion that supernatural beliefs might have their origins in real-life experiences, regardless of whether such experiences are genuinely 'paranormal' or not. Hufford writes:

> The primary theoretical statement of the [experience-centred] approach might be roughly summed up as follows: some significant portion of traditional supernatural belief is associated with accurate observations interpreted rationally. This does not suggest that all such belief has this association. Nor is this association taken as proof that the beliefs are true... (Hufford, 1982, p. xviii)

So the idea here, in the context of the Bristol Spirit Lodge, is that their 'ethno-metaphysics' (Hallowell, 2002, p. 20), comprising their folk-models of consciousness, is founded upon rational interpretations of experiences had during séances and in the process of mediumship development. That is not, as Hufford states, to say that such experiences are genuinely of a paranormal nature (though they could be), but just to suggest that their experiences have validity in themselves, and that such beliefs are not to be lightly brushed aside as necessarily irrational or unfounded (Turner, 1993, p. 11; Bowie, 2013), indeed they may be able to tell us something of interest about the nature and phenomenology of human consciousness, and about the relationship between consciousness and the physical body (Peres *et al.*, 2012; Hunter, 2013a).

A Brief History of Spiritualist Mediumship

The Spiritualist movement has many historical predecessors in the form of, amongst other historical seers and prophets, the Eighteenth Century Swedish mystic and scientist Emmanuel Swedenborg, whose journey's through the spirit world while in a trance state seemed to pre-empt the Spiritualist movement by almost a century (Van Dusen, 1994). The craze for animal magnetism, also known as mesmerism, in the early Nineteenth Century also pre-empted, and was eventually subsumed by, the Spiritualist movement. Patients undergoing mesmeric treatments often seemed to exhibit extrasensory powers while in the mesmeric trance (Inglis, 1989, pp. 46-60), and some even claimed to be in contact with spiritual beings.

The Spiritualist movement, as a distinct phenomenon, however, didn't officially take shape until March 31st 1848 when, in the small town of Hydesville in New York State, the home of the Fox family became the locus of some unusual psychokinetic activity (Doyle, 2006; Pearsall, 2004, pp. 29-33; Melechi, 2008, p. 161; Byrne, 2010, p.18). The Fox's were plagued by perplexing anomalous bangs and knocks on the walls and ceiling of their modest wooden house. In an effort to make sense of what was going on the two youngest sisters of the family, Kate and Margaret, began to address the knocks as though they were being produced by an invisible intelligence. The sisters soon realised that they could communicate with this apparently invisible agent through a simple code of knocks, one for 'Yes' and two for 'No,' and in this way discovered that the mysterious knocker was the spirit of a pedlar by the name of Charles Rosma, who had been murdered in the house some years before the Fox family moved in (Bednarowski, 1980, p. 213; Gauld, 1982, p. 3; Taves, 1999, p. 166; Pearsall, 2004; Stemman, 2005, p. V; Blum, 2007; Warner, 2008, p. 221; Byrne, 2010; Moreman, 2010, p. 161). This would come to be known as the 'spiritual telegraph.'

News of the Fox sisters and their apparent ability to communicate with invisible spirits spread rapidly across the United States and Europe leaving a trail of individuals discovering their own ability to communicate with the dead (Nelson, 1969, p. 5). By 1853, only five years after the movement's birth in New York State, Spiritualism had become a religion, and spread across the Atlantic to secure a firm foothold in Britain with the establishment of the first Spiritualist Church in the small town of Keighley in Yorkshire (Doyle, 2006, p. 84; Nelson, 1969, p. 91). Before long the manifestations of spirit communication began to diversify, evolving from simple question and answer sessions with knocks, through experiments with Ouija boards and automatic writing to full trance communications utilising deep altered states of consciousness, and eventually to the alleged materialisation of spirits from the mysterious semi-physical substance known as 'ectoplasm' (Moreman, 2010, p. 161).

The earliest form of Spiritualist mediumship, comprising raps and knocks, evolved into what would later be called 'physical mediumship,' defined by Jon Klimo as the purported ability of certain mediums to 'channel unknown energies that affect the physical environment in ways that can be directly experienced by persons other than the channel' (Klimo, 1987, p. 200). Perhaps the most influential innovator in early physical mediumship was the Scottish-born American medium Daniel Dunglas Home (1833-1886). After an early life allegedly filled with spiritual visions and premonitions, Home conducted his first séance at the age of eighteen and swiftly gained a reputation as a powerful medium. By 1856 Home was conducting séances in Britain. Séances with Home were said to feature a wide range of inexplicable phenomena, from communications with spirits while the medium was in a deep trance state, to the materialisation of hands and heads, and the levitation and apportation (spontaneous appearance) of objects. In 1868 he performed his most famous paranormal feat - the levitation of his body horizontally out through a third-story window at Ashley House in London. (Doyle, 2006, p. 99; Lamont, 2006, pp. 185-187).

In 1874 Home's mediumship received further support with the publication of a positive report by physicist Sir William Crookes. Using specially designed laboratory equipment Crookes tested Home's ability to change the weight of physical objects and to play tunes on an accordion suspended out of reach in a cage (Lamont, 2005, pp. 204-207; Alvarado, 2006, p. 142; Melechi, 2008, pp. 198-200). Arthur Conan Doyle considered Home to be something of a virtuoso in that he was proficient in four different forms of mediumship: the direct voice (whereby spirits communicate verbally independent of the medium), trance mediumship (whereby spirits communicate verbally through the body of the medium), clairvoyance (the ability to see visions of the spirit world, the future and distant locations) and physical mediumship (the ability to psychically manipulate physical objects) (Doyle, 2006, p. 106). Home's abilities form the core phenomena of physical mediumship, even today.

Owing to numerous exposures of fraudulence, especially after the foundation of the Society for Psychical Research in 1882, physical mediumship slowly declined in popularity to be replaced with somewhat more refined forms of clairvoyant and trance mediumship, which came to be known as 'mental mediumship' (Neher, 1990, p. 207). Three of the most influential and rigorously investigated mental mediums, Leonora Piper (1857–1950), Gladys Osborne Leonard (1882-1968) and Eileen J. Garrett (1893-1970), would enter into a deep trance state during which ostensible spirits would communicate through their inert bodies giving apparently veridical information under controlled conditions to sitters and psychical researchers alike. This is referred to as 'trance mediumship.' Today, Euro-American society is perhaps most familiar with 'platform mediumship.' This is the kind of mediumship that you will find in the Spiritualist churches, as well as on television programmes and theatre stages, and is often referred to as psychic or clairvoyant (or clairaudient, clairsentient, etc.) mediumship. Platform mediums do not usually enter into a trance state (at least not a particularly deep one), and the spirit communications they receive are often highly symbolic, requiring interpretation by both the medium and the person to whom the message is directed.

By the late 1950s physical mediumship was virtually extinct in the United Kingdom, though there were several exceptions including the physical mediumship of Helen Duncan (1897-1956) and Minnie Harrison (1895-1958), amongst a few others. It wasn't until the 1990s that an interest in physical mediumship returned to the popular consciousness (Foy, 2007).

A reinvigorated interest in physical mediumship developed after the publication of Montague Keen and David Fontana's *The Scole Report* by the Society for Psychical Research in 1999, and the popularised version *The Scole Experiment*, also published in the same year. Montague Keen, one of the parapsychologists who investigated the group on behalf of the Society for Psychical Research, outlines the basic claims made about the Scole experiments, he writes:

> Based on two years of regular séances, the Group's chief claims were that they had established contact with a 'team' of spirit communicators ... These had been accessed through ... a husband and wife team, both of whom entered swiftly into deep trance, remaining thus throughout the proceedings, of which they retained no conscious recollection. The purported discarnate contacts had facilitated the manifestation of spirit lights, moved furniture, created apports (objects appearing from no known source and by no known means), displayed shadowy figures described as angelic forms, and produced films, allegedly employing a novel form of energy not involving the traditional ectoplasmic extrusions ... (Keen, 2001, pp. 167-168)

Regardless of whether or not the phenomena witnessed at Scole were genuinely paranormal, the popularisation of the case led to the emergence of new experimental home-circles devoted to the development of physical mediumship, with circles often employing séance procedures influenced by the Scole group's set-up (Hunter, 2012). It was at one of these new private home-circles that my main fieldwork informant, Christine, first became acquainted with mediumship.

Into the Field:
Contemporary Trance & Physical Mediumship in Bristol

The Bristol Spirit Lodge was established in 2005 as a centre for the development of trance and physical mediumship when Christine, who describes herself as a mother and housewife in her mid-sixties, became convinced of the reality of spirit mediumship following a physical mediumship séance at *Jenny's Sanctuary*, a well known Spiritualist circle in Banbury. She had been invited to the séance by a friend and, not knowing what a physical mediumship séance was, decided to go along to find out. During the séance, conducted in a plain room with about 30 sitters, Christine saw bright lights floating and flashing around the séance room, heard numerous disembodied voices, whistles and loud bangs coming from all corners, witnessed a 'partly materialised something,' and, to cap it all off, heard a voice that she recognised as belonging to her deceased father. In a short self-published autobiography Christine describes the profound effect of this séance experience on her worldview:

> I now had no option but to believe that something very serious was happening. I felt sick with the sudden shock …
> I knew I couldn't ignore reality … There are no boundaries.
> We simply cannot see all that exists. I needed to somehow

persuade my mind to accept this fact completely; otherwise
I would close my mind, whilst at the same time knowing
that my previous belief was incorrect. I had believed that
when we died we were dead. I needed to get a grip if I was
to learn from the experience that had been offered to me
[in] the séance ... at Banbury (Di Nucci, 2009, pp. 23-25)

Prior to her life-changing séance experience, Christine claims that
she was uninterested in religious and spiritual matters, jokingly
describing herself as a 'devout atheist.' She claims no psychic
abilities and recalls only two possible paranormal experiences
from her youth. She does recall an invisible friend she had during
a period of family disruption, but interprets this as nothing
more than a 'psychological crutch,' seeing no reason to consider
it a hint at her future interest in spirit mediumship. She was,
however, particularly interested in the developments of modern
science, having read Stephen Hawking's popular *A Brief History
of Time* (1988), and journalist Lynn McTaggart's pop-science
(some might say pseudoscientific) book on quantum physics and
consciousness, *The Field* (2001). Her autobiography describes
how she attempted to interpret the experiences she had while in
the séance room through the lens of her interest in science, which
she has characterised as a 'DIY house-wifey awareness of science'
(Interview with Christine, 25/02/2013). She now has a great
enthusiasm for mediumship, a fact alluded to by the sheer amount
of time she spends in her Lodge with developing mediums - by
now she has taken part in over one thousand séances.

The Lodge itself is a wooden shed in Christine's back
garden. Originally, while still based in Bristol, the Lodge was
constructed, using £2,000 of her savings, according to simple
rules recommended by Ron, the circle leader at Jenny's Sanctuary.
It was important to Christine that the Lodge be built with love,
and that it be imbued with positive emotions. To this end all
the materials used to construct it were blessed, kissed and treated

with great respect. It was important to Christine that the Lodge only be associated with 'positive energies,' so as to avoid the risk of attracting negative entities during séances. The Lodge was aligned so that the séance cabinet, a curtained off corner of the room in which the medium sits while in trance (a direct descendant of the spirit cabinets used by physical mediums in the late Nineteenth and early Twentieth centuries), was located in the North corner, a position deemed conducive to the flow of vital 'energies' necessary for the successful development of physical mediumship.

All mediums at the Lodge are working towards the manifestation of various physical phenomena including levitation, transfiguration (the appearance of spirit faces over the face of the entranced medium), ectoplasmic materialisation, dematerialisation of the body and psychic surgery, and all of this under the direction of their discarnate spirit teams. However, due to the difficulties associated with the production of such seemingly outlandish phenomena (which only highly developed mediums are allegedly able to produce), the majority of séances held in the Lodge are trance sessions, during which the medium enters into a trance state and allows members of their spirit team to communicate with the sitters (Gauld 1982:29). Spirit teams at the Lodge generally consist of between six and sixteen individual spirits with distinctive and consistent characters, ranging from children who died in the Nineteenth century, Victorian undertakers, through Native American chiefs and Chinese philosophers. Individual members of each medium's spirit team are usually differentiated through the use of distinctive bodily postures and exaggerated vocalisations that allow them to be recognised as distinct personalities (Hunter, 2013b), and each spirit usually works towards the production of a specific physical phenomenon, depending upon their own interests. This emphasis on trance mediumship, or channeling (Klimo, 1987; Brown, 1997), locates the practices of the Bristol Spirit Lodge firmly within the remit of the anthropological debate over spirit possession (Lewis, 1988, p. 24).

Mediumship and the Development of Folk Models of Mind & Matter

As we have already seen, the Lodge was established specifically so that Christine could apply her 'house-wifey DIY knowledge of science' to understand the experiences she had during the séance in Banbury. Mediumship development at the Lodge can, therefore, be thought of as an on-going experiment in which both mediums and sitters construct their own understandings of the nature of consciousness and reality. The following extract from an interview with Christine demonstrates how belief at the Lodge is not a fixed position, but rather represents an ongoing process of learning, interpretation and re-interpretation. Indeed, in a recent interview Christine explained how she has a problem with the word 'belief' being applied to her, explaining how she thinks she is 'generally mistrusting' and that without evidence she has 'difficulty believing in anything.' Her conclusions about the nature of mind and matter, therefore, are founded upon her own experiences with mediumship. She says:

> [Mediumship] expands the thinking. It certainly expands the possibilities. I wasn't thinking any of this when I started six years ago. You learn all the time, I mean I'm doing three, four, Séances a week and have over a thousand Séances with all different people, all different mediums and all different situations. I am fascinated by it still. I am not one least bit satisfied that I've learned anything. I want more! Yeah, I want more and more and more. Because it's just a bigger subject than any other I've hit on (Interview with Christine 16/06/2012).

A few of the key ideas that, according to my interview data, have arisen from this experimental process of experiential learning include the idea that consciousness can survive the death of the physical body, that personhood is partible, that the body is permeable, that reality is non-physical, and that consciousness is a fundamental property of the universe. We will now explore these themes through extracts from interviews with members of the Bristol Spirit Lodge.

Interview Extracts and Commentary

The following extracts are taken from interviews with mediums and sitters at the Bristol Spirit Lodge between 2011-2013, and have been transcribed directly from audio recordings. Through looking at some of the ideas concerning the nature of consciousness and the body, as well as descriptions of interactions with spiritual beings, it is hoped that we will begin to see the emergence of key features of the ethno-metaphysical system of the Bristol Spirit Lodge.

1) Survival of Consciousness after Death.

In this extract from Sandy, a nutritional therapist in her late forties and medium at the Lodge, describes how her experiences developing mediumship over the past four years, have led her to a firmer understanding that personal consciousness survives the physical death of the body:

> Um, I'm much more relaxed ... I've been able to think about what I believe in. It never occurred to me before, I just didn't think about it. And, uh, it's changed the pace of my life. It's changed, um, my knowledge of continuation, after we've died, and it's given me comfort in that way. The funny thing was before it ever happened, um, I knew my brother and my grandmother still existed, but it never occurred to me that anybody else did either. Because they

were the only two people I knew who'd died, then I knew
they were still about, but that's as far as I'd ever thought it,
I'd never looked into any of it ever, I'd just never considered
any of it ever (Interview with Sandy 23/03/2011).

It was only after being introduced to mediumship by Christine,
and subsequently developing trance mediumship herself, that
Sandy came to realise that consciousness survives after the death
of the body. Similarly, in this quotation from Emily, a 33 year
old mother of two and office worker who has recently begun to
develop physical mediumship, explains how her experiences with
mediumship have led to a reassurance of her own belief in survival:

I think it has proven that there is more to 'life' and I
guess I'm not worried about death ... I also feel like I
am contributing to getting the message and something
evidential 'out there' to help people believe in the reality
of continuing life, as I believe this to be, and come closer
to understanding what exists around them. I feel that it's
amazing and it should be shared! (Interview with Emily
12/02/2013).

Emily first became seriously interested in mediumship following
a health scare that prompted her to question the possibility of life
after death. Her experiences with mediumship development have
helped to diminish her concerns about dying.

2) Spiritual Augmentation

One of the most interesting ideas that has emerged, in my
opinion, is that spiritual beings can be useful, that they can
actually help in everyday life in a variety of ways. I refer to this
as an augmentation. In her study of Afro-Cuban Spiritism,
for example, Diana Espirito Santo argues that mediumship is

a 'type of partnership between a person and a series of spirits' and that the 'person' of the medium is a 'meeting-ground for the unique abilities of each of the spirits belonging to her spiritual cordon' (Espirito Santo, 2011, p. 102). Spirit mediumship can be thought of, therefore, as a process whereby the medium's person is expanded through the incorporation of other spiritual beings, thus creating what could be considered a composite, or multiple, personhood. Here Sandy explains how the spirits help her to keep a clear mind, assisting in the recall and implementation of knowledge and information:

> [The spirits] help me keep a clearer mind, and therefore I am able to make better decisions. I can utilise information that I've got ... I did a degree in nutritional medicine, years ago I was a nurse and a mid-wife, and there's a lot of information in my head somewhere, but I can actually tap in on information that I've not used in years and years and years ... the knowledge is mine but it can be used more efficiently (Interview with Sandy 23/03/2011).

Simlarly Christine explains how she interacts with her spirit guide Fuzzy Critter (also known as FC). Fuzzy Critter plays an important role in the organisation of the séances at the Lodge, and directs Christine on occasion in order to get the 'energies right.' She explains:

> As time when on in trusting Fuzzy Critter, and these telepathic voices, I did get to a point where I knew it was separate from me ... It was a separate personality. The words he uses are better than mine ... his language is different to mine ... His general way of working, it's not me, in fact sometimes I'll argue with him ... I have a sense, he seems to approach me from this side of my shoulder, this side of my head [left]. I, in my own mind, feel that he's a bit like a fluffy

owl siting on my shoulder … Sometimes it's annoying if I'm doing housework and he wants to communicate with me, and I get this feeling. It's a bit like having something playing with your hair, or whispering in your ear when you're trying to do something (Interview with Christine 18/11/2009).

For Sandy and Christine, then, spiritual beings provide a practical service through giving advice and helping to focus lines of thought and inspiration, perhaps echoing the classical notion of the daemonic muse. Transpersonal psychologist Alex Rachel has even gone so far as to speculate on the possibility that human consciousness has evolved along side, and under the symbiotic influence of, non-physical entities (Rachel, 2013). Christine recently explained the importance and practicality of this symbiotic relationship between spirits and the living, and how the modern world has forgotten something fundamental:

> Mankind [is] missing something that is their natural right … The world is crap and we are missing a link that we are entitled to … Ancestors can offer their advice, their support, for real (Interview with Christine 25/02/2013).

3) Porous Bodies and Field-like Selves

These kinds of experience appear to hint at a model of personhood that is somewhat different to the usually assumed 'Western' model of the person, which Clifford Geertz defines as:

> … a bounded, unique, more or less integrated motivational and cognitive universe, a dynamic center of awareness, emotion, judgment and action organized into a distinctive whole and set contrastively against other such wholes and against its social and natural background (Geertz, 1974, p. 31)

Experiences with mediumship would appear, therefore, to lead towards a different perspective on the nature of the person, one that has classically been labelled a 'Non-Western' model of personhood, which is contrasted with the Western model, as outlined above, in that the person is conceived as porous and susceptible to the influence of external agents (Steffen, 2011; Smith, 2012, p. 53). This conception of the person as porous comes across most strongly in Lodge members' descriptions of the body. Christine says:

> I think we just flow through each other. Or, we've got very blurred edges, we appear to be solid, but only our eyes are seeing this solid, this light reflection which causes us to appear solid. We're not. So, our boundaries aren't where we think they are. We are here to experience whatever this is, this life-form, this stage of life is. We are here … to experience, or to perceive things as solid and individual and it's a very little tiny part of a very big life. I think. Possibly (Interview with Christine 16/06/2012).

Christine conceives of the boundaries of the person as extending beyond the confines of the physical body, which itself only *appears* to be solid. According to this perspective the 'solid' and the 'individual' are, to a certain extent, illusionary. With a porous body, then, it is possible for things to flow in and out of the person. Anthropologist Fiona Bowie has characterised this through describing the body, in the context of Spiritualist trance séances, as a 'shared territory, holding the physical life-force of the medium and the conscious intelligence of visiting spirits' (Bowie, In Press, p. 14). In further discussions, Christine has described her model of consciousness as being somewhat 'like an onion,' that is 'a whole split into millions and trillions of consciousnesses that can act together' (Interview with Christine 25/02/2013). This kind of pluralistic understanding of consciousness and the person recurs throughout the ethnographic literature (see, as one such example, Roseman on the structure of the self among Senoi Temiar, which is described as consisting of 'a number of potentially detachable selves' 1990, p. 227).

Here, as another example of understanding the body as permeable, Emily describes the sensation of spirit beings moving into her 'personal space' as she waits to go out into the Lodge to practice her mediumship:

> Then usually around the table while we are waiting for the start I will feel a presence around me kind of like an enveloping feeling, the first thing I feel is as if a friend is standing unseen nearby. I have an awareness of there being someone there, near me, that is a friend. I then feel them come closer into my personal 'space' in some quiet gentle way (Interview with Emily 13/02/2013).

Emily's description of a sense of presence, unseen but felt, suggests a model of the self as a non-physical field expanding outwards, into which other entities can pass. In this extract from an interview with another medium, Rachael, who has been attending the Lodge for just over one year, she explains how before developing mediumship she would frequently experience unusual, and often unpleasant, sensations of spirits moving through her body. She explains:

> When they actually make a personal entrance into your body, that's pretty bizarre. It would normally happen, um, in the middle of the night I'd wake up and there was something, it's a sort of odd feeling, it's like, um, if you can imagine taking off a polo necked jumper, but from inside yourself. It's like something's pulling, it's kind of gone in, and then it's kind of pulling out, and it's, oh, I can't explain it, but it's the weirdest, weirdest feeling.

But it's quite horrible … It happened, um, on about three occasions through my thirties, and in the end I got talking to a medium and she said it sounds like a spirit entity in you, or something passing through you, and she said to contact the local Spiritualist church, but, I did that, but nobody there seemed to feel the same kind of thing: with mental mediumship it all seems to be outside of the person coming in through the mind and talking, it wasn't, with me it's a very physical thing … (Interview with Rachael 16/06/2012).

For Rachael the process of developing mediumship allowed her to come to terms with experiences that had previously been disturbing. Where once the experience of spirits moving through her body had been unpleasant and spontaneous, it is now both deliberately induced and enjoyable. She explains how mediumship development has made her 'soft and squidgy' and 'more open to other people' (Interview with Rachael, 25/02/2013).

There is also a belief amongst Lodge members that the physical body itself can, on occasion, dematerialise completely. This extract from a report by Jerry (a regular sitter and developing medium at the Lodge), on witnessing a physical mediumship demonstration, describes his difficulty in coming to terms with the apparent dematerialisation of the medium's physical body:

I've been trying to think of words to adequately describe what I felt and saw, but it's impossible really. I was sitting next to the cabinet, so when I was asked by Yellow Feather to move in front of the cabinet I was able to do this quite easily, despite it being in blackout conditions at the time. When Yellow Feather asked me to feel the chair, where [the medium] had been sitting, he wasn't there! His chair was empty! The spirit team

had, they said, dematerialised him. I found this hard to
believe. But [the medium] is a big lad and I was sitting
right beside the cabinet, and no-one walked past me. So
where was he? (Jerry, October 2011)

All of this seems to suggest that the classical anthropological
distinction between Western and Non-Western personhood
conceptions is overly simplified, and that there are huge
variations in the way that consciousness and the body are
understood and experienced even within a single 'dominant'
culture. This is not the same as saying that the members of
the Bristol Spirit Lodge necessarily partake of a socio-centric
conception of the self, as perhaps exemplified by the frequently
cited example of Japanese notions of an 'interdependent' self
'as part of an encompassing social relationship [in which] one's
behavior is determined, contingent on, and, to a large extent
organized by what the actor perceives to be the thoughts,
feelings, and actions of others in the relationship' (Markus &
Kitayama, 1991, p. 227). It is not this kind of social-self concept
that I am referring to, because in most cases the members of
the Lodge appear to possess what might be considered a normal
'Western' notion of the self in terms of kinship relationships
and everyday social interactions. Where they differ is in the
porosity of the self: the belief that the self can be influenced by
non-physical entities, that the physical body is not permanently
bounded and may be entered by non-physical beings as well as,
on occasion, dematerialising completely, and that the self can
leave the physical body during altered states of consciousness.
What we seem to be dealing with, then, is a greater degree of
intra-cultural variation in experiences and concepualisations
of self and body than the standard Western/Non-Western
dichotomy seems to allow for (Spiro 1993, pp. 144-145), and
this calls for further investigation (Lillard, 1998).

4) Panpsychism

The final aspect of this ethno-metaphysical system that I want to touch upon is the notion of 'panpsychism,' broadly defined as the idea that consciousness is inherent in all matter (Velmans 2007, p. 279). Here Christine explains her understanding that even seemingly inert tables possess an element of consciousness:

> It's funny because ... I think that table has an element of consciousness in it. I think it belongs to something. I think it's part of something. I think it's got vibrations. It's got a something. I don't know how aware it is, but people, or certain psychics, can pick up the memory of that table - the history of that table, the tree it belonged to. You know, if you get sensitive enough you can do all that stuff. I can't, but it has a being, a something. That table does! If that's got consciousness, that's it, it's beyond me, it really is beyond me where it starts, where does it come from? I don't know where it comes from, I haven't a clue, and it gets more and more complicated as you look into it and wonder about it ... I don't know what consciousness is and I've got no idea. I don't know where it comes from. I definitely, I think it's everywhere, but, everything is conscious to different degrees ... maybe it collects together and becomes stronger. I don't know (Interview with Christine 16/06/2012).

Christine's experiences assisting the development of mediums at the Bristol Spirit Lodge have ultimately led her to an understanding of consciousness as a fundamental property of reality, and as ubiquitous throughout matter. This understanding has emerged from a combination of anomalous experiences in the séance room, and the metaphysical teachings of the spirits she converses with through entranced mediums. For Christine, séance phenomena are an expression of the fact that matter and energy are the same thing. Consciousness, as an aspect of physical existence, therefore, must also be energy, and so consciousness must be present in everything to a greater or lesser extent. She explains how mediumship is simply the 'energy of people that have died interacting with the energy of people who are alive' (Interview with Christine 25/02/2013).

Preliminary Conclusions

The often cited distinction between so-called 'Western' and 'Non-Western' models of the self and person appears to represent an overly simplistic dichotomy that does not fit with the ethnographic data (La Fontaine, 1985; Spiro, 1993). To assume that there is a neat divide between 'bounded' and 'porous' models of the person, and to suggest that these represent discrete 'Western' and 'Non-Western' categories, is an oversimplification of something that is far more fluid and varied. Experiences with mediumship development in sub-urban Bristol, for example, have led my fieldwork informants to develop models of personhood that would classically have been defined as 'Non-Western.' What we appear to be dealing with, therefore, is a much greater degree of intra-cultural variation in understandings about the nature of consciousness and its relation to the body than the standard dichotomy seems to allow for, and this variation derives, to a large extent, from personal experience (Luhrmann, 2012, xxii).

In the context of the Bristol Spirit Lodge, mind and matter are causally interconnected and frequently overlapping. Discarnate, non-physical, spirits can interact with physical bodies, and the material world can be influenced by conscious intention, for example in the practice of psychic surgery. Ectoplasm represents a half-way substance between the physical and the non-physical: it is believed to be extruded from the physical body so that it can be manipulated by non-physical spirits. The human body can, on occasion, even be dematerialised completely under the influence of spiritual entities, and consciousness can exist beyond the confines of the physical brain. All of this suggests a hugely different conception of the nature of the 'self' to the often assumed 'bounded, unique...distinctive whole' (Geertz, 1974) of the Western notion of the self.

To conclude, it is clearly important to take experience seriously in the study of folk-psychology, ethno-metaphysics and supernatural belief. Through attempting to understand the experiential foundations of belief in, for example, survival of consciousness after death, the permeability of the body and pluralistic models of the self, we can move towards a more nuanced understanding of different cultural and sub-cultural systems. Ideas that might, at first glance, appear outlandish need not necessarily be classified as irrational or unscientific, but can be understood as logical conclusions drawn from first-hand personal experiences interpreted rationally (Hufford, 1982; Turner, 1993; Bowie, 2013). Once we are able to move beyond the hegemonic dismissal of alternative modes of understanding the relationship between the mind and the body, we open ourselves up to a much wider range of possibilities regarding the nature of consciousness (Cohen & Rapport, 1995, p. 13; Samuel & Johnston, 2013).

References

Alvarado, C.S. (2006). Human radiations: Concepts of force in Mesmerism, Spiritualism and psychical research. *Journal of the Society for Psychical Research, 70* (884), 138-162.

Bednarowski, M.F. (1980). Outside the mainstream: Women's religion and women religious leaders in nineteenth century America. *Journal of the American Academy of Religion, 48* (2), 207-232.

Blum, D. (2007). *Ghost hunters: The Victorians and the hunt for proof of life after death.* London: Arrow Books.

Boddy, J. (1988). Spirits and selves in Northern Sudan: The cultural therapeutics of possession and trance. *American Ethnologist, 15* (1), 4-27.

Bourguignon, E. (1973). *Religion, altered states of consciousness and social change.* Columbus: Ohio State University Press.

Bourguignon, E. (1973). A framework for the comparative study of altered states of consciousness. In E. Bourguignon (Ed.) (1973). *Religion, altered states of consciousness and social change* (pp.3-38). Columbus: Ohio State University Press.

Bourguignon, E. (2007). Spirit possession. In C. Casey & R.B. Edgerton (Eds.), *A companion to psychological anthropology* (pp.374-388). Oxford: Blackwell Publishing Ltd.

Bourguignon, E. Bellisari, A. & McCabe, S. (1983). Women, possession trance cults, and the extended nutrient-deficiency hypothesis. *American Anthropologist, 85* (2), 413-416.

Bowie, F. (2013). Building bridges, dissolving boundaries: Towards a methodology for the ethnographic study of the afterlife, mediumship and spiritual beings. *Journal of the American Academy of Religion, 81* (3), 698-733.

Bowie, F. (In Press). 'Material and immaterial bodies: Ethnographic reflections on a trance séance.'

Bowker, J. (1973). *The sense of God: Sociological, anthropological and psychological approaches to the origin of the sense of God.* Oxford: Clarendon Press.

Boyer, P. (2001). *Religion explained: The human instincts that fashion gods, spirits and ancestors.* London: William Heinnemann.

Braude, S. (1988). Mediumship and multiple personality disorder. *Journal of the Society for Psychical Research, 55* (813), 177-195.

Brown, M.F. (1997). *The channeling zone: American spirituality in an anxious age.* Harvard: Harvard University Press.

Budden, A. (2003). Pathologizing possession: An essay on mind, self and experience in dissociation. *Anthropology of Consciousness, 14* (2), 27-59.

Byrne, G. (2010). *Modern Spiritualism and the Church of England, 1850-1939.* Woodbridge: The Boydell Press.

Cardeña, E., Van Duijil, M., Weiner, L.A. & Terhune, D.B. (2009). Possession/trance phenomena. In P.F. Dell & J.A. O'Neil (Eds.), *Dissociation and the dissociative disorders: DSM-V and beyond* (pp. 171-184). New York: Routledge.

Carrazana, E., DeToledo, J., Tatum, W., Rivas-Vasquez, R., Rey, G. & Wheeler, S. (1999). Epilepsy and religious experience: Voodoo possession. *Epilepsia, 40* (2), 239-241.

Cohen, A.P. & Rapport, N. (1995). Introduction: Consciousness in anthropology. In A.P. Cohen & N. Rapport (Eds.), *Questions of consciousness* (pp. 1-18). London: Routledge.

Cohen, E. (2008). What is spirit possession? Defining, comparing and explaining two possession forms. *Ethos, 73* (1), 101-126.

Csordas, T.J. (1987). Health and the holy in African and Afro-American spirit possession. *Social Science and Medicine, 24* (1), 1-11.

Dawson, A. (Ed.) (2011). *Summoning the spirits: Possession and invocation in contemporary religion.* London: I.B. Tauris.

Di Nucci, C. (2009). *Spirits in a teacup: Questioning the reality of life after death has led one housewife along an adventurous path towards discovery.* Bristol: Bristol Spirit Lodge.

Doyle, A.C. (1926 [2006]). *The history of Spiritualism, vol. 2.* Fairford: The Echo Library.

Emmons, C.F. (2008). On becoming a spirit medium in a "rational" society. *Anthropology of Consciousness, 12* (1), 71-82.

Espirito Santo, D. (2011). Process, personhood and possession in Cuban Spiritism. In A. Dawson (Ed.), *Summoning the spirits: Possession and invocation in contemporary religion* (pp. 93-109). London: I.B. Tauris & Co. Ltd.

Foy, R. (2007). *In pursuit of physical mediumship.* London: Janus Publishing.

Fry, P. (1986). Male homosexuality and spirit possession in Brazil. *Journal of Homosexuality, 11* (3-4), 137-153.

Gauld, A. (1982). *Mediumship and survival: A century of investigations.* London: Granada Publishing Ltd.

Geertz, C. (1974). 'From the native's point of view': On the nature of anthropological understanding. *Bulletin of the American Academy of Arts and Sciences, 28* (1), 26-45.

Giles, L. L. (1987). Possession cults on the Swahili coast: A re-examination of theories of marginality. *Africa: Journal of the International African Institute, 57* (2), 234-258.

Goff, A.C., Brotman, A.W., Kindlon, D., Waites, M., and Amico, E. (1991). The delusion of possession in chronically psychotic patients. *The Journal of Nervous and Mental Disease, 179* (9), 567-571.

Gomm, R. (1975). Bargaining from weakness: Spirit possession on the South Kenya coast. *Man, 10* (4), 530-543.

Guthrie, S. (1980). A cognitive theory of religion. *Current Anthropology, 21* (2), 181-203.

Guthrie, S. (1993). *Faces in the clouds: A new theory of religion.* Oxford: Oxford University Press.

Hageman, J.H., Peres, J.FP., Moreira-Almeida, A., Caixeta, L., Wickramasekera II, I, & Krippner, S. (2010). The neurobiology of trance and mediumship in Brazil. In S. Krippner & H.L. Friedman (Eds.), *Mysterious minds: The neurobiology of psychics, mediums and other extraordinary people.* Oxford: Praeger.

Hallowell, A.I. (2002 [1960]) Ojibwa ontology, behaviour, and world view. In G. Harvey (Ed.), *Readings in indigenous religions.* London: Continuum.

Halloy, A. (2010). Comments on "The mind possessed: The cognition of spirit possession in an Afro-Brazilian religious tradition" by Emma Cohen. *Religion and Society: Advances in Research, 1,* 164-176.

Hawking, S. (1988). *A brief history of time: From the Big Bang to black holes.* London: Bantam Books.

Hufford, D.J. (1982). *The terror that comes in the night: An experience-centred study of supernatural assault traditions.* Philadelphia: University of Pennsylvania Press.

Hunter, J. (2011). Talking with spirits: Anthropology and interpreting spirit communication. *Journal of the Society for Psychical Research, 75* (904), 129-142.

Hunter, J. (2012a). *Talking with spirits: Personhood, performance and altered consciousness in a contemporary Spiritualist home-circle.* Unpublished M.Litt Dissertation, University of Bristol.

Hunter, J. (2012b). Contemporary physical mediumship: Is it part of a continuous tradition? *Paranthropology: Journal of Anthropological Approaches to the Paranormal, 3* (1), 35-43.

Hunter, J. (2013a). Introduction: Taking experience seriously. *Paranthropology: Journal of Anthropological Approaches to the Paranormal, 4* (3), 3-8.

Hunter, J. (2013b). 'Numinous conversations: Performance and manifestation of spirits in spirit possession practices.' In A. Voss & W. Rowlandson (Eds.), *Daimonic imagination: Uncanny intelligence.* Cambridge: Cambridge Scholars Press.

Inglis, B. (1989). *Trance: A natural history of altered states of mind.* London: Grafton Books.

Keen, M. (2001). The Scole Investigation: A study in critical analysis of paranormal physical phenomena. *Journal of Scientific Exploration, 15* (2), 167-182.

Klimo, J. (1987). *Channeling: Investigations on receiving information from paranormal sources.* Los Angeles: Jeremy P. Tarcher.

La Fontaine, J.S. (1985). Person and individual: Some anthropological reflections. In M. Carrithers, Collins, S. & Lukes, S., (Eds.), *The category of the person: Anthropology, philosophy, history* (pp.123-140). Cambridge: Cambridge University Press.

Lamont, P. (2005). *The first psychic: The peculiar mystery of a notorious Victorian wizard.* London: Abacus.

Lewis, I. M. (1971). *Ecstatic religion: An anthropological study of spirit possession and shamanism.* London: Penguin Books Ltd.

Lewis, I.M. (1988). *Religion in context: Cults and charisma.* Cambridge: Cambridge University Press.

Lewis-Fernandez, R. (1992). The proposed DSM-IV trance and possession disorder category: Potential benefits and risks. *Transcultural Psychiatry, 29,* 301-317.

Lillard, A. (1998). Ethnopsychologies: Cultural variations in theories of mind. *Psychological Bulletin, 123* (1), 3-32.

Luhrmann, T.M. (2012). *When God talks back: Understanding the American evangelical relationship with God.* New York: Alfred A. Knopf.

McTaggart, L. (2001). *The field: The quest for the secret force of life.* London: Harper Collins.

Melechi, A. (2008). *Servants of the supernatural: The night side of the Victorian mind.* London, William Heinemann.

Moreira-Almeida, A., Neto, F.L., & Cardeña, E. (2008). Comparison of Brazilian Spiritist mediumship and dissociative identity disorder. *Journal of Nervous and Mental Disease, 196* (5), 420-424.

Moreman, C.M. (2010). *Beyond the threshold: Afterlife beliefs and experiences in world religions.* London: Rowman & Littlefield.

Nelson, G.K. (1969). *Spiritualism and society*. London: Routledge & Kegan Paul Ltd.

Obeyesekere, G. (1984). *Medusa's hair: An essay on personal symbols and religious experience*. Chicago: University of Chicago Press.

Ong, A. (1988). The production of possession: Spirits and the multinational corporation in Malaysia. *American Ethnologist, 15* (1), 28-42.

Oohashi, T., Kawai, N., Honda, M., Nakamura, S., Morimoto, M., Nishina, E., Maekawa, T. (2002). Electroencephalographic measurement of possession trance in the field. *Clinical Neurophysiology, 11* (3), 435-445.

Pearsall, R. (2004). *The table-rappers: The Victorians and the occult*. Stroud: Sutton Publishing.

Peres J.F, Moreira-Almeida A., Caixeta L., Leao F., Newberg A. (2012). Neuroimaging during trance state: A contribution to the study of dissociation. *PLoS ONE, 7* (11), 1-9.

Rachel, A. (2013). Daimonic ecologies: An inquiry into the relationships between the human and nonphysical species. In A. Voss and W. Rowlandson (Eds.), *Daimonic imagination: Uncanny intelligence* (pp. 321-339). Newcastle upon Tyne: Cambridge Scholars Publishing.

Rasmussen, S.J. (1994). The 'head dance,' contested self, and art as balancing act in Tuareg spirit possession. *Africa: Journal of the International African Institute, 64* (1), 74-98.

Roseman, M. (1990). Head, heart, odor, and shadow: The structure of the self, the emotional world, and ritual performance among Senoi Temiar. *Ethos, 18* (3), 227-250.

Roxburgh, E. & Roe, C. (2011). A survey of dissociation: Boundary-thinness, and psychological wellbeing in Spiritualist mental mediums. *Journal of Parapsychology, 75* (2), 279-300.

Samuel, G. & Johnston, J. (2013). *Religion and the subtle body in Asia and the West: Between mind and body*. Abingdon: Routledge.

Schmidt, B. & Huskinson, L. (2010). *Spirit possession and trance: New interdisciplinary perspectives*. London: Continuum.

Skultans, V. (1974). *Intimacy and ritual: A study of Spiritualism, mediums and groups*. London: Routledge & Kegan Paul.

Smith, K. (2012). From dividual and individual selves to porous subjects. *The Australian Journal of Anthropology, 23*, 50-64.

Solomon, G & Solomon, J. (1999). *The Scole Experiment: Scientific evidence for life after death*. London: Judy Piatkus.

Spiro, M. (1993). Is the Western conception of the self 'peculiar' within the context of the world cultures? *Ethos, 21* (2), 107-153.

Steffen, V. (2011). Intrusive agents and permeable selves: Spirit consultation in Denmark. In S. Fainzang & C. Haxaire (Eds.), *Of bodies and symptoms: Anthropological perspectives on their social and medical treatment*. Tarragona: Publicacions URV.

Stemman, R. (2005). *Spirit communication: A comprehensive guide to the extraordinary world of mediums, psychics and the afterlife*. London: Piatkus.

Taves, A. (1999). *Fits, trances and visions: Experiencing religion and explaining experience from Wesley to James.* Princeton: Princeton University Press.

Taves, A. (2006). Where (fragmented) selves meet cultures: Theorising spirit possession. *Culture and Religion, 7* (2), 123-138.

Turner, E. (1993). The reality of spirits: A tabooed or permitted field of study. *Anthropology of Consciousness, 4* (1), 9-12.

Van Dusen, W. (1994). *The presence of other worlds: The psychological/spiritual findings of Emanuel Swedenborg.* West Chester: Chrysalis Books.

Velmans, M. (2007). The co-evolution of matter and consciousness. *Synthesis Philosophica, 22* (44), 273-282.

Warner, M. (2008). *Phantasmagoria: Spirit visions, metaphors, and media into the twenty-first century.* Oxford: Oxford University Press.

Wilson, P. J. (1967). Status ambiguity and spirit possession. *Man, 2* (3), 366-378.

Wilson, D.G. (2013). *Redefining shamanisms: Spiritualist mediums and other traditional shamans as apprenticeship outcomes.* London: Continuum.

Zingrone, N. (1994). Images of woman as medium: Power, pathology and passivity in the writings of Frederic Marvin and Cesare Lombrosso. In L. Coly & R.A. White (Eds.) *Women and parapsychology: Proceedings of an international conference* (pp. 90-123). New York: Parapsychology Foundation.

Table tipping exercise at the Arthur Findlay College, Stansted, England. Photograph by Shannon Taggart.

Cyber Psychics: Psychic Readings in Online Social Spaces

Tamlyn Ryan

Since the Internet was launched into the public domain in the mid 1990s, people have been using the web to find information and be sociable with others. Indeed, people have shaped internet technologies so we can do 'just about everything we do in real life, but we leave our bodies behind' (Rheingold, 2000, p.xvii). Psychic readings, which have taken place in real life for centuries, also take place in online social spaces. Certainly, psychic reading is a huge commercial venture (see Carrette & King, 2004; Wooffitt, 2006) and there is an abundance of websites dedicated to telling people their futures for the price of a premium rate telephone call. Yet there are numerous online social spaces where budding psychics and mediums meet to exchange psychic readings for free, integral to what they consider to be their spiritual lifestyle (Ryan, 2008). However, whilst sociologists of e-religion have studied world religions, sects and new religious movements comprehensively since the advent of the Internet, the spiritual nature of psychic readings online has up until now remained overlooked.

This chapter introduces the vast world of the cyber psychic by considering the various ways in which members of the psychic-spiritual milieu use social media to engage in psychic reading practice. Virtual community message board forums and chat rooms provide excellent spaces in which developing psychics and mediums can find support from others of like minds. As well as virtual communities, more recently psychics and mediums have been utilising social networking sites such as Facebook to not only find others with similar interests but also to offer and deliver their psychic readings. What follows is an introduction into psychic-spiritual practices online including an example of a participant observation of a synchronous psychic development circle which took place via a chat room. Drawing upon prior personal experience of an offline circle, the author provides a comparison between the offline and online psychic development circles in order to consider the motivating factors behind contributing to free psychic reading exchange in online social spaces. The chapter concludes that social media applications available on the Internet provide the spiritual seeker ample opportunity to engage in a reciprocal form of mutual support and psychic reading exchange. Moreover, being able to do this supports the spiritual seekers' goal of becoming a more spiritual person.

The Psychic-Spiritual Milieu

Typically, psychics and mediums are interested in a wide range of spiritual topics. Indeed, the different techniques employed in psychic readings, and the corresponding eclecticism of spiritual interests are characteristic of the cultic milieu and strongly associated with the beliefs and practices of the New Age Movement (see Campbell, 2002). Such interests are many and varied, incorporating for instance, theosophical teachings from Christianity, Buddhism, Taoism or Hinduism. Similarly, spiritual interests may also include a fascination with fairies, angels, American Indians, crystals, auras and divination techniques such as the I-Ching, Tarot, palmistry or psychometry. Although some mediums and psychics like to distance themselves from the negative stereotypes associated with the New Age Movement, their spiritual interests are an important part of their everyday lives. To them, being able to help other people with their skills is paramount to what they term their spiritual work (Ryan, 2008). Furthermore, there is a belief that they are working for Spirit. Indeed, many mediums and psychics call their skills a 'gift' from Spirit, and believe their life's purpose is to use that gift to help others (Wooffitt, 2006).

Yet, despite a growing interest in psychic and spiritual matters, such beliefs and practices remain marginalised and open to ridicule from dominant cultural conventions. However, as Campbell (2002) notes in regards to the wider cultic milieu, there appears to be a common consciousness and a sense of mutual sympathy and support amongst individuals who follow cultic or New Age interests. Indeed, individual members of the milieu are united within some sort of community or, "common ideology of seekership" (Campbell, 2002). This may also apply to what could be regarded as a smaller, more specific section of the wider cultic milieu which, placing emphasis on the spiritual orientations of psychic practices, may be more suitably termed the psychic-spiritual milieu (Ryan, 2008). Within the psychic-spiritual milieu there exists a common consciousness which fosters a supportive network in which developing psychics and mediums may use their psychic skills to help others as well as learn about themselves as spiritual people. As will be discussed, the Internet provides ample opportunity to expand this supportive network. First however, we may briefly consider the tools and techniques of psychic practitioners.

Psychic Practices: Tools and Techniques

Wooffitt (2006, p.1) defines the apparent abilities of psychics (and mediums) as being able to "communicate with the dead…acquire information by psychic powers…gain personal or intimate knowledge of people and events from the arrangement of tarot cards, or the lines in the hand, or simply by holding personal belongings". Thus, contemporary psychics 'read' for their clients (sitters) using different techniques. The Parapsychological Association (PA) have collated these various techniques under the concept of 'psi phenomena', a term used to denote activity related to paranormal cognition (e.g. extrasensory perception, ESP) and paranormal action (e.g. psychokinesis). Clairvoyance and precognition are used by the PA to denote the specific activities that take place during a psychic reading. Clairvoyance is defined as the "acquisition of information concerning an object or contemporary physical event". In terms of precognition, the PA defines this as, "a form of extrasensory perception in which the target is some future event that cannot be deduced from normally known data in the present". However, it is important to note that amongst the psychic-spiritual milieu, clairvoyance is often used to refer to a number of psychic abilities such as mediumship, visions and psychic dreams.

Mediumship

Meanwhile, defined as "the alleged ability to receive communications from people who have died", mediumship is considered as being distinct from the abilities of a psychic (Fontana, 2005, p.91). Psychics often rely on intuition or extra-sensory perception and they may use tools such as Tarot cards and crystal balls to help them perceive information. Mediums however claim to receive their information from speaking directly to spirits in the spirit world, or via their 'spirit-guide' (Fontana, 2005). There are two particular ways in which a medium is said to receive information from spirit – physical and mental mediumship. Physical mediumship is also known as trance, or transfiguration mediumship whereby the mediums body is said to be temporarily inhabited by a spirit to produce psychokinetic effects such as 'raps' (knocking) or manifestations of spirit (Fontana, 2005; see also psychics.co.uk). Mental mediumship, meanwhile, involves the medium communicating with spirits to pass on messages to the people they are reading for (sitters).

Messages may be received in different ways: clairvoyance, clairaudience and clairsentience. As already noted, clairvoyance, "clear-seeing", relates to the medium seeing images. Meanwhile, clairaudience, or "clear hearing" relates to messages heard by the medium and clairsentience, or "clear sensing", involves the medium having impressions placed on them by spirit, usually in relation to the spirit's characteristics. Mediums will typically experience just one of these skills, although it is not uncommon for them to use a combination of these abilities. Many mediums will train in a psychic development circle organised by a church affiliated with the Spiritualist National Union. Spiritualism first became popular during the late nineteenth century (see for instance Hunt, 2003; Fontana, 2005; Gilbert, 2008). Today however, whilst the Spiritualist church development circle remains a popular way to develop mediumship, there are numerous independent psychic and mediumship development circles and groups across the country. Having the supportive environment in which to explore and develop ones psychic abilities is considered important for budding psychics and mediums. Such groups are not easy to locate however. The Internet has helped to make the psychic-spiritual community more accessible to seekers wishing to find online groups that foster this supportive environment.

The Psychic-Spiritual Milieu in Cyberspace

Although early writings about the Internet may now be considered a little over-optimistic or technologically deterministic, the impact of new internet technologies on all factions of social life cannot be overlooked (Dawson and Cowan, 2004). Whilst premium-rate telephone psychic "hotlines" are advertised widely on the Internet, the interests, beliefs and practices of the psychic-spiritual milieu have a significant presence on the Internet (Ryan, 2008). New and alternative forms of religion and spirituality have made use of the Web to provide information and promote services relating to their practices. Moreover, as an important communication tool, the Internet provides ample opportunity to network and interact with others who share specific interests. Particularly, social media such as virtual communities and social networking sites (SNSs) afford seekers of psychic-spirituality the opportunity to socialise with like-minded individuals. Social media is also being used by those wishing to engage in psychic reading practice.

Social Media and Psychic Readings

Of specific interest in this chapter are those psychic readings which are exchanged for free via social media. Virtual communities and groups based on psychic interests within social networking sites (such as that on Facebook) constitute a significant portion of the online psychic-spiritual milieu. They offer spaces in which seekers of psychic-spirituality may meet others who share similar interests or who have had similar experiences. Within the psychic-spiritual milieu there are numerous virtual communities that utilise either synchronous or asynchronous means of communicating, although often both will be available.

For instance, Craig and Jane Hamilton-Parker founded their very successful web community www.psychics.co.uk in 1998. Since then, the community has grown rapidly and the website content has evolved extensively. The website itself has a busy synchronous chat forum with several chat rooms, as well as an asynchronous discussion board forum. The community side of the website is well organised. There is an obvious hierarchy to membership status with general visitors to the chat room and the online community discussion boards, whilst those who pay a subscription to the site may access extra features, including psychic development classes. The regular chat room based "psychic reading sessions" are scheduled where registered members of the site can attend and wait to see if they will receive a reading. Whilst membership to all web communities fluctuate over time, psychics.co.uk is still highly regarded as an online social space in which one may learn the skills of mediumship and find others of like-mind.

Meanwhile, psychic and mediumship readings are freely offered on many other websites such as InspiredofSpirit.com (see also, www.spiritualforums.com; www.mysticboards.com). Established in 2004, the activity on this website centres chiefly on an active message board community. There is also an active chat room within which scheduled psychic development circles and real time psychic and mediumship readings take place. Classes in Tarot reading and other related psychic-spiritual interests are also conducted via the chat room. Asynchronous (non-real time) readings are freely offered on the community message boards, which are monitored to ensure the safety of all participants. What is especially important is that the sitter is requested to provide detailed feedback of their reading in exchange. This allows the budding psychic or medium to review the progress of their online psychic development.

Reading Online: Experiences

Readers from one chat room recounted their experiences in the pilot study for my doctoral research (Ryan, 2008). For instance, one reader told how reading asynchronously via a message board is often much easier as it gives the recipient time to digest what is being said before giving what is hoped to be detailed feedback.

Feedback from recipients of readings is considered crucial to the development of one's psychic or mediumship skills. Meanwhile, another reader spoke about his experiences of reading in real time synchronous communication via MSN Messenger (now Windows Live Messenger) and within various psychic chat rooms across the Internet. He recounted how when he first started to use the Internet for psychic readings, he was very uncertain as to how it could work, believing that the recipient would have to be present. Yet, he soon discovered that the images and messages he received from spirit came in just the same way as if conducting the reading in the presence of the sitter. However, he did point out one key difference in reading online in real time compared with a face to face reading:

> ...Online is very time-consuming...if I am reading face to face then I realise I may be reading the message slightly incorrectly...if that is the case it is very quick to establish. Online also relies on my typing,,,,Another storr.[sic] (Keith, male aged 49)

Social Networking Sites

Whilst virtual communities remain popular, in recent years social networking sites (SNSs) such as MySpace and Facebook have proved even more so (Ellison, Steinfield & Lampe, 2006). Indeed, this chapter would remain incomplete if SNS, in particular Facebook (currently the most popular SNS with over 500 million active members), remain unmentioned. SNSs enable users to create personal profiles and build social networks (Boyd & Ellison, 2007). On Facebook, connections are usually made with friends and family members, but there is potential to extend networks to complete strangers who are added to the users "friends" list. Social networks are then visible to their "friends" and they also have the option of allowing "friends of friends" to see their network so more connections can be made. How connections are made within the psychic-spiritual milieu, and how SNSs are important in the construction and management of psychic-spiritual identity form the basis of part of my doctoral research and will be discussed in future publications. Facebook however, offers ample opportunity for developing and practicing psychics and mediums. Facebook groups, for example, provide specific places for group discussion on spiritual topics as well as a space in which budding psychics and mediums can offer readings for free in much the same way they do in virtual community message board forums. Facebook is also an excellent tool for self promotion.

Studying the Psychic-Spiritual World

Whilst studies of religious virtual community have shed light on specific practices of mainstream religions (see for instance, Campbell, 2005; Hutchings, 2007), the practices in which members of the psychic-spiritual milieu engage in online social spaces remains unknown. To date, the author is not aware of other academic research relating to psychic-spiritual practices in online social spaces. However, sociological research has been carried out into psychic practices offline. Whilst some time ago Jorgensen (1992) conducted a three-year participant observational study of the 1970s esoteric milieu for his doctoral research. During this time he took on the role of practitioner of the Tarot, offering readings at numerous psychic fairs taking place at the time, in an area known as The Valley. Whilst his research gave him ample opportunity to consider the social organisation of psychic readings, Jorgensen noted how his role as practitioner of the occult Tarot lacked what he considered to be a closer association with a more personally meaningful "occult knowledge of reality".

In the 1970s, interest in paranormal and psychic phenomena was not widely accepted. In contrast, such interests are less of a taboo today. Indeed activities such as ghost vigils, mediumship and psychic/holistic fairs are very popular in the twenty first century. Indeed, it could be argued that the Internet has facilitated the growth in popularity of these activities. Thus, Jorgensen's study of the 1970s esoteric milieu, some twenty years before the Internet became available to the general public, could be considered to be somewhat outdated.

In an attempt to update Jorgensen's research however, the researcher set out to examine closely the more subjective and intrapsychic experience of this phenomenon, benefiting from being immersed in the experience itself. A keen personal interest in psychic spirituality and involvement in the psychic-spiritual culture for the last ten years afforded the researcher the prior "insider" knowledge useful for gaining the in-depth perspective Jorgensen felt was missing from his own study (see Anderson, 2006). Thus, the present study involved the researcher taking on the role of cyber psychic, participating in online psychic reading exchange within a synchronous psychic development circle.

Methodological and Ethical Concerns

Studying the online psychic-spiritual milieu requires the researcher to take into account a number of considerations. Firstly, the ontological status of paranormally derived cognition and the researchers own particular epistemological position. Despite her own experience within the psychic-spiritual culture online, an agnostic approach was adopted for this study. Whilst being able to participate as fully as possible by drawing on prior beliefs and experience, the researcher "steps out of" the research setting in order to examine it critically (Davies, 1999; Chang, 2008). Further thought on the researcher's personal epistemological leanings is discussed elsewhere. Secondly, one is also required to consider carefully the research design and ethical concerns for online research (see Hine, 2000).

The question: what is different about researching online social spaces? is a good place to begin thinking about issues such as whether informed consent is required and to what extent participants can expect a degree of privacy given the public nature of most online interaction. Agencies such as the British Sociological Association (BSA), the Economic and Social Research Council (ESRC) and the Association of Internet Researchers (AoIR) have addressed the need to develop a standardised set of ethics. However, the development of ethical guidelines for online research is especially complex, given that the Internet is in a constant state of flux and technological change (Berry, 2004). Researchers must allow for flexibility in the design of online research methods and ethical approaches, particularly as guidelines concerning internet research are still in development (BSA, 2002).

Indeed, the issue of informed consent in online participant observational research has caused significant debate. It may be argued here that information online can be considered to be in the "public domain". The premise is that behaviour in a public space, for instance a public house, can be observed without the need for the researcher to disclose their true identity or seek permission to observe others (see Hilbert, 1980; Homan, 1980 for discussion). Recent guidelines from the ESRC (2010) address this issue:

> Information provided in forums or spaces on the Internet and Web that are intentionally public would be valid to consider "in the public domain", but the public nature of any communication or information on the Internet should always be critically examined, and the identity of individuals protected unless it is critical to the research. (ESRC, 2010, section 1.3.2.5)

In regards to the study situations discussed in this chapter, all participants were aware they were being observed for research purposes.

Participant Observation: In-Depth Participation

The study involved participant observation of a synchronous chat-room based psychic development circle. The researcher undertook the role of "participant as observer" (Gold, 1958), and was able to draw on prior experience and personal interest in psychic-spiritual development. For a period of nine months (June, 2009 – March, 2010), she participated in a weekly synchronous psychic-spiritual development circle, held in a chat room created on wireclub.com. The two hour circle took place Monday evenings between the hours of 8pm and 10pm. On average, there were three other participants each week. Chrissie, aged 52, ran the circle, recruiting the other participants via her Facebook status message. Unemployed, Chrissie has been a Spiritualist medium for over twenty years. Whilst she regularly gives mediumship demonstrations in Spiritualist churches and centres near her home, she is also a psychic artist. Meanwhile, the other two regular participants were John, aged 38 and Janey, aged 34. Other, occasional, participants included Karen and June, both aged 48 and Todd, 29. During the circle, the researcher would be seated at a dining room table working on a laptop computer. Interaction within the weekly circle was conveniently transcribed digitally as the chat room event unfolded, whilst fieldwork notes were written up during and afterwards.

The study was concerned with extrapolating the key similarities and differences between the online development circle and its offline counterpart. The researcher had had prior experience in participating in an offline psychic spiritual development circle intermittently for a period of five years prior to commencing her doctoral research. The offline circle would take place in the home of the organiser Marianne, a spiritual practitioner who has been running development classes and psychic development workshops for about fifteen years. The various participants in her classes come from a variety of backgrounds and, whilst classes consisted mainly of women aged between 25 and 55, there were male attendees on several occasions.

A typical class would take place in Marianne's study. Attendees would sit in a semi-circle facing Marianne who sat at the front. Behind her, on top of a bookcase full with books relating to holistic therapies and esoteric subjects, sat a vase of fresh flowers and several lit tea-light candles. The room was also lit by a small lamp in the far corner. The walls of the room were bare apart from a 10" by 10" black and white photograph of a Buddha. In contrast to the researcher being seated at her dining table in front of a computer screen, in Marianne's circle, she was seated on a plastic garden chair in a dimly lit room. The location of the researcher in relation to other participants in the psychic development circle however, did not impede upon her involvement. However, despite the difference in setting there are basic similarities and differences between offline and online psychic development circles that are unpacked in following section, along with a consideration of the motivating factors behind individual participation in online psychic development.

The Online Psychic Development Circle

Psychic development circles provide an environment in which those wishing to build on their psychic and mediumship skills can find support off others who may have more experience. The two circle settings the researcher participated in shared some similarities typical to the development circle. For example each followed a particular procedure. Both circles began with an opening prayer or ritual and involved various exercises based on meditation and visualisation techniques before ending in a closing prayer or ritual. The opening prayer or ritual is an important component of the psychic or spiritual development circle as it sets the scene for the work that members of the circle intend to engage in (for instance see Hunter, 2010). In a study of online Pagans it was found that the opening ritual is "first and foremost, a mode of paying attention" (Smith, 1987 in Cowan, 2005, p.137). Setting the scene through an opening ritual or prayer, whether on or offline, is accepted amongst participants as a signal to "pay attention" and "be present", for instance, for the following two hours. Furthermore, the opening prayer acts as a request to God, Spirit or other preferred supernatural entity, to protect members of the circle whilst they work psychically, for instance, in Pagan and Wiccan rituals, such as 'drawing the circle', by invoking the Spirit guardians of the elements (Earth, Air, Fire, and Water). This has the same effect as the opening prayer within the psychic development circle; those participating in the ritual will feel protected by the spirit guardians they have invited into the circle. The belief is that if one works without psychic protection, one is vulnerable to attack from darker spirit forces (e.g., see Bloom, 1997). Prayers are also used as a way of invoking protection by a supernatural entity, purportedly an angel, spirit guide or other such "positive force". The following is an example of one of the prayers used to start the online psychic development circle. The prayer is similar to that used in a Spiritualist church:

> Chrissie: Dear Divine Spirit, guides, helpers and family
> Chrissie: i ask you tonight to draw close to us as we join here
> Chrissie: to develop in the way that you feel we need to
> Chrissie: we accept your wisdom and your teachings and in return we ask for you help to understand the lessons that are shown to us

Chrissie: please place a blanket of protection around us
whilst we work
Chrissie: Amen
Janey: amen
John: amen
Tamlyn: amen
Todd: amen

Thus, the performance of an opening ritual, whether visual or textual, does something. It acts to signify that what will happen from this point for the next two hours will be devoted to the purpose of the gathering. The reply of "amen" acts in acknowledgement from the other participants that they understand what they are required to do.

Meanwhile offline in the circle organised by Marianne, the opening ritual was very different, and very visual. But it still did something. Marianne would begin the evening's proceedings by opening her arms out widely to the sides, and each participant would do the same. Participants of the group would then take a deep breath in and then, whilst drawing arms together again, bringing their hands together as if in prayer, would breathe out and visualise the room filling with white light. Marianne and the participants would then bow their heads over their hands in acknowledgement that they were now starting spiritual work. The commencement of spiritual work would depend on the context of the circle. Typically in Marianne's offline class, discussion would centre on how each participant was feeling and how their week had been in general. Marianne and the other members of the class would listen to whoever was talking with minimal interruption.

Only when each participant had spoken would Marianne then use the information people had shared to begin a discussion. Usually, this would entail discussing an issue somebody had had during the week, and offering potential solutions based on Marianne's intuitive feelings about the situation. Sometimes,

Marianne would suggest that a member of the circle required healing, for instance, and then a short healing ritual would take place, usually by way of a visualisation exercise. Time would then be taken for a meditation. Marianne would guide participants of the circle into a meditation by instructing them through a visualisation. After around two minutes she would stop talking and allow everyone to continue with their meditation to explore their own visualisations. The meditation would typically take around twenty minutes.

Online however, the period of discussion concerning how each person was would typically be limited to small-talk engaged in whilst waiting for all participants to join the chat session. Once she was satisfied that everyone was present in the chat room, Chrissie would announce that she would say the prayer. Following on from the prayer, Chrissie would offer some philosophical thought based on her own preparation for the circle that evening. A short meditation would then follow. The example below illustrates Chrissie introducing some philosophical reflection before giving instructions on the evening's meditation exercise:

> Chrissie: tonight i am inspired to talk to you about dont laugh.... winnie the pooh
>
> Chrissie: you see within the woods, especially the 100 acres woods, you are never truly alone
>
> Chrissie: for within the woods is an energy and a wisdom that can only be imagined though books, listening to guides talking in trance through mediums or funny enough through cartoons
>
> Chrissie: you see there is always someone around for those poor cartoon characters, you never see them truly alone forever do you
>
> Chrissie: they have a happy bunny come jump on their laps, or a bird will fly and sing a song before landing on their shoulders

Chrissie: there is also a great healing that takes place and then everyone starts singing and dancing...

Chrissie: and everyone starts to feel great.... but even in cartoons, a sadness will return briefly as the main characters have to decide how to sort out their problems

Chrissie: but they know this time around that they dont have to sort it out on their own

Chrissie: sometimes they just have to sleep on it... goldilocks

Chrissie: sometimes they need to arrange a great party and make a dress or get pumpkins to turn in to carriages

Chrissie: but they always find a way in the end

Chrissie: and the message here tonight is.... so can you

Chrissie: you too can draw upon all the energy and the friendships and get the support if you truly need it...

Chrissie: so now we shall go into meditation

Chrissie: this is what i would like you all to do

Chrissie: we are going to walk into the 100 acre woods and we will look around until someone comes and meets us... spend some time with them and ask them for some words that could help you and ask them for a gift and then come back here

Chrissie: in about 3 or 4 mins... please let me know when you are back

The key difference between both the online and offline context of the circle is the length of time allowed for the meditative exercise. Being co-present in intimate surroundings, the offline circle is able to engage in a relatively lengthy meditation. Online however, without the physical proximity and trust that can build quicker in the offline circle, twenty minutes is a long time to ensure participants will remain attentive during the exercise.

Sustaining attention in the online circle can be difficult, however, and this provides us with a point of departure in terms of how the online differs to the offline circle. The World Wide

Web offers a vast world of entertainment and information that offers easy distraction. The following extract is an example of this. During an exercise in which John is connecting to a spirit that Chrissie, a spirit artist, has drawn, Chrissie is somewhat annoyed by the discovery that Todd appears to be otherwise engaged on Facebook:

> Chrissie: Todd why are you on facebook?
> Todd: i am off it now
> Chrissie: i did ask you to close the window earlier
> Todd: k
> Chrissie: so Todd now i'll ask who you think this portait is for in the group and you would have lost your connection
> John: feel something -a tingling in the same area, by the side of the head now
> Todd: i think it is for Tamlyn to
> Chrissie: if you were at a church circle, you wouldnt go out of the building and i ask the same here please

It is expected that if one is to be present in a circle, then one participates fully. As noted by Chrissie, if Todd was sitting in an offline development circle such as that held regularly in Spiritualist churches he would be required to stay present within the circle at all times. Todd's distraction however does not faze the others in the group. One could imagine if this had happened in a co-present group, other members would be distracted and this would be seen as an interruption of the "energy" within the circle.

Spiritual and psychic development work, in both online and offline contexts, depend heavily on the full participation of those present. As already discussed, those who attend circles such as these do so to find support amongst others who they perceive to be of like mind. Indeed, despite the weak ties within the online group (or indeed the offline circle), there is reciprocal support amongst participants (Lange, 2007; Wellman & Gulia, 1999).

There is an unspoken agreement that those participating in such groups will both give and accept a degree of support from others. Furthermore, key to finding this support is being able to trust in the other participants.

Sitting in an offline circle, each participant is physically aware of the others in the group. Facial expressions and voice intonation aid communication and trust can build more readily. Online, however, each participant has only the textual contributions from other people. Indeed, they have to trust that those others are who they say they are (see Donath, 1999). Furthermore, this online context requires each participant to be attentive to the needs and contributions of the others – the prayer and the exercises help to instil a sense of common identity and shared vision or goal (Philipsen, 1992). Thus participants in the online circle recognise that, as in an offline circle, it is time to work together to progress spiritually.

Working together in a circle relies on each member being willing to co-operate and participate in what is happening. It could be argued that this requires considerably more effort in an online situation (e.g., see Donath, 1999). Certainly, the prayer of protection and the meditation exercise go a considerable way toward ensuring that participants are ready to engage in the activities. However, we may consider in more depth the motivating factors involved in psychic development practice online. Kollock (1999) wonders how online communication can facilitate such sharing and cooperation amongst complete strangers. Examining why people are happy to cooperate with one another in anonymous online social spaces, he concludes: "There are fundamental features of online interaction which change the costs and benefits of social action in dramatic ways" (Kollock, 1999, p.221). In considering the motivating factors behind people engaging in knowledge sharing in online social spaces, he concludes that people engage in online knowledge sharing economy because they get something out of it.

Using the notion of 'gift exchange', Kollock notes how online gift exchange, the gift of digital information, is more generous and much more risky. He argues that online, people freely give advice (a form of knowledge) without necessarily expecting anything back. Within both the on and offline psychic development circle, advice is given from the interpretation of messages supposedly from Spirit. However, the key difference is that the online circle is free. Offline, classes such as the one organised by Marianne may incur a fee of around £8 per class. We may ask then, what else could encourage people to engage with strangers in online social spaces in this way?

For an explanation, we could consider the notion of seekership (Campbell, 1992) and how seeking to identify with others is the key motivational factor at play here. Seeking support for their spiritual beliefs and practices online allows members of the psychic-spiritual milieu to begin to identify with others who they perceive to be 'more spiritual'. By participating – sharing knowledge – in online social spaces they become more fully socialized within a network, internalising the shared language and goals of the wider milieu. Members of the milieu seek identification with more established members to ensure that what they believe in and what they are practicing is correct, and they are thus developing spiritually in the correct way. Chiu, Hsu and Wang (2006) studied motivations for knowledge sharing in virtual communities. They state: 'People who come to a virtual community are not just seeking information or knowledge and solving problems; they also treat it as a place to meet other people, to seek support, friendship and a sense of belongingness' (Chiu et al., 2006, p.1874).

The Internet provides the ideal social space in which people seeking companionship may find some sense of belonging and identification with others who share their interests (e.g., see Baym, 1998; Chiu et al., 2006; Evans, 2003; Kling, 1996; Nettleton et al., 2002; Rheingold, 1994; Watson, 1997). Within the psychic-spiritual milieu and its principle of epistemological individualism, it is important for members to seek out others for reassurance and identification. However, in online social spaces, members of a social network need to participate in and contribute to knowledge sharing in order for the community or network to sustain. This is a two-way relationship. In order for a person to feel a sense of belonging within that community or network, they must be rewarded in some way for their contribution (Wellman & Gulia, 1999). Thus, on the individual level, seekers are looking to identify with others with whom they can form a reciprocal relationship of support. However, this relies on the wider group dynamics in supporting that relationship of reciprocity (Kollock, 1999).

The shared vision of the psychic-spiritual development circle is for those who are participating to feel as if they are in a supportive environment with like minded people. The goal, meanwhile, is to take part in regular sessions in the hope that within time, individuals will begin to feel as if they are progressing spiritually. By engaging in reciprocal support over time, participants will begin to feel as if they helping others (Kollock, 1999) – the ultimate goal of being a spiritually minded person (Ryan, 2008). In this way, they also feel as if they are needed, that they are making a difference to someone else's life (Baym, 2010). Thus, it may be suggested that not only do seekers engage in psychic reading online to practice their skills, but they do so in order to identify with others and find belongingness (Chiu *et al.*, 2006). Furthermore, they regard helping others in their own spiritual development (by offering mutual support), as part of being a spiritual person – what they are indeed seeking to be.

Conclusion

This chapter has considered how the Internet and its various social media applications may be used in the practice of psychic reading. Using the psychic development circle as an example, the online and offline contexts of psychic development were discussed. In particular, it may be suggested that the online social environment provides the spiritual seeker ample opportunity to find others of similar interests. Being able to identify with others is important in the life of the seeker. However, more than this, the online spiritual context – the psychic development circle, provides a unique setting for reciprocal support. It is this opportunity for mutual support which ultimately allows the individual spiritual seeker to not only feel as if they are receiving the guidance they are seeking but that ultimately, they feel able to help others in their own spiritual and psychic development. People are motivated to engage in psychic development online to not only find support but offer support to others (Kollock, 1999; Wellman & Gulia, 1999). In turn, this makes them feel like they are needed (Baym, 2010); that they are doing something useful and they are helping others. In psychic-spiritual terms, they are able to help others progress on their spiritual journey. Thus, the practice of free psychic reading exchange online supports the spiritual seekers need to feel that they are becoming a spiritual person.

References

Anderson, L. (2006). Analytic autoethnography. *Journal of Contemporary Ethnography, 35*, 373-395.

Baym, N. K. (1998). The emergence of community in computer-mediated communication. In S. Jones, *Cybersociety: Computer-mediated communication and community* (pp.35-68). Thousand Oaks, CA: Sage.

Baym, N. K. (2010). *Personal connections in the digital age.* Cambridge: Polity.

Berry, D. M. (2004). Internet research: Privacy, ethics and alienation: an open source approach. *Internet Research 14* (4), 323-332.

Bloom, W. (1997). *Psychic protection: Creating positive energies for people and places.* London: Piatkus.

Boyd, D. M., & Ellison, N. B. (2007). Social network sites: Definition, history and scholarship. *Journal of Computer-Mediated Communication, 13* (1), 210-230.

British Sociological Association, BSA. (March, 2002). Statement of ethical practice for the British Sociological Association. Available online at <http://www.britsoc.co.uk/user_doc/Statement%20of%20Ethical%20Practice.pdf> [accessed 16/05/2008].

Campbell, C. (2002 [1972]). The cult, the cultic milieu and secularization. In J. Kaplan and H. Lööw (Eds.). *The cultic milieu: Oppositional subcultures in an age of globalisation.* Walnut Creek, CA: AltaMira Press.

Campbell, H. (2005). *Exploring religious community online: We are one in the network.* New York: Peter Lang.

Carrette, J., & King, R. (2005). *Selling spirituality: The silent takeover of religion.* London: Routledge.

Chang, H. (2008). *Autoethnography as method.* Walnut Creek, CA: Left Coast Press Inc.

Chiu, C. M., Hsu, M. H., & Wang, E. T. G. (2006). Understanding knowledge sharing in virtual communities: An integration of social capital and social cognitive theories. *Decision Support Systems, 42,* 1872-1888.

Cowan, D. E. (2005). *Cyberhenge: Modern pagans on the Internet.* London: Routledge.

Davies, C. A. (1999). *Reflexive ethnography: A guide to researching selves and others.* London: Routledge.

Dawson, L. L., & Cowan, D. E. (2004). Introduction. In L. L. Dawson and D. E. Cowan (Eds.), *Religion online: Finding faith on the Internet* (pp. 1-16). London: Routledge.

Donath, J. S. (1999). Identity and deception in the virtual community. In M. A. Smith and P. Kollock (Eds.). *Communities in cyberspace.* London: Routledge.

Ellison, N., Steinfield, C., & Lampe, C. (2006). Spatially bounded online social networks and social capital: The role of Facebook. In *Proceedings of the Annual Conference of the International Communication Association,* 2006.

Economic and Social Research Council (2010). Framework for research ethics (FRE). Available from <www.esrc.ac.uk> [Accessed 05/06/2010].

Evans, K. (2003). The significance of virtual communities. *Journal of Social Issues 2* (1). available online at <http://www.whb.co.uk/socialissues/indexvol2.htm> [accessed 15/07/2010].

Fontana, D. (2005). *Is there an afterlife: A comprehensive overview of the evidence.* Hants, UK: O Books.

Gilbert, H. (2008). *Speaking of spirits: Representations and experiences of the spirit world in British spirit mediumship.* Unpublished Doctoral Thesis, University of York.

Gold, R. L. (1958). Roles in sociological field observations. *Social Forces, 1* (4), 217-223.

Hilbert, R. A. (1980). Covert participant observation: On its nature and practice. *Journal of Contemporary Ethnography, 9* (1), 51-78.

Hine, C. (2000). *Virtual ethnography.* London: Sage.

Homan, R. (1980). The ethics of covert methods. *The British Journal of Sociology, 31* (1), 46-59.

Hunt, S. (2003). *Alternative religions: A sociological introduction.* Aldershot, Hants: Ashgate.

Hunter, J. (2010). Contemporary mediumship and séance groups in the UK. *Psychical Studies: The Journal of the Unitarian Society for Psychical Studies, 76,* 7-13.

Hutchings, T. (2007). Creating church online: A case-study approach to religious experience. *Studies in World Christianity, 13*(3), 243-260.

Jorgensen, D. L. (1992). *The esoteric scene, cultic milieu, and occult tarot.* London: Garland Publishing.

Kenworthy, D. (1998). *A 1-900 Psychic Speaks.* Charlottesville, VA: Hampton Roads Publishing Company Inc.

Kling, R. (1996). Social relationships in electronic forums: Hangouts, salons, workplaces and communities. In Kling, R (Ed.). *Computerization and controversy: Value conflicts and social choices* (2nd ed.). San Diego: Academic Press.

Kollock, P. (1999). The economies of online cooperation: Gifts and public goods in cyberspace. In M. A. Smith and P. Kollock (Eds.), *Communities in cyberspace.* London: Routledge.

Lange, P. (2007). *Fostering friendship through video production: How youth use YouTube to enrich local interaction.* International Communication Association Conference, May 27, 2007 San Francisco, California.

Nettleton, S., Pleace, N., Burrows, R., Muncer, S., & Loader, B. (2002). The reality of virtual social support. In S. Woolgar (Ed.), *Virtual society? Technology, cyberbole, reality.* Oxford University Press: Oxford.

Philpsen, G. (1992). *Speaking culturally: Explorations in social communication.* Albany, NY: SUNY Press.

Rheingold, H. (1994). *Virtual community: Finding connection in a computerized world.* London: Secker & Warburg.

Rheingold, H. (2000). *The virtual community: Homesteading on the electronic frontier.* London: MIT Press.

Ryan, T. (2008). *Cyber psychics: An exploratory study of psychic spirituality in cyberspace.* Unpublished MA Dissertation, University of York.

Wellman, B. & Gulia, M. (1999). Virtual communities as communities: Net surfers don't ride alone. In M.A. Smith and P. Kollock (Eds.), *Communities in cyberspace.* London: Routledge.

Watson, N. (1997). Why we argue about virtual community: A case study of the phish.net fan community. In S. Jones (Ed.), *Virtual culture: Identity and communication in cybersociety.* London: Sage.

Woodruff, F. (1998). *Secrets of a telephone psychic.* Oregon: Beyond Words Publishing.

Wooffitt, R. (2006). *The language of mediums and psychics: The social organization of everyday miracles.* Hampshire: Ashgate.

Mambo Carmen becomes possessed by the Loa Gede at a Voodoo ceremony in Brooklyn, NY.
Photograph by Shannon Taggart.

SPIRIT POSSESSION
IN EAST AFRICA

BARBARA STÖCKIGT

There are centuries old therapeutic practices that have been, and still are being, applied successfully in non-European contexts (see Ellenberger, 1985), in particular, healing through the use of trance states and spirit possession. Such practices play a significant role in the traditional healing rituals of Africa, but are seldom, if ever, included in natural science oriented psychotherapy methods. In consciousness research, trance and possession states are referred to as altered states of consciousness (ASCs). It is possible to distinguish between pathological and non-pathological ASCs. The spiritual and shamanic trances of the healer, employed during healing rituals, can be labeled non-pathological, for example, and may be contrasted with the states of consciousness associated with schizophrenia, which can be considered pathological in nature (see Scharfetter, 1990). While in Western societies ASC are predominantly the remit of psychiatry, ASC are institutionalized in up to 90% of non-European cultures, and are often held to be desirable states with positive applications (see Bourguignon, 1973). Such directed therapeutic use of ASC has traditionally been employed for centuries, but has largely been forgotten in modern Euro-American societies. In traditional cultures ASC are generally used to heal people, and there is a wealth of knowledge concerning how ASC can be triggered and put to use.

The contents of this chapter are drawn from my doctoral thesis, which pursued the question of how the treatment and cure of the pathological ASC of a psychotic person can be initiated by the non-pathological ASC of the traditional healer. In an attempt to promote the exchange of different medical systems, the views of the healers with whom I worked are of central importance in this study. The secondary questions of this research are concerned with whether healing by ASC includes effective cross-cultural factors, and if our Western psychotherapy can be broadened by this (see Stöckigt, 2011). The study employed qualitative research methods, because of their emphasis on the subjectivity of social interactions and the complexity of personal experience.

In 2005 I undertook six-months of field-based research in East Africa, mainly in three different regions of Kenya (Nairobi, Western Kenya, Coast region), where 23 individual interviews with spiritual healers from six different ethnic groups (Swahili, Zigula, Nyamwezi, Mijikenda, Luo, Luyia) were carried out. The interviews were structured with reference to Flick's (1995) *episodic interview* and Spradley's (1979) *ethnographic interview.* Four of the interviewed healers were women, 19 were men. Ethnographic participant observation was employed throughout the research period (see Flick, 1995). In addition to the interviews, I attended treatments of psychological disorders (amongst others), demonstrations of various spiritual techniques, and spirit possessions performances.

From this initial fieldwork twelve interviews were selected, transcribed and analyzed. The analysis is based on a circulatory deconstruction, as proposed by Jaeggi, Faas & Mruck (1998). This open, and at the same time transparent, procedure leaves room for the development of new theories, and thus meets the requirements of the research data (see Jaeggi *et al.*, 1998). The selection of the interviews for analysis was based on their quality (for example the recording quality, openness of the healer in the interview context, and so on), region or ethnic group, and gender of the healer. Interviews with female healers were selected preferably with the aim of approximating the gender balance. Three interviews with female healers were therefore selected. In total three interviews with healers of each ethnic group of the Luo, the Luyia, the Mijikenda and the group of healers from the coastal region (Swahili, Zigula, Nyamwezi) were selected.

This field research, with its specific research questions, led me very quickly into the world of spirits. In this chapter, therefore, I would like to emphasise the importance of spirits in relation to traditional African healing systems.

The Spiritual Healer

In African traditional healing systems there is no uniform classification of types of healers. In a publication of the WHO a traditional healer is defined all in all as follows: 'A traditional healer is defined as an educated or lay person who claims an ability or a healing power to cure ailments, or a particular skill to treat specific types of complaints or afflictions and who might have gained a reputation in his own community or elsewhere. They may base their powers or practice on religion, supernatural experience, apprenticeship or family heritage' (Ahmed *et al.*, 1999, p. 79).

The term shaman was rarely used by the interviewed healers themselves, yet many parallels can be seen. Shamanism is a ubiquitous phenomenon in cultures which assume an animist world view (see Schenk & Rätsch, 1999; Walsh, 1998). According to Krippner a shaman offers 'spiritually-oriented services that other people are unable to provide' (Krippner, 1999, p. 72), and Eliade coined the description of the shaman as the great master of ecstasy (see Eliade, 1975). Following Eliade's classification, the majority of the interviewed traditional healers in this study can be seen as shamans, as they induce an ASC in themselves, in the sense of ecstatic possession trance, and use it for healing purposes.

According to the interviewed healers' own descriptions, the category of traditional healer is divided into spiritual healer and herbalist. The spiritual healer works with spirits, amongst other things. Herbalists, on the other hand, do not, and are often very keen to stress this fact. They are limited to the use of herbal medicines.

Except for one, all interviewed healers came from healer families. For ten of the spiritual healers, their healing gift was first revealed by a serious illness. Four of them explicitly reported psychological problems. In most cases, the disease persisted until the healing gift was recognized and accepted, but if the spirits were not listened to the illness would recur. The initiation is an important aspect of the development of the healing gift. In most cases, the initiation consists of two stages. In the first stage the initiate is purified and the spiritual gift is proclaimed. The ancestral spirits are called to welcome and accept the initiate. In the second stage the initiate has to prove his spiritual gift, and through this shows that he has been initiated into the mysteries of the spiritual world.

An initiation transcends time and space. It covers the past as well as the future, and empowers the healer to see other places (including visionary capabilities, clairvoyance, and distant healing). Through the initiation consciousness is expanded, and reality is experienced in a novel way. The boundaries of personhood become more permeable and allow contact with a transcendental and spiritual world (see Katz & Wexler, 1989). Initiation can be dangerous and, according to a female healer, can even mean the death of the initiate. While the risks are minimized through mentoring and guidance of the initiates, they are also taken into account in order to obtain greater knowledge. Only through the willingness to look death in the eyes, and through the experience of rebirth, can the initiate achieve a new level of consciousness. If an initiation is successful, the initiate has changed sides, '...from being a patient or sufferer to mastery over the source of affliction, and becoming a healer...' (Janzen, 1992, p. 89).

Once the initiate has passed the initiation, he is protected by his healing spirits. During the often long initiation process the character and the social behavior of the initiates are tested. He is instructed in his duties, obligations and rules by the elders, and they continue to advise and support him after the initiation. It is not only about gaining healing powers, but offering them to one's community and integrating them in a social network (see Katz & Wexler, 1989; Krippner, 1999). An initiation requires not only personal and family qualities, but also sacrifices (including money), a willingness to follow a particular life path, and courage.

The Psychotic Person

The term *psychosis* was not common to all interviewed healers. The more colloquial term *madness* was therefore used during interviews, enabling each of my informants to understand.

The symptoms of psychoses can vary greatly and often depend on the cause. The description of the symptoms of most of the spiritual healers is very clear and detailed, and shows many similarities to descriptions of Western medicine and comparative cultural studies (see Edergton, 1966; Leff, 1981; Machleidt & Calliess, 2004: WHO, 1979). They most closely resemble psychoses from the schizophrenic group. In addition, dissociative disorders, mood disorders, anxiety disorders, adjustment disorders, organic mental disorders, and mental disorders due to psychoactive substances can be outlined by the symptoms and causes listed. However, it has to be considered that a transfer of the description of *madness* by the spiritual healers to classification systems like ICD-10 WHO (1997), or the DSM-IV American Psychiatric

Association (2001), which were developed in the Euro-American culture, has significant limitations in different cultural contexts (see Machleidt & Callies, 2004). One's own cultural limitations should always be considered before attempting to classify disease phenomena from other cultures.

All spiritual healers named abnormalities in social behavior as a symptom. Nine spiritual healers emphasized aggressiveness. Strange and sometimes striking social behavior can occur, for example: unpredictability, avoidance of social contact and/or eye contact, neglect, ruthlessness and lack of cooperation, running away, nudity and sexual disinhibition. The sufferers may attract attention through bizarre gestures and sudden laughter which is incomprehensible to others, logorrhoea [incoherent talkativeness] and apparent self-talk. Psychoses can also be manifested in apathetic, dull and dumb behavior. Even suicide can occur. The literature confirms these numerous examples of striking social behavior (see Edergton, 1966; Maithya, 1996; Pfeiffer, 1994). Three spiritual healers mentioned precursors, or warning signs, of the later psychosis, including abnormal dreams and physical symptoms (such as headaches, dizziness, memory disturbances, noise and light sensitivity and changes in eating habits). None of the spiritual healers named delusion as a symptom, and few healers mentioned hallucinations. In contrast to a rational-technical world view, hallucinations and delusions are not always seen as pathological, but can be interpreted as real according to traditional African ideas (see Pfeiffer, 1994).

As in Western medicine the spiritual healers described a multifactorial etiology of psychoses. Almost all spiritual healers named physical (accidents, serious infectious diseases and so on), psychological (too much thinking, for example) and social (e.g. poverty) causes. Various causes may coexist. Furthermore, in contrast to Western medicine all interviewed healers mentioned spiritual causes and witchcraft. Spirit possessions and witchcraft may not only lead to psychological disorders, but can equally result in physical or social problems (see Abbo, 2003: Peltzer & Ebigbo, 1989: Swantz, 1990).

A spirit or demon possession often signifies punishment and persecution by the spirits, having done wrong by oneself or by a family member, such as theft, murder or a lack of respect for a deceased family member. The spirit possession is thus to be understood as the highest moral authority within the social structures and one can deduce that a psychotic person can bear the guilt of his state himself. Through possible punishment for acts within the family, strong family ties become obvious, which can represent both maintenance and restriction for the individual, especially from a Western point of view (see Maithya, 1996; Peltzer & Ebigbo, 1989: Pfeiffer, 1994). Certain other acts may also lead to spirit possession: if you have disturbed a ritual at specific locations (such as trees or ruins), or by meeting certain animals, (such as snakes). Furthermore, a psychological and physical disorder can exist because of a possession by healing spirits, signifying the existence of a spiritual gift. The healing spirits want to get attention through the disease or punish the afflicated if they are not listened to.

Witchcraft and curses are of great importance in the understanding of disease in East Africa. They emphasize social relations; for curses always come from a person and target somebody else, and thus represent disturbances in the social environment (see LeBeau, 1996). All spiritual healers clearly distinguished witchcraft from spirit possession by ancestral and healing spirits. It is obvious that all spiritual healers have knowledge about witchcraft, since all state that they can treat it. The transitions between intentional harm to a person and benefit or cure of a person by witchcraft can be quite fluid. One healer (Mijikenda), for example, mentioned justified witchcraft in the case of theft, and another healer (Luyia) even mentioned witchcraft as one of the spiritual talents. Witchcraft is often practiced in secret and has great power over people, resulting in varied fear responses throughout Africa. It gives those who use it, and those who fight it, great influence, which can lead to abuses on both sides. Taboos and discrimination exacerbate these phenomena (see Mbiti, 1969). Spiritual healing techniques for the benefit of the people and magical practices like witchcraft to the detriment of people are seldom distinguished between. This is one reason, among others, why spiritual healing processes are often discredited and their potential is misconstrued.

Some causes, in particular witchcraft and spirit possession as a result of one's own fault, can support stigma of mental illness and fear of it. Two healers emphasized not to touch any of their patients, so that no spirit or curse can take possession. Maithya confirms this when he writes that almost 80% of psychiatric patients [in Bungoma district, Kenya] are encountered with anxiety and avoidance, which can lead to mentally ill family members being kept hidden (some even in chains) in houses, where they will not receive traditional nor Western medical treatment at all (see Maithya, 1996; Pfeiffer, 1994).

The Nature and Meaning of Spirits

All spiritual healers agree that spirits are a natural creation of God, and a matter of course like God himself. They are everywhere, were always there and there are so many that it is impossible to mention them all. Spirits are part of the cosmic order and are involved in a hierarchy. One can recognize monotheistic (God the Creator as the supreme authority), animistic (deities in nature) and manistic (veneration of ancestors) elements. Everything, even the mundane, is under the influence of the transcendent and divine. As a spiritual healer one acts as an intermediary between spirits and humans, so spirits are intermediaries between God and man (see Scharfetter, 1992). Ancestral spirits are taken for granted by all spiritual healers. They must be honored by the living, and often certain skills, such as a healing gift, are inherited from them.

The relationship between humans and spirits is not always harmonious, and power plays no small role in it. As described earlier, spirits want to influence people. They can try to take possession of people, by lying in wait for them or seducing them, for instance. Even spiritual healers do not call their spirits too often, since possessions sap their strength. Conversely, people can control spirits (see Mbiti, 1969). The ability to control his healing spirits, and master them, distinguishes him and allows for the collaboration of the spiritual healer with his healing spirits (see Eliade, 1975; Walsh, 1998). However, this power can also be abused, and can go so far that people hold spirits as slaves, as one healer described. The question as to whether the spiritual healer controls his healing spirits or the other way around, cannot be answered unequivocally (see Findeisen, 1960). It is true that the spiritual healers call their healing spirits and deal with them, but they also have to listen to their messages and provide them with regular gifts, often in the form of animal sacrifices, in order to keep themselves out of trouble, as claimed by all interviewed healers. The relationship between humans and spirits is thus quite ambivalent.

Spirits have no form, they are invisible, like the wind. They can, however, take on different forms, including human and animal forms, and hide behind it and try to gain power over people. A healer (Luo) claimed that the spirit of a psychotic patient turns into a lion's spirit, which explains his dangerous nature. On the other hand, another healer (Mijikenda) called his healing spirit a lion spirit, which highlights its strength. The lion is one of the strongest animals in Africa and is a symbol of power. Another healer (Luo) mentioned a snake spirit being one of his spiritual advisers. The snake is a symbol of fertility, wisdom, immortality and healing in many of the world's cultures (see Heinze, 2000). Animal spirits can therefore be dangerous seducers, helpers and spiritual advisers.

Spirits have their own characters, their own signs (greeting, songs, incense), are often assigned a natural element like water, earth, fire, air, and have different tasks to perform. Spirits cannot do everything, but they are omnipotent in their respective specialization. According to a healer of the Luyia, the seven colors of the rainbow are linked with the seven spiritual talents and certain spirits. God will act directly through the medium *Omufumu* (using the naming in Luyia), a plant spirit through the diviner *Omuliuli*, a water spirit through the rain-maker *Omukimba*, an animal spirit through the priestly adviser *Omukambisi*, and an earth spirit through the blacksmith *Omwiranyi*. The prophetic visionary *Omungoosi* comes directly from the sun. It was only the talent of the circumcisor *Omukhebi* that was not related to a spirit, and this was most likely due to the fact that it was forgotten in the interview context, rather than there being no equivalent.

All spiritual healers agree that spirits are found in specific locations, often in impressive places in nature, such as caves, large (baobab) trees, cliffs, forests and ruins. The Mijikenda call these spirit-places *Mzimo*, and there are precise rules regarding how and whether such a place can be entered or not. There are certain groups of spirits, such as spirits of the sea or the sun, local spirits of an ethnic group, or foreign spirits (see Janzen, 1992). The night runner (in Luo *Jajuok* in Luyia *Omubini*), is mentioned by some healers as a special group of spirits that can be inherited. They fall upon the sleeping person causing nocturnal restlessness, but are otherwise harmless.

Several healers described groups of spirits occupying a hierarchy. Thus, one healer (Mijikenda) mentioned four categories of spirits: God is directly followed by *Malaikas* (all following names in Swahili), which are blessed beings similar to archangels, followed by *Djinnis* and *Shetwanis*, also called *Shetani* (see Swantz, 1990), and *Masheitani* (see Janzen, 1992; Yassin, 2003). In the lowest rank are the *Kibwengos*. *Kibwengos* are small spirits. They are used as messengers and like to annoy people and ambush them. To each *Malaika* belongs a *Djinni*, a *Shetwani* and a *Kibwengo*. The good *Malaikas* and their followers can be found on the right (e.g. right side of the body), the evil on the left. The association of positive or negative qualities to the right or left side is often also seen in divination, for instance with regard to the side onto which the animal sacrifice falls when it dies.

The spiritual healers generally distinguished between good and evil spirits. Only one healer (Mijikenda), however, stressed that a spirit is bad, meaning that it is harmful to people if not listened to, or if his demands are not fulfilled. So long as they are respected and attended, all spirits are friendly towards humans. Another healer of the Mijikenda ethnic group explains that evil spirits were expelled from paradise because they would not listen to God, like the fallen angel Lucifer in Christianity. Evil and satanic spirits, or demons, are called *Ashantanis* in Swahili, and *Jojiende* in Luo. They often hunt people without any reason. Hunting spirits are called *Kimimakombe* in Luyia. A healer (Luyia) claimed that childless people, people who got struck by lightning, and people who commit suicide are possessed by satanic spirits and their names may not be passed on in the family. On the other side of this dual system are the good spirits, which of course includes the healing spirits, in Swahili *Ruhani*, in Luo *Juogi* and in Luyia *Kimisambwa*.

The dualistic and hierarchical structures of all ethnic groups I have studied are found again in many traditional cultures around the world (see Halifax, 1983), and even have parallels in the world religions, especially Islam and Christianity. Throughout the research, however, the observation was made that Christianity has little acceptance for traditional world-views. Throughout my field research I did not come across a single Christian traditional healer. By contrast, Islam is not in conflict with traditional beliefs, as seen in the development of the Swahili culture. Thus, all interviewed healers of the coast, as well as the Mijikenda ethnic group, are Muslims. In this regard, Mbiti writes: 'Mission Christianity has come to mean for many Africans simply a set of rules to be observed…' (Mbiti 1969, p. 233), and 'Another area of ready agreement between Islam and traditional concepts and practices is in matters of divination and magic.' (Mbiti 1969, p. 251).

According to Giles, however, one can detect some discriminatory aspects of the hierarchy of spirits among the Swahili. She divides spirits into a group of Islamic, civilized spirits of the coast, and the group of uncivilized Bantu-spirits inland (see Giles, 1999). Accordingly, the Islamic spirits are mostly good, strong and pure and the Bantu-spirits wild and impure. This corresponds with the descriptions of several healers of the coast, which support the fact that *Ruhanis* are good spirits, angels and healing spirits, whereby the word *Ruhani* is of Arab origin (see Yassin, 2003). Thus, in the different groups of spirits one can recognize a symbolic expression of cultural and historical identity and social structures in the ritual hierarchy (see Giles, 1999).

Communication of the Spirits in the Healing Ritual

The traditional African treatment of mental disorders is extensive. All spiritual healers mentioned spiritual methods, except for one the use of phytotherapy and most of the rest also use sociotherapy. In addition, relaxation, further advice and nutrition were mentioned. In African traditional medicine therefore, the biological, sociological and psychological treatment principles of Western psychiatry are included (see Kutalek, 2003). A further level of meaning in the treatment is given by the spiritual dimension, which is taken for granted in traditional African societies, while in Western medicine it does not exist (see Katz & Wexler, 1989).

Spiritual treatment assumes that there are supernatural powers that can heal, and which expand the capacity of the spiritual healer beyond personal knowledge and techniques. Further, because of the chaos created by illness the order and harmony in the cosmic structure is supposed to be restored through the spiritual healing ritual. Through his spiritual abilities, the spiritual healer is an intermediary and traveler between the human and nonhuman worlds (see Scharfetter, 1992). This dynamic, inseparable relationship between man and transcendent forces allows healing (see Katz & Wexler, 1989). The complexity of traditional healing rituals is beyond the scope of the current chapter (but see Stöckigt, 2010), rather, the focus is on the communication of the spirits during the spiritual healing ritual.

Spiritual healers call on their healing spirits when they need more information and are not making headway with the treatment. Several healers insist that this should not be done often, because healing spirits are difficult to deal with and take energy from the healer while possessing him. To call the healing spirits, spiritual healers usually use incense, fire, drums, rattles, songs, prayers, and go to holy places. However, the healing spirits can also possess the spiritual healer without being called, for example, if their instructions were not followed. Signs of their coming vary and are usually physical, for example, a feeling of heaviness or lightness, tremor, dizziness, or emotional fluctuation, such as for example sudden tears. In most cases the healers referred to dream-like states, some to loss of control, and others described themselves as mad. One female healer spoke of an extreme alertness. During the spirit possession many spiritual healers experience a complete or partial amnesia. As a result of this amnesia, assistants are very important to the healers, enabling them to pass on the instructions of the healing spirits after the possession.

The spiritual healers primarily employ a form of ecstatic trance. Trance-inducers are primarily rhythmic sounds and movements, physical exhaustion in long healing rituals and altered respiration, as well as the influence of smoke. The possession states are usually characterized by a heightened consciousness, and go beyond the boundaries of time, space and matter which are characteristic of everyday consciousness. During the possession the healing spirits talk and sing through the spiritual healer, they know everything and give instructions for treatment. In the possession the healing spirits have a body and a form and therefore the ability to exert influence on the physical world.

With the same methods with which the healing spirits are called, especially by the rhythm of the drums and the singing of certain songs, the spirits are lured out of the patients. Drums and animal sacrifices serve in general to please the spirits. Spirits seldom show themselves, because they are most vulnerable when visible and thus reveal their secrets. The length of time it takes for spirits to reveal themselves in the patient depends on their strength and also on the strength of the healing spirits. When the spirits of the patients appear, the healing spirits can make contact with them. First, the healing spirits calm down the spirits inhabiting the patient, they talk to each other, the spirits of the patient can speak out regarding their demands and wishes, they may even dance together. The patient may, or must, act out the symptoms of his mental illness in the healing ritual and meets in the spiritual healer someone who can understand him, which often leads to an emotional release and a sense of relief (see Machleidt & Peltzer, 1997). Through the ritual, he is forced '...to come out of his prison to full self-expression' (Janzen, 1992, p. 129). The meeting of the spirits, or the behavior of those in possession trance (e.g. spiritual healer and patient), is characterized by strong expressions and emotions, which would often not be accepted in normal social structures (see Leff, 1981).

After the spirits of the patient have received presents (such as candy or animal sacrifice), and their demands have been met, the healing spirits ask them to leave the patient. Since all spirits are fighting for influence over people the spirits are not always easily chased away. Then the healing spirits threaten the spirits of the patient and possibly even beat them, expecting the patient to receive the blows. Spirits can also be chased away by plant toxins, or be lured into objects, which are then ritually destroyed. Thus the ability to meet the needs of the spirits on the one hand and to show power and strength on the other plays an important role in spiritual healing rituals. If the healing spirits said and did what they wanted to, or the spiritual healer is satisfied with their information, they leave the spiritual healer. Some interviewed healers said that they feel a little dizzy or tired after a possession; others said that everything is as usual.

The possession of the spiritual healer by his healing spirits signifies that healer and patient meet in an altered level of consciousness, whereby the spiritual healer can induce the ASC himself and the patient does not. In this way the spiritual healer is now able to understand the meaning of the disease and to respond to it and, vice versa, the patient has the ability to communicate his (psychotic) experiences (see Machleidt & Peltzer, 1997). This communication in an ASC between the spiritual healer and psychotic patient can be described as state-specific communication according to Tart's model. If one assumes that qualitative and quantitative shifts of consciousness take place in an ASC, it is also obvious that the communication in the ASC assumes new forms, which those not experiencing an ASC will be unable to understand (see Tart, 1987).

Outlook

The encounter of spiritual healer and patient in an ASC is central in spiritual healing, and is very different to the practice of Western psychotherapy. Apart from concepts of transpersonal psychology and hypnotherapy, ASC are mostly classified as pathological in Western medicine. While spiritual healers deal with ASC, and use them for healing purposes, ASC are usually seen as frightening, leading to pathological disintegration, in Western cultures (see Bourguignon, 1973; Dittrich, 1996).

Whether spirits exist or not cannot be answered definitively, because the idea of spirits is closely associated with world views and this research is not about to pass judgement on whether a particular world view is right or wrong. At the same time, spirits are described all over the world. In many religions and cultures, present and past, spirits are understood as divine or transcendent beings which act as an intermediary between God and man. There are worldwide descriptions of nature spirits, elemental spirits, ancestral spirits, guardian spirits, angels, demons, goblins, the Holy Spirit, and so on. Helping/healing, harmless or hazardous properties are awarded to them (see Halifax, 1983; Scharfetter, 1992). In recent centuries, especially in Western industrialized countries, religion has lost this emphasis and its importance, but spirits still survive in folk beliefs, fables, fairy tales and myths (see Jung, 1968).

In Western psychology and medicine, spirits are mostly seen as outwardly projected parts of the personality, which, among other things are reflected amongst others in hallucinatory psychoses and dissociative disorders (e.g., see Ndoye, 2006). Jung, however, goes beyond the individual, and speaks of archetypes of the collective unconscious. In this regard, he describes internal impulses, which arise from a source outside the control of our consciousness. According to Jung, these inner impulses and forces are described in mythology as gods, spirits and demons and are still as active as ever (see Jung, 1968).

These internal impulses, or internal sources, seem to convey a wisdom beyond the personality and ego. This is also known as the inner voice, inner teacher, or higher self. This wisdom is often associated with intuition. Whether these sources are within us or outside us cannot be proved (see Walsh, 1998). That there is no separation between vitalising spirit and dead matter, subject and object, inside and outside, has not only been discussed for a long time in religions, philosophies and mythologies, but also in natural sciences such as quantum physics, where the universe is described as a cosmic web of relationships and interactions (see Capra, 1987).

But even without being able to, or wanting to, make a final statement about the existence of spirits, it is very likely that in rational dominated industrial societies sources of knowledge beyond the rational mind are underestimated, as are spiritual healers or shamans, who were among the first to explore and use these treasures (see Walsh, 1998). Dealing with ASC is a central gateway to this treasure of expanded knowledge.

References

Abbo, C. (2003). *Management of mental health problems by traditional healers in Kampala district.* Unpublished manuscript, Makerere University Kampala.

American Psychiatric Association (2001). *Diagnostical and statistical manual of mental disorders – DSM-IV.* Göttingen-Bern-Toronto-Seattle: Hogrefe.

Bourguignon, E. (1973). *Religion, altered states of consciousness, and social change.* Columbus: Ohio State University Press.

Capra, F. (1987). Moderne Physik und östliche Mystik. In R. N. Walsh and F. Vaughan (Eds.), *Psychologie in der Wende.* Bern/München/Wien: Scherz.

Dittrich, A. (1996). *Ätiologie-unabhängige Strukturen veränderter Wachbewusstseinszustände.* Berlin: Verlag für Wissenschaft und Bildung.

Edergton, R. B. (1966). Conceptions of psychosis in four east african societies. *American Anthropology, 68* (2), 408-425.

Eliade, M. (1975). *Schamanismus und archaische Ekstasetechnik.* Frankfurt a. M.: Suhrkamp.

Ellenberger, H. F. (1985). *Die Entdeckung des Unbewussten.* Zürich: Diogenes.

Findeisen, H. (1960). Das Schamanentum als spiritistische Relgion. *Ethnos 3-4,* 192-213.

Flick, U. (1995). *Qualitative Forschung.* Hamburg: Rowohlt.

Giles, L. L. (1999). Spirit possession and the symbolic construction of Swahili Society. In H. Behrend and U. Luig (Eds.), *Spirit possession, modernity and power in Africa* (pp.142-164). Oxford: James Currey Ltd.

Halifax, J. (1983). *Schamanen: Zauberer, Medizinmänner.* Heiler. Frankfurt a. M.: Insel.

Heinze, R.-I. (2000). Serpent mythology in healing rituals: A cross-cultural survey. In S. Krippner and H. Kalweit (Eds.), *Jahrbuch für transkulturelle Medizin und Psychotherapie 1998/99 (pp.25-42).* Berlin: Verlag für Wissenschaft und Bildung.

Jaeggi, E., Faas, A., & Mruck, K. (1998). *Denkverbote gibt es nicht! Vorschlag zur interpretativen Auswertung kommunikativ gewonnener Daten.* (2. überarbeitete Fassung). Forschungsbericht aus der Abteilung Psychologie im Institut für Sozialwissenschaften der Technischen Universität Berlin, Nr. 98-2.

Janzen, J. (1992). *Ngoma: Discourses of healing in central and southern Africa*. Berkeley: University of California Press.

Jung, C. G. (1968). *Der Mensch und seine Symbole*. Olten: Walter.

Katz, R., & Wexler, A. (1989). Healing and transformation: Lessons from indigenous people. In K. Peltzer and P. O. Ebigbo (Eds.), *Clinical psychology in Africa* (pp.19-43). Nigeria: Chuka Printing Company Limited.

Krippner, S. (1999). Close encounters of the shamanic kind: From meetings to models. In A. Schenk and C. Rätsch (Eds.). *Was ist ein Schamane? Schamanen, Heiler, Medizinleute im spiegel westlichen Denkens. Curare: Sonderband*: 13. Berlin: Verlag für Wissenschaft und Bildung.

Kutalek, R. (2003). Medizinische Systeme in Afrika. In K Greifeld (Eds.), *Ritual und Heilung: Eine Einführung in die Medizinethnologie*. Berlin: Reimer.

LeBeau, D. (1996). *Health, illness and witchcraft*. Unpublished manuscript for the PAAA/AASA conference, University of South Africa, Pretoria.

Leff, J. (1981). *Psychiatry around the globe. A transcultural view*. New York: Marvel Dekker, Inc.

Machleidt, W., Calliess, I.T. (2004). *Psychiatrisch-psychotherapeutische Behandlung von Migranten und transkulturelle Psychiatrie*. In M. Berger (Ed.), *Psychische Erkrankungen: Klinik und Therapie* (pp.1161-1183). München: Urban & Fischer.

Machleidt, W, & Peltzer, K. (1997). Ein Heilungsritual zur Behandlung psychisch Kranker bei den Tumbuka in Südostafrika: Die Chilopa-Zeremonie. In K. Hoffmann & W. Machleidt (Eds.), *Psychiatrie im Kulturvergleich*. Berlin: Verlag für Wissenschaft und Bildung.

Maithya, H. M. K. (1996). Mental healthcare in pluralistic healthcare system: Some evidence from Babukusu of Bungoma District. *Social Behaviour and Health*, Monograph 3 (June), 19-27.

Mbiti, J. S. (1969). *African religions and philosophy*. Nairobi: East African Educational Publishers Ltd.

Ndoyé, O. (2006). Vorstellung eines Besessenheitsrituals: >Ndoep< aus dem Senegal. In E. Wohlfahrt and M. Zaumseil (Eds.), *Transkulturelle Psychiatrie: Interkulturelle Psychotherapie* (p.25). Heidelberg: Springer Medizin.

Peltzer, K., & Ebigbo, P. O. (1989). *Clinical psychology in Africa*. Uwani, Enugu: Chuka Printing Company Limited.

Pfeiffer, W. M. (1994). Die Stellung des psychisch Kranken in anderen Kulturen. In F. J. Illhardt and W. Effelsberg (Eds.) *Medizin in multikultureller Herausforderung* (p.327). Mainz: Gustav Fischer.

Scharfetter, C. (1990). *Schizophrene Menschen*. München: Psychologie Verlags Union Urban & Schwarzenberg.

Scharfetter, C. (1992). Der Schamane: Das Urbild des Heilenden. In K. Hauck (Ed.), *Der historische Horizont von der Spätantike zum Frühmittelalter* (pp.422-432). Göttingen: Vandenhoeck & Ruprecht.

Schenk, A., & Rätsch, C. (Eds.) (1999). *Was ist ein Schamane? Schamanen, Heiler, Medizinleute im spiegel westlichen Denkens. Curare: Sonderband: 13*. Berlin: Verlag für Wissenschaft und Bildung.

Spradley, J.P. (1979). *The ethnographic interview*. New York: Holt, Rinehart & Winston.

Stöckigt, B. (2010). Behandlungsmethoden traditioneller Heiler in Ostafrika. In W. Machleidt and A. Heinz, A. (Eds.). *Praxis der interkulturellen Psychiatrie und Psychotherapie*. München: Urban & Fischer in Elsevier.

Stöckigt, B. (2011). *Begeisterte Welten: Traditionelle Therapien von Psychosen in Ostafrika*. Frankfurt a.m.: Peter Lang.

Swantz, L. (1990). *The medicine man among the Zaramo of Dar es Salaam*. Uppsala: The Scandinavian Institute of African Studies in cooperation with Dar es Salaam University Press.

Tart, C. (1987). Bewusstseinszustände und zustandsspezifische Wissenschaften. In R. N. Walsh and Vaughan, F. (Eds.). *Psychologie in der wende* (pp.227-243). Bern/München/Wien: Scherz

Walsh, R. N. (1998). *Der Geist des Schamanen*. Frankfurt a. M.: Fischer.

WHO (1997). Dilling, H., Mombour, W., Schmidt, M. H. (Eds.), *Internationale Klassifikation psychischer Störungen. ICD-10, Kapitel V (F)*. Bern – Göttingen – Toronto – Seattle: Hans Huber

Yassin, A. (2003). *Conflict and conflict resolution among the Swahili of Kenya*. Unpublished manuscript: University of London, School of Oriental and African Studies.

An experienced Mãe-de-santo incorporates her Caboclo (spirit of a native Brazilian) in a ceremony in the forests of northern Rio de Janeiro. Photograph by Diana Espírito Santo.

Developing the Dead in Cuba: An Ethnographic Account of the Emergence of Spirits and Selves in Havana

Diana Espirito Santo

This chapter, based on over twenty months of ethnographic fieldwork in Havana, carried out between August of 2005 and July 2011, is about Cuban mediums, loosely defined as Spiritists, and their relationships to their spirits. More specifically, it is about how they learn to become mediums through the development of these spirits, a process referred to as desarrollando muertos in Cuba, which literally means 'developing the dead'. I will start with a brief story – a story of 'encounter.'

Introduction: Leonel's Story

Leonel was seven years old when he first showed signs of being a strange child. He began to have sudden and violent seizures, as well as exhibiting an unusual restlessness and inability to sleep. At the time, Leonel's father, an agronomist, was mobilized by the government in the provinces, and spent large amounts of time away from home, which left his mother, Virginia, to handle the situation by herself. Both Leonel (senior) and Virginia were committed revolutionaries. They too had taken part in the literacy campaigns of the early 1960s, believed in the ideals of the socialist project and, as many white folk in their position, had limited or no contact with the religious world, regarding it as a mostly 'African' supersitition. Worried sick, Virginia took Leonelito to all the psychologists and psychiatrists she could find, from clinic to clinic, and from hospital to hospital. His eventual diagnosis was epilepsy, and he was soon loaded with medication. Still, he would have uncontrollable seizures, sometimes at home, and sometimes at school. His restlessness did not disappear; instead, Leonelito would sit up for hours at night fiddling with his toys and apparently talking to himself. He wouldn't let Virginia sleep. She was desperate.

One day, on one of the hospital visits, Virginia sat with her small son in the waiting room, and next to her was an older woman, a lady who was accompanying her granddaughter. What she told Virginia would change the course of Leonel's life from that moment on. She said the medicine that Leonel was being given was slowly killing him, that what he had was not epilepsy, but an urgent need to 'develop his spirits'. She told Virginia that they were wasting their time at the hospital, since what she needed to do was to take him to someone who could really attend to him, for he was born to be a 'cabeza grande' (which literally means, big head). In retrospect, Virginia understood that this lady was a medium, but because of her ignorance of all things 'religious' back then, she had barely understood what she had meant. For a moment, she was alarmed to think that her son's head was going to grow unusually large! But the woman had then explained that Leonel was born to do great things in the religious field, for he had very powerful *muertos* (dead) guiding him, and that his seizures were spiritual, not medical in nature.

Virginia returned home in a state of bewilderment and shock, but she was willing to listen to the advice that she had so coincidentally happened upon. She contacted the only person she could think of that might be able to help: an old uncle of hers who had always claimed to 'see' things. At her uncle's counsel, Virginia took Leonel to a woman who would become his first *madrina*, his spiritual Godmother. In effect, this woman confirmed the spiritual diagnosis she had heard at the hospital. Leonel was a natural medium, and unless this mediumship was worked, he would only suffer further, for these entities needed to be acknowledged and put to good use. Virginia began to drop him off at the madrina's house on a regular basis, and together they began the development process, first identifying, and then establishing rudimentary communication with Leonel's spirits. Leonel remembers that he was made to concentrate, sometimes for hours, in front of her spiritual altar, to which the dead would come, focusing his thoughts on nothing else but the retrieval of information. He had found the whole thing intolerable at first.

Virginia confesses that she worried obsessively about Leonel's health at this time, since the seizures had not disappeared altogether, and particularly because she now knew that they were episodes of temporary and uncontrolled possession. He was a small child and these frequently left him distraught and physically sick. She explains that all his spirits wanted to come to him, and that they were simply too strong for a fragile body of barely ten years of age. Francisco, for example, was one such spirit. Francisco had been an African slave in Cuba; he had been kidnapped from his home in Africa, enchained, and brought to the New World at the age of seventeen. He had lived until an old age, and was, at one point, a free man, but the experience of slavery had left his body doubled up, and his feet bent and damaged. He could also be aggressive, the bitterness of his savage and inhumane treatment having been burned into his manner. Virginia recalls that when Francisco possessed Leonel, as a child, Leonel would exhibit these very same physical, and often temperamental, characteristics, as if a giant weight had been placed on his shoulders, making him crippled. Leonel would become Francisco, and Virginia knew all too well how dangerous this could be.

When I met Leonel, he was forty-five years old. As with all religious Cubans, he had seen his fair share of obstacles throughout the early decades of the Revolution and when he encountered the need to be initiated in santería (Cuba's popular religion of the 'orichas,' or 'santos'), at the age of seventeen, he had done so in secret. Leonel was, by now, a knowledgeable and experienced *santero*, as well as a medium. Finding himself with no viable state work at the beginning of Cuba's notorious 'Special Period' crisis (after the collapse of the Soviet Union and its economy, on whom Cuba was heavily dependent), Leonel had begun to consult professionally, using a variety of oracles, including cowrie shells, and performing *misas espirituales*, spiritist rituals in which one collectively prays, sings, and incorporates the dead, so that these can pass on their messages and receive 'light.' Francisco had become a regular part of his life, a spirit of 'the house,' as he described it, routinely coming down during trance sessions.

As time had gone by, Francisco had calmed down, and no longer damaged Leonel's body. He was put to 'work' at misas and was at peace with his role as Leonel's main 'work spirit.' Eventually he did not need to possess Leonel anymore in order to communicate with him, for the two had become part of each other to the extent that Leonel could understand him in his thoughts, and sometimes even dreams. Francisco's visibility had also increased during the years. Leonel had made him a 'representation,' which was in fact a life-size, fully clothed version of this old man, to which he talked and placed offerings of cigars, rum or food. For both Leonel, and his now elderly parents, Francisco was family, as well as being Leonel's spirit. I understood that this spirit was 'present' in Leonel, as well as in his house. As were other spirits now, such as that of an Arab astronomer, who had begun to inform and guide his interest in astrology, which he was teaching and practicing with great success at the time I met him. Francisco had passed to Leonel much knowledge of witchcraft and ritual protection, perhaps when he had most needed it. But now, he had also given way to other important spirits.

Expanding Selves

The story of Leonel's illness is typical of many individuals' first encounter with their gifts for spiritual mediation. While not all signs of mediumship are that dramatic – visions, dreams, and premonitions are also common indications of a latent need to develop as a medium – the solution is not perceived to be exorcism, but rather an acceptance of these newly discovered properties of the individual's own functioning, which manifest physically at first, but which are crucial to the broader religious community in the long-run. Normality and tranquility are regained for all those involved when the individual's true nature is revealed and accepted, and quite often resistance is futile. Indeed, in Cuba, developing mediumship involves embracing a sort of 'unboundedness', for the medium must cease to be only him or her, and instead cater to the perspectives that gradually emerge through his or her mediation, namely, those of the spirit guides – known simply as 'muertos'. The spirit medium's endeavor, and the self that she produces in it, is, in this sense, an extended one, challenging both notions of possession as dissociation (Levy et al., 1996), culturally sanctioned or otherwise, and understandings of trance – as an altered state of consciousness – as prior to the experience of 'spirits' proper (Bourguinon, 1976; Crapanzano & Garrison, 1977).

In this chapter I explore a specific concept of 'self' as it is manifest among spirit workers in a popular Cuban-Creole practice in Havana known as 'espiritismo', or 'espiritismo cruzado' (literally translating as 'crossed spiritism', cf. Bermudez, 1967; Bolivar, Gonzalez & del Rio, 2007; Mederos & Hodge Limonta, 1991; Millet, 1996), one that enables a theorization of the complexity of the spirit-person relation in terms that in my view most resemble those of the mediums who experience such a relation. More specifically, I will argue that this spiritist 'self' is essentially multiple in as much as it encompasses the very spirits that are developed and worked as part of a medium's career, and that become, through their enactment in the social realm, social selves in their own right. My contention, in understanding the experience of a trainee medium in Cuba, is that the learning process is one best characterized by the expansion of oneself in a given social and religious environment, where the medium brings into existence a series of voices that are at once an intrinsic and emerging part of her, and a set of carefully constructed relationships through time. A person's first encounter with the spirit world becomes, then, a fundamental point of departure for this understanding, as this is the first encounter with her own multiplicity, often a traumatic or bewildering one. A medium is simply not a medium without her spirits, to whom she responds and adjusts herself. The first step in such a task is the acceptance that the borders of her own agency do not end with her skin, but are co-extensive and respondent to a spirit world that must be acknowledged and respected as part of her own life and capacity for effect; the second step is to enable these selves (spirits) to exist socially, out there. This ethnographic approach, which stresses the ontogeny of spiritual development as an encompassing, self-constructing process, begs the question of where we situate the 'reality' of spirits, which in the Cuban case reduces neither just to bodily dispositions, nor to cultural representations.

In their introductory chapter to a volume on new perspectives in the study of spirit possession, Huskinson and Schmidt critically argue for approaches that neither dichomotize spirit phenomena into possession/trance categories, nor takes interpretation as a platform from which to articulate certain ethnocentrisms common to the history of the spirit possession literature. Rather, they say, spirit possession is a tricky subject matter because it is so widely misunderstood (2010, p. 12). Advocating a type of hyper relativist position which they draw close to 'perspectivism,' Huskinson and Schmidt say the 'key is to be more receptive to that which is unfamiliar or in apparent opposition to our preconceived ideas: to open up dialogues with unfamiliar disciplines that may offer important insights into our own' (ibid), and thus learn from them. Fair enough. But having earlier argued – in part, following Lambek (1989) – against stringent or dichotomous definitions of possession and trance, whereby the 'biological' experiences are somehow universal, in contrast to the culturally-overdetermined 'possession' bit, the authors seem to shy away precisely from exploring exactly how the two relate. Perhaps countering traditional prejudices, as they advocate (ibid: 11), may also mean going beyond a position of absolute relativism, and into something softer. In particular, that does not dissociate the 'ability' or 'capacity' for spirits from the bringing into existence of a particular kind of person, with a particular kind of physiological patterns, consciousness, attentiveness, and 'habits of the body' (see Samuel, 2010, p. 39). For Samuel, to take into consideration a mind-body complex in an understanding of spirit possession in mediation means acknowledging that 'this complex is itself not ultimately separable from its cultural and physical environment' (2010, p. 40). In my view, a balanced account of spirit possession, mediation and communication requires first and foremost a consideration of the person, not simply ideologically, as a 'category' or idea of self (Mauss, 1985) informed by culturally-specific understandings that are more or less shared, nor just phenonemologically, as a constellation of dispositions and modes of attention (Csordas, 1990), but as the site of multiple agencies – visible and invisible – which become grounded in and as forms of self-awareness, knowledge-generation, and biography.

   In his account of spirit possession in Niger, Paul Stoller describes that for the Songhay, spirits are 'carried' by their mediums at all times; their presence is both a source of pride and a burden (1989, p. 49). In Cuba, by contrast, all persons are thought to have muertos, spirit guides, although developing them as tools for serving others is a burden only some are called to. Like Songhay mediums, espiritistas too, are connecting devices between worlds, even if those worlds are not conceived as existing separately. And while they are not in 'existential limbo' (ibid, p. 50), as Stoller states for the mediums in Niger, they too have been frequently faced with the socially and physically disrupting aspects of their relationships to the spirits. Indeed, we could say that these characteristics of spirit contact find strong continuities with other spirit cults world-wide, where mediums' and healers' lifestories often suggest that 'selfhood is paradoxically both plural and integral' (Willis, 1999, p.150), becoming apparent, among other things, through illness. In Cuba, as we saw from the story of Leonel, it is often by virtue of potent forms of first impact that espiritistas acknowledge not simply the processual, ongoing and reconstructive nature of their expanded self, but also its precariousness and constant need for nurture and work. But espiritistas are not just bridges or 'channels' (Brown, 1997). They become the embodiment of their spirits. These spirits may be priests or monks, nuns, priestesses of African religion or healers; they may be slaves, or emancipated slaves; creoles, intellectuals of past centuries, casino owners from a recent past; indigenous peoples and native americans; gypsies, Arabs, Lebanese, Chinese, and members of other communities with historical labor ties to the island; artists and cabaret dancers, doctors, devout Catholics, Haitians, Mexicans, and sorcerers, among others – in sum, an 'inventory' (Garoutte & Wambaugh, 2007, p. 160) of peoples some more generic than others. If a person's spiritual-make up is on the one hand absolutely unique to him or her, on the other it is also clearly a refraction of historical processes that transcend the individual, and yet emerge from his or her existence as a social being at a particular point in time.

Spiritists in Havana

Espiritistas integrate an organic web of Afro-Cuban religious practitioners and clients that are characterised by their high pragmatism and ability to transit easily between spaces and ritual roles. Along with its sister cults of Santería (see Brown, 2003; Wirtz, 2007), a religion associated with Yoruba influences that worships the oricha gods, and Palo Monte (see Figarola, 2006; Ochoa, 2010), Cuba's Bantu-Congo derived set of magical practices, espiritismo furnishes the spiritual-seeker in Havana with mechanisms by which to diagnose ailments, ostacles and enemies, and to recover from them or act upon them. While espiritistas do not wield any traditional oracle as such, in contrast to santeros for example, whose oracular craft requires of them extensive knowledge of myths and divination signs, espiritistas are 'seers', glimpsing present and future through recourse to myriad forms of informal divination, such as cards, stones, shells, and glasses of water, as well as sensory and imagistic modes of knowledge-retrieval. Orozco and Bolivar (1998, p. 288) claim espiritismo to be Cuba's most widespread spirit mediumship practice, and they are probably right. Cuba's official ideological stance towards religious practices has precluded, at least until recently, the reliability of statistical data on religious affiliation (see Ayorinde, 2004, for an account of the Revolution's relations with religious believers and institutions over time). But ethnography points to the existence of a fluid, non-institutionalised, domestic form of religious experience, whereby experts are widely sought on matters that range from the purely mundane to the life threatening. In a world where the spirits of the dead are paramount – practitioners of most Afro-Cuban religious 'branches' must acknowledge their ancestors' wishes, as well as those of their spirit guides, before any ritual step is taken – espiritista mediums are consulted almost universally. That religion in Havana is also, for the most part, deeply implicated in the experience of political, economic, and other unavoidable social processes (Argyriadis, 1999; Holbraad, 2005), should alert us not only to the dangers of considering spirit phenomena in isolation (as a curiosity that exists unto itself), but also of locating it analytically under the cognitive category of 'belief.' Religious technologies work, particularly in the Afro-Cuban religious field, because they 'resolve', as people say (Hagedorn 2001, p. 212). And espiritismo arguably 'resolves' by providing the means by which religosos can construct themselves and their destinies through increasing knowledge of their muertos and the potentialities they carry forth.

Cuban espiritismo is an umbrella term that embraces a variety of interrelated models of spirit mediumship, and their corresponding assumptions and philosophies of engagement. While in the eastern provinces of Cuba are known for the prevalence of a spiritist variant called 'cordón' (Garcia Molina et al., 1998; Martinez & Sablón, 2001), largely considered to be heavily influenced by both Cuba's indigenous and folk Catholic roots, in Havana espiritismo divides itself mainly according to more or less doctrinal forms. On the one hand, espiritistas 'cientificos' (scientific spiritists) form themselves around a cluster of organized, albeit small-scale, groupings that promote the 19th century notion that spiritism is science, morality and philosophy, and that define their purpose in opposition to what they regard as the unnecessary ritualism and materialism of the Afro-Cuban religious complex (see Espirito Santo, 2010, 2011). On the other, the so-called espiritistas 'cruzados' form an extensive city-wide web of semi-isolated practitioners – generally immersed in other Afro-Cuban religious engagements – who mostly consult from home and who participate sporadically in the collective rites of misas espirituales (spiritist masses), whereby the dead are summoned and incorporated in lively possession ceremonies. But as Román has argued, a neat division between the two 'types' is inaccurate and unhistorical (2009). While 'cientificos' have been relatively successful at projecting themselves as an elite, or at least as proponents of a 'purer,' more rational, version of espiritismo, their temples and centres are just as fascinating for their syncretic and diverse histories as they are for their science-wielding discourses. Indeed, with regards to 'development' as a medium, all espiritistas acknowledge that they work with one and the same stata of metaphysical entities. What differs is the weight, moral and otherwise, placed on particular learning and ritual techniques. In this chapter I have chosen to focus on the more diffused, and to some extent, less exclusive forms of espiritismo, but this is no way disqualifies some of the observations that I will be making from being generalized to all spirit mediums.

All forms of Cuban spiritism derive in part from North American spiritualist movements, with which the island had contact due to its geographical proximity, but in particular, from their counterparts in France, from where some of the founding texts of European spiritism were imported from the mid-1800s onwards, namely, Allan Kardec's. Kardec (born Leon Hypolite Denizard Rivail, 1804-1869) was a pedagogue-turned-religious entrepreneur at a time when Europe was in the grip of Comte's positivism, one that fostered a growing enthusiasm for the idea that the 'immaterial' could become a scientific field of inquiry (see Sharp, 1999, 2009). Urged by his curiosity about the growing number of paranormal claims and séances in France, Kardec began visiting mediums known to close friends, prepared with a notebook and a list of penetrating questions that he would pose to the spirits in cross-examinational style. At the end of two years of investigation, Kardec had not only encountered the same spirits repeatedly through different mediums, whom he examined incessantly, but had found that the messages were invariably directed at him, taking on a much graver tone in his presence. In one of these sessions, Kardec was visited by an enlightened spirit who ordered him to adopt a *nom de plume* and begin the process of publishing the volumes of notes and supernatural interviews he had amassed during this experimental time. His first book,

Le Livre des Esprits was published in 1857, followed by *The Book of Mediums* in 1859, and *The Gospel According to Spiritism* in 1864, by which Kardec's interpretation of spiritism amassed an astounding popular following.

What lay behind these lengthy volumes was the development of an elaborate cosmological map which Kardec claimed he had been the recipient of through his extensive communications with the beyond. His philosophy proposed that a person's spirit did not just survive his or her physical demise, but that there would be a continuous interaction between the living and the dead to the extent that the latter can shape the former's actions and decisions, coercing or influencing human affairs. Kardec posited a theory of repeated reincarnation and karmic debt, and explained illness and adversity in terms of 'tests' or 'trials' in one's life mission. As one evolved morally and intellectually, he claimed, one would climb higher in a kind of ladder where the highest scale was populated only by saints and other inaccessible wise men. In this new 'scientific' religion, there were no superior races or sexes but rather individual spirits on singular trajectories of evolution. Importantly, Kardec's spiritism rejected a hegemonic relationship to the divine, as well as the existence of heaven or hell. It also embraced a fundamental right to understand and experience it on a personal and empirical level. Given its familiarity with prior movements that had swept Europe such as Mesmerism and Swedenborgism (Abend, 2004, p. 509), it is unsurprising that spiritism found an easy home among the European middle-classes, bored by dogma and enchanted by the promises of scientific inquiry on a larger, more transcendent scale (see Washington, 1995).

Spiritism was 'transported' to Latin American countries through colonial affiliation to particular European nations, such as Spain and Portugal, only a few years after Kardec generated his principal body of work. This occurred, in great part, through illegal importation of spiritist texts via traveling elites and intellectuals, using unofficial translations. While in Cuba it was among the large creole middle-classes that a 'scientific,' or 'Kardecist' spiritism was to find its first basis of support (many of whom were independence-supporters whose faith in the Church system had waned considerably after it had sided with the Spanish colonial empire during the first independence wars), it soon became the case that espiritismo acquired a more healing oriented flavour, especially as it spread to the poorer eschelons of Cuban urban and rural society, acquiring the 'colors of its Creole environment' (Brandon, 1997, p. 87). Indeed, the appearance of spiritist technologies in Cuba proved to be immediately effective to practitioners of the largely underground, persecuted Afro-Cuban religions, particularly Santería and Palo Monte. While 'Kardecist' institutions proliferated in the new Republic after 1902, federations and societies emerging country-wide to defend a new 'scientific' spiritual practice with a doctrinal basis, santeros, paleros and other religious folk began to appropriate spiritist concepts of evolution, spirit classification, and reincarnation, as much as spiritists began to work within certain Afro-Cuban ritual parameters and specifications. Espiritismo seemed to perfectly plug in the gap left by the anihilation of African ancestor cults in Cuba (Brandon, 1997, p. 78), as well as furnishing its wider cosmos with an ontological – as well as moral – frame or continuum along which the entities, spirits, and gods of the dominant Afro-Cuban religious branches (or Reglas) could be classified under a single roof (Palmié, 2002, p. 192), articulating their existence in terms of the other. Since its basic rite, the misa espiritual, did not logically exclude any spirits, as Brandon (1997, p. 87) argues: 'in Cuba Kardec's spirit guides frequently embodied the popular stereotypic images of Cuban ethnic, racial, and professional groups. Not only did Cuban espiritistas in their mediumistic trance manifest spirit guides that resembled themselves, both physically and in temperament, but both black and white mediums manifested spirit guides who were *Africanos de nación* – Lucumí, Mandinga, Mina, and Congolese tribesman who had suffered and died in slavery (Cabrera, 1971, pp. 64-65). None of this was in Kardec' (Brandon, ibid). Nowadays spiritists fulfill such a vital function in their Afro-Cuban religious milieu that some authors posit that their misas are simply not performed if not as an integral part of an Afro-Cuban religious rite (Castellanos & Castellanos, 1992, p. 195). While this may be an exaggerated claim, for spiritist ceremonies are organized for a wide range of reasons, from light-giving masses for the deceased to exorcistic cleansing rites, espiritistas work under many of the same assumptions and constraints as their Afro-Cuban religious counterparts, making divisions between them more a matter of ritual roles and expertise than belief-systems.

In the contemporary religious landscape in Havana, espiritista mediums cater to a variety of needs. The most important of these is the identification a person's so-called cordón espiritual. While religious ancestors and the spirits of deceased family members play a crucial role in the lives of those who follow Afro-Cuban religiosity more generally, at the very constitution of a person are a group of protective spirit guides who are inextricably linked to his or her own life path, and have been so since the moment of their birth. This set of spirits, known in Cuba as one's *cuadro* or *cordón espiritual* – or simply, one's *muertos* – functions to both watch over and direct the individual's actions and choices during the course of their material existence. The relationship between protected and protectee, however, is subtle and complex. The 'human' characteristics of the spirits who act as guides can, for the most part, be deeply implicated in the individual's own psyche and motivational impulses. Apart from constituting potential tools of 'battle,' these entities come equipped with their own biographical histories, including specific knowledges and skills, inclinations, as well as biases and limitations. They too, have lived lives and died deaths, and can overlap with the individual in any number of personal traits, physical and psychological. But this influence is far from top-down or unilinear. Rather, there is a continuous feedback process occurring between the person and her guides which means that neither one's spirits are necessarily permanent or established, but constantly build on each other, emerging from each other's mutual influence. So, while an individual is conceived to be the potential recipient of his spirits' talents or flaws, as well as whims or desires, in as much as she may bring them forth through her actions in the world, this need not mean that all their respective characteristics be cultivated. Yosleny (not her real name), for example, a girl in her twenties, was told once that she has a spirit of a sexually permissive woman in her cordón, but that she does not lend herself to the same behavior because she has refused to 'give way' to the potential influence of this entity in her own psyche. José (not his real name), by contrast, claims that acknowledging the presence of an artist muerto in his cordón has done much to bring about his success as a painter. Spiritist rites are by and large exercises of observing and identifying such entanglements, building a basis of information that will serve as the starting point for other forms of existential and even religious engagement, so that, for example, a person will only be allowed to become initiated in Palo Monte if they have a spirit in the cordón who 'knew of those things' and who wills it.

In a more general sense, mediums clarify the state of an individual's relationships and their potential future, perceive and pass on knowledge regarding the existence of jealous neighbors or competitive co-workers, determine whether the individual is being followed by any unwanted spirits or *enviaciónes* ('low' spirits) and associate him or her with this or that oricha-santo (in Santería), generally creating a portrait which the client takes away with them, to build on in subsequent consultas, or with subsequent espiritistas. In short, they form part of a spiritual community widely characterised in Havana by its logics of instrumentalism, pragmatism, and to some extent ritual accumulation (Argyriadis, 1999, 2005), but more significantly, cross-referentiality, in which the ritual niches of the cults of Espiritismo, Santería, Ifá, and

Palo Monte are largely interdependent and inclusive. Espiritistas stand out on account of what many regard as their innate skills or 'grace', often described as coming from God. But while most mediums would see themselves as somehow 'special – they can 'see', 'hear', 'feel' or 'dream' – mediumship is itself not seen simply as a gift, internal to a person or otherwise. It is instead seen as a set of special relations that cannot be located exclusively inside the person/body of the medium herself. In this sense, mediumship is more about having the ability to fruitfully engage in these relations with the spirits, than about any pre-given sensitivity or talent. Categorized only loosely by Cuban mediums as being of more or less 'light,' 'clarity,' 'knowledge,' and 'evolution', 'good' or 'bad,' – terms that can also refer to the spirit's ability to 'get things done' or to 'see' further; and 'education' – the dead are regarded as virtually human in their wishes, need for attention, faults and vices, kindness or charity. Knowing how to unfold and manifest their presence in one's life, as a medium, requires engaging with and catering to these same idiosyncrasies, often in a clearly material way.

Learning, Materializing, Coming into Being: Eduardo and Olga's House

A few months after I arrived in Cuba in 2005, I met two of the people that would become my most trusted and valuable informants, as well as my friends and mentors. It was in their spacious and airy apartment in Habana Vieja, with their *ahijados* (godchildren), that I was to watch and understand the dynamics of *desarrollo* more systematically. Eduardo and Olga not only dedicate themselves to the spiritist labor on a full-time basis, working misas espirituales throughout Havana in order to earn a living, but regularly gather, in their own home, a varied group of men and women who are in need of desarrollo as mediums themselves. These misas are referred to in Havana as *escuelitas* (little schools), and their purpose is to provide a relaxed ritual space in which to work and develop one's muertos.

Development is considered to be a lengthy affair that may take years to fully come into effect. Neophyte mediums, as well as non-mediums, are thought to have disorganized and sometimes anarchical and whimsical spirits in need of hierarquization. While at times this anarchy means the medium is more vulnerable or insecure – for, as spiritists say, an army of disorganized soldiers is hardly expected to successfully fight a battle – at others it may cause physical and mental disturbance, particularly if possession is uncontrolled or involuntary. *Darles un ordén*, a phrase much heard among spiritist godmothers and fathers, means working towards an effective structuring of each spirit's task and place in the person's cordón espiritual. Another fundamental trope is that of 'education'. Undeveloped spirits are often described as being in need of educación, tantamount to manners, sociability, civility. At home, developing mediums are encouraged to build small altars, essentially a spirit's first port-of-call in the communication process. Composed rudimentarily of several glasses of water and a crucifix laid out on a white mantel or cloth, and often surrounded by diverse spirit representations such as dolls, statuettes and icons, as well as saints' images and photos of deceased family members, it is at the altar, or *bóveda espiritual*, that a neophyte forges the first connection to her cordón; where he or she becomes permeable and receptive, like water. It is unsurprising that altars grow and complexify over time, for they are collages of tradition set in by the paths of personal experience, each one different to the next. As the medium expands, so does her bóveda, to an extent. As Bettelheim notes, 'altar construction is fluid, mixing a variety of religious systems and iconographies and inventing new ones' (2005, p. 314), yielding entirely personal assemblages. As with Leonel (above), mediums must learn to evoke their spirits' presence at the bóveda, namely, by praying, talking, lighting candles and placing gifts such as flowers. The primary device of such forms of development is the process of materialization – that is, of achieving the *acercamiento*, or 'coming closer' of, these same muertos, so that they take on visibility, tangibility, and consequence in the lives of those they protect. In misas espirituales this process is taken to an extreme, for the spirits are summoned to literally become their mediums; that it, so become social creatures. While the collective performance of songs both enables and 'clothes' the spiritual experience – for the words of these songs invariably refer to the spirit's group identity, and in that sense, mimicks them into existence – a spirit's need for social recognition is most evident through possession episodes.

Cuban spiritists refer to the act of incorporating their entities as 'bajando muertos' (to make the dead come down). Conscious or not, possession is not conceived of as a state of substition of selves, but rather as a process of allowing an immediate and unambiguous co-presence of personalities during a given amount of time. Bajando muertos is thought to be one of the main means by which spirits become aware of themselves and their import in productive ways. Through bodies spirits are mirrored, sung to, and tamed of their coarseness or aggression. We could say that spirits become real – both to themselves and to their social actors and audience – when they are put to work in a public setting through the medium; and this can only be achieved via a series of material correspondences that speak to their existence in a given social sphere, such as that of a misa. To call forth a spirit, is, in many senses, to visually and materially represent it, to recreate it, at that moment, and from that moment onwards. To 'develop' is exactly this: to discern, evoke, and embody the identities of one's spirits in as much a social manner as possible – to endow the spirit with life. This idea was driven home to me over the months that I spent participating in, and observing, Eduardo and Olga's misas. Among other things, I became gradually familiar with the regular appearance of some of their own spirits.

While her husband's [mental] mediumship functions entirely within the threshold of the conscious, he 'sees' and 'hears,' Olga is an experienced and graceful trance medium, who not only consistently 'passes' her own spirit guides – an *Indio* (indigenous spirit) and an *Africana* (a spirit of African descent) – but also her husband's, who relies on her *materia* (matter, body), to communicate with or receive counsel from his own entities in more direct forms. Eduardo's predominant *espiritu de trabajo* (work spirit) is a wise and religiously savvy old African man called Ta José, who had been a *brujo* (a sorcerer) in life, and with whom he shares a caring and respectful relationship. Olga routinely falls into trance with Ta José, especially when he needs to transmit an urgent message to Eduardo; and after many years, he slips easily into her body, and out again. When he descends, this spirit takes on a slow and deliberate posture, speaking quietly and directy, as an elderly man would do, and passes on his advice kindly but sternly, to both Eduardo and his medium, Olga, often on what to do to resolve a particular problem. Eduardo not only listens patiently and obeys but also has for Ta José a particular straw hat, a red scarf, as well as a cane, which he unfailingly retrieves and proceeds to accomodate on his spirit, as soon as he arrives. But there were many other entities in (and of) the house, and to each one of these, another particular ritual of hospitality would be performed.

On one occasion, for instance, I was fortunate enough to witness the appearance of another of Eduardo's main spirits - the spirit of a strong gypsy patriarch. Eduardo had induced Olga into trance, and she had eventually succumbed to this rather 'macho' spirit, who was at once horrified at finding that he was wearing a skirt, and, moreover, that his dagger was not in place. His hands kept clumsily searching for it on his body, but all he would find would be Eduardo's wife's hips and her jangling bracelets. Eduardo explained to the spirit that he was now in his *caballo's* (literally meaning 'horse,' the medium) body, and that she was naturally fond of wearing jewelry. He placed a bandana on the spirit's head, in what seemed to be an attempt to make him feel more 'manly,' tying it at the back. But the spirit continued to feel Olga's skirt restlessly, tugging and pulling at it, as if he were pulling up his falling trousers. He was loud and rough spoken, and paced around the room in giant steps, making Olga look rather awkward, in her tiny frame. "Carajo!" (shit!), the spirit exclaimed in occasional spurts of aggression, looking down at us, challengingly. He asked for *vino seco*, bitter wine, and Eduardo offered him some beer and menthol cigarettes instead, both of which he repeatedly replaced throughout the duration of the trance, to keep up with the gypsy's alarming rate of consumption. The patriarch remained for a long while – he drank and smoked.

When he began to insinuate a mood for flamenco dancing, moving his torso in this way and that, stomping the floor with his feet in cadence, we all started to clap, encouraging his performance. Music was put on the tape player in the next room – the sound of Gypsy Kings filled the air – and it was then promptly switched off, as the spirit had shown contempt for it. Before he left, he passed on messages to each one of us in turn, and gave Eduardo a solid man-hug, tapping his shoulders in a farewell gesture. Then he was gone. Olga was startled for a few minutes, and she sat down recovering, sweating, and unaware of the events that had just unfolded during the previous hour. As usual, she retained no memory of her activities during trance, only that she had not been entirely 'present,' and that her body had taken on a life of its own.

During my time at Eduardo and Olga's *escuelita*, I understood that the couple had come to know their spirits to such an extent that very often they were already privy to when exactly these would make an appearance at one of their misas. And they would be ready. The fans, the shawls, the hats, the drinks, and the cigarettes they would have for their various spirits were all small and modest tributes prepared beforehand to compensate such efforts. A means not only of accommodating these entities in 'skins' not of their own – of molding or 'dressing' them to the circumstances (or the circumstances to them) – but also of paying homage to them, of showing gratitude for their hard work.

But Eduardo and Olga's house in itself was a testament to the spirit's omnipresence in their lives. It was, after all, a *casa religiosa* (a religious house). Small tables and specially arranged room corners were set out with elaborately dressed dolls, representing their spirits, and adorned with their respective gifts and attributes: tarot cards, jewelry, hand fans, lipsticks, perfume, honey and flowers for the female spirits, especially the gypsies; coconut shells with strong rum or aguardiente, miniature tools and weapons, red and black scarves, and cigars for the male spirits, especially the Africans. Statuettes and other small plaster and ceramic figures were also visible throughout the flat, some of them suggesting the presence of Arab or Indian spirits, with bows and arrows, others in the shape of some of Cuba's most venerated saints, such as the Virgen de Regla or the Caridad del Cobre. These were not objects to be contemplated but engaged, cared for, pleaded with, giving birth in this way to a sustained and respectful interaction of mutual reciprocity. Indeed, representations did more than merely represent. They were, in effect, instruments of spiritual sedimentation – that is, means by which a spirit's presence in a medium's social and material life could be generated, consolidated and maintained. They were grounding mechanisms for the spirit in question, points of objectification. Havana's religious houses are replete with such visual references. From Buddhas, Krishnas, Native-Americans and Catholic saints to plaster-caste African figures: the muertos of any given house generate a plethora of seemingly discrepant representations via their historical and biographical specifics, in Cuba known as 'corrientes.' While many spirits come bearing African ancestry, and thus corrientes that remit to Santería or Palo Monte for example, others manifest Asian, European or

Middle-Eastern qualities which must rendered palpable in their representations and the nature of their offerings. In this sense, Bettelheim's observation that as the spiritist 'accumulates power through experience, the altar accumulates objects' (2005, p. 315) has it in reverse: it is much more the case that as the altar and its surrounding representational spaces grow, the more an essentially creative control is achieved over a spirit collective, which is none other than an expanding self-system. Development is not just reflected in the complexification of a house's material culture, but often a consequence of it. Indeed, I came to understand that the power of mimicry in espiritismo lies at the very core of its efficacy.

At the end of my fieldwork period in Havana, and at the insistence of Eduardo and Olga, I decided to represent a spirit of my own cordón – a streetwise and seductive gypsy woman – whom Eduardo claimed was simply aching to have more potency and influence in my life. At his escuelita he would never fail to remind me that if I offered her a representación she would be more likely to help me, especially in matters of love, which he and Olga identified as one of my key failings or osogbos (which in Santería and its divination branch of Ifá, means curse or bad luck). That this spirit came with the corriente de Ochún (the oricha of fertility and sensuality) further proved their point: I needed to make her more consequent in my life, or risk facing the almost impossible task of finding a stable relationship. I decided to invest in this suggestion, and acquired a doll from a woman in Centro Habana who dresses and sells all manner of dolls and icons for religious purposes. She came with a frilly yellow print dress, a bandana with a large flower, loopy earings, as well as a series of necklaces and pendants, and was subsequently 'baptized,' spiritually, by Eduardo, in a ceremony dedicated to honouring and thanking my spirits. The consecration involved, among other ritual acts, the pouring of a small amount of specially prepared water over her head, just as one would do with a child at a church. He assured me that representing one of my most important spirits was crucial in working towards a much needed spiritual order, for I needed to be able to see her in physical form, as well as imagine her presence.

The point is not only that material representation fortifies the spirit: it is also that it allows for a more tangible space of contact and effect on a daily basis, between the medium and her spirit, which is it itself what leads to its fortification. Indeed, what the baptism suggests is that the spirit comes into being on a different scale when it is formally recognized in such ways – it gains a name, a presence in the house, a face and a body. Matter, in the form of dolls, icons, images, or saints' figures, does not just stand for spiritual beings and their essence, and neither does it simply contain them; these objects also are these essences, in ways that are comparable to the individual's own spiritual overlap in trance or in mediumistic moments. Leonel, for example, refers to his life-size doll as Francisco; he does not make a distinction between Francisco-the-real-spirit, and Francisco-the-representation. The two have, to some extent, coalesced in the creation and existence of his image in material form. Moreover, Leonel's Francisco became Francisco on the day of his formal christening: 'he was now baptized, created,' Leonel explained to me once, 'he could now go to church and assert his presence; he now had life.' A representation can become, in his words, 'a cell-phone to the dead.'

Towards a Synthesis

William James noted that we have as many selves as there are others who accord us recognition and carry our image in their mind (James, 1950, cited in Jackson, 1998). The philosopher and social psychologist George H. Mead built upon this key idea by positing the immanently social nature of minds and selves, in particular their emergence in social experience and interaction through the mediation of symbols and gestures. Selfhood, argued Mead (1962), is the ability of an organism to become an object to itself, a feat possible only by social encounter and communication through language. A thinking 'self,' in this light, is first enacted, not pre-given, since it is only by virtue of our embodied sociality that we can acquire self-reflexivity and auto-determination. In the field of religious experience we can translate these insights in any number of ways. For instance, both Taussig (1993) and Kapferer (1979, 1995) posit the role of performative mimesis in the creation of cosmology and presence (see also Schiefflin, 1985). Cuban espiritismo is a prime example of this process. Possession rites, but also the forms of materiality that are implicated in a given spirit's becoming, are not reflective of a pre-existing cosmos but central to its production on a immanent plane of existence, in turn, providing spaces from which it may be differentiated, organized, empowered, or transformed. These forms of production are indissociable from those of the self, for only through its material recreation does the person's extended self-system, comprising of her spirits, afford change and growth. In Cuba spirits are not just assumed but worked into being through varying performative, material, somatic and imagistic technologies. We would be missing the point if we ignored the fact that for mediums, too, spirits are nothing if not social creatures, made real via their materialization in the world, among the living, and through the living. An undeveloped spirit is, I was often told, a 'sleeping spirit,' mute and impotent to effect positive influences in the lives of those it protects. From the perspective of Cuban spiritists, then, the dead gain in power, and thus presence, as they increasingly engage with the material and social world. To develop spirits is to create selves where they can be seen and act back, via their ability to be seen, touched, interacted with, and even smelt.

Michael Lambek tells us that the phenomenon of spirit possession instrinsically 'raises questions that are provocative for all of us as human beings, questions pertaining to such things as the sources of human agency, or the relationship between action and passion, or autonomy and connection, in selfhood' (1998, p.104). For many of us, it seems to me, these questions are a direct result of the sheer alterity of such experiences, or 'beliefs', to which we, as anthropologists, have limited access. But while spirit posession is clearly an interesting arena in which to formulate new concepts and debates on self and agency, it has instead traditionally served more as a stage for conceptual projection, rather than inspiration. There is nothing that brings out the positivist in us quicker than to talk of ghosts, says Stephan Palmié (2002), borrowing a phrase from Francoise Meltzer (1994).

This issue goes to the core of our relationship – as anthropologists of religious phenomena – to our informants' statements and accounts. And it is a highly problematic one, for they are often problematic statements, from our 'rationalist' (and rather disenchanted) point of view. Palmié argues that 'we cannot seem to resist transcribing spirits, gods, or the world of witchcraft into codes that satisfy our deeply held beliefs that stories in which they figure are really about something else: category mistakes, faulty reasoning, forms of ideological mis-recognition, projection of mental states, and so on, figments of individual or collective imagination that may be profitably analyzed in terms of their psychological or social functions but that cannot be taken literally as referents to a reality that is really "out there"'(2002, p. 3). Notions of 'belief' make it difficult to understand the role of spirits 'out there,' where Cubans themselves place them.

But Cuban espiritismo does not make it difficult for us to bypass these notions. It points us in a different direction, namely, toward the field of behaviour, action, and intersubjectivity as critical to the affirmation of spirits' existence in a person's life.. The question I have been asking implicitly in this chapter is how spiritist self-awareness comes about. I argue that answering it involves understanding how the 'links' in the system that is the mediumistic task – spirits – become autonomized and objectified as social entities with agency and consequence, not inside minds, but in a tangible social space. The spirit identification process is one that always implicates others who perceive, witness, confirm and convince the medium of the veracity of her spirits. Misas espirituales, in this light, are above all rituals geared towards the social exhibition and legitimization of one's spirits, designed to empower both the medium via the performance of particular songs and prayers associated with their spirits' identities, and the entities themselves, through the production of trance. The act of representation through images and dolls is another instance of the kind of materialization processes imperative to desarrollo, which in the end, is geared to making visible one's spirit guides, of recreating their presence among people. In his essay, 'The Will to Believe' (1897), William James proposes that a religious belief can bring into existence that which is the object of belief, by bringing into existence some effect in the lives of the believers. Beliefs can become facts when these are acted upon. Among Cuban espiritistas, the same is true: only when acted upon, materialized, acknowledged, and socialized, do spirits begin to exist for their mediums; until then, they are merely untapped potentialities – shadows of selves.

Acknowledgements

This chapter is based primarily on my PhD research work, made possible by a grant from the Economic and Social Research Council. I also thank the Royal Anthropological Institute and University College London's graduate school for smaller grants. More recent work in Cuba has been made possible by Portugal's Fundação para a Ciência e Tecnologia, with the support of my host institution from 2009-12, the Instituto de Ciências Sociais (ICS) of the University of Lisbon, and from 2012 to now, the Centre for Research in Anthropology (CRIA), at the New University of Lisbon (UNL). I am especially grateful to Leonel and his family, and to Eduardo and Olga and their muertos.

References

Abend, L. (2004). Specters of the secular: Spiritism in nineteenth-century Spain. *European History Quarterly 34* (4): 507-534

Argyriadis, K. (1999). *La religión à la Havane. Actualité des représentations et des pratiques cultuelles Havanaises.* Paris: éd. des Archives contemporaines.

Argyriadis, K. (2005). El desarrollo del turismo religioso en la habana y la acusación de mercantilismo. *Desacatos 18*: 29-52

Ayorinde, C. (2004). *Afro-Cuban religiosity, revolution, and national identity.* Gainesville: University Press of Florida

Bermúdez, A. A. (1967). Notas para la historia del espiritismo en Cuba, *Etnologia y Folklore, 4*, 5-22.

Bettelheim, J. (2005). Caribbean Espiritismo (Spiritist) altars: The Indian and the Congo. *The Art Bulletin 87* (2): 312-330

Bolivar, N., González, C., & del Rio, N. (2007). *Corrientes espirituales en Cuba.* Havana: Editorial José Marti.

Bourguignon, E. (1976). *Possession. Chandler & Sharp series in cross-cultural themes.* San Francisco: Chandler & Sharp Publishers.

Brandon, (1997). *Santeria from Africa to the New World: The dead sell memories.* Bloomington, IN: Indiana University Press.

Brown, D.H. (2003). *Santeria enthroned: Art, ritual, and innovation in an Afro-Cuban religion.* Chicago: The University of Chicago Press

Brown, M.F. (1997). *The channelling zone: American spirituality in an anxious age.* Cambridge, MA & London: Harvard University Press

Castellanos, J. & Castellanos, I. (1992). *Cultura Afrocubana 3: Las Religiones y las Lenguas.* Miami: Ediciones Universal.

Crapanzano, V. & Garrison, V. (Eds.) (1977). *Case studies in spirit possession.* New York, London: Wiley

Csordas, T. (1994). *The sacred self: a cultural phenomenology of charismatic healing.* Berkeley, CA; London: University of California Press

Espirito Santo, D. (2010). Spiritist boundary-work and the morality of materiality in Afro-Cuban religion. *Journal of Material Culture, 15* (1), 64-82.

Espirito Santo, D. (2010). 'Who else is in the drawer?' Trauma, personhood and prophylaxis among Cuban scientific Spiritists. *Anthropology & Medicine 17* (3): 249-259

Figarola, J. J. (2006). *La Brujería Cubana. El Palo Monte.* Santiago de Cuba: Editorial Oriente

Garcia Molina, J. A., Garrido Mazorra, M. M. & Frainas Gutierrez, D. (1998). *Huellas Vivas del Indocubano.* Toronto: Lugus Libros

Garoutte, C. & Wambaugh, A. (2007). *Crossing the water: a photographic path to the Afro-Cuban spirit world.* Durham & London: Duke University Press

Hagedorn, K. J. (2001). *Divine utterances: The performance of Afro-Cuban Santeria.* Washington, DC: Smithsonian Institution Press.

Holbraad, M. (2005). Expending multiplicity: Money in Cuban Ifá cults. *Journal of the Royal Anthropological Institute, 11* (2): 321-254.

Huskinson, L., & Schmidt, B. E. (2010). Introduction. In L. Huskinson and B. E. Schmidt (Eds.) *Spirit Possession and trance: New interdisciplinary perspectives* (pp. 1-15). London, NY: Continuum

Jackson, M. (1998). *Mimica ethnographica: Intersubjectivity and the anthropological project.* Chicago, IL: University of Chicago Press.

James, W. (2000). *Pragmatism and other writings.* London: Penguin Classics. (Orginally published 1897).

Kapferer, B. (1979). Mind, self and other in demonic illness: The negation and reconstruction of self. *American Ethnologist 6* (1): 110-133

Kapferer, B. (1995). From the edge of death: Sorcery and the motion of consciousness. In A. P. Cohen & N. Rapport (Eds.). *Questions of consciousness* (pp. 134-152). ASA monographs 33: Routledge

Lambek, M. (1998). Body and mind in mind, body and mind in body: Some anthropological interventions in a long conversation. In M. Lambek and A.Strathern (Eds.), *Bodies and persons: Comparative perspectives from Africa and Melanesia* (pp. 103-123). Cambridge: Cambridge University Press.

Levy, R., Howard, A. & Mageo, J.M. (1996). Gods, spirits and history: a theoretical perspective. In J. M. Mageo & A. Howard (Eds.) *Spirits in culture, history, and mind* (pp. 11-28) London & New York: Routledge

Mead, G. H. (1962). *Mind, self and society from the standpoint of a social behaviorist.* Chicago, IL: University of Chicago Press. (Orginally published 1934).

Martinez, C. C. & Barzaga Sablón, O. (2000). *El Espiritismo de Cordón: un Culto Popular Cubano.* Havana: Fundación Fernando Ortiz

Mauss, M. (translated by W. D. Halls) (1985). A category of the human mind: the notion of person; the notion of self'. in M. Carithers, S. Collins and S. Lukes (Eds.), *The category of the person: Anthropology, philosophy, history* (pp. 1-25). Cambridge: Cambridge University Press

Mederos, A. A., & Limonta, I. H. (1991). *Los llamados cultos sincréticos y el espiritismo.* Havana: Editorial Academia.

Millet, J. (1996). *El espiritismo: Variantes Cubanas.* Santiago de Cuba: Editorial Oriente.

Ochoa, T. R. (2010). *Society of the dead, Quita Manaquita and Palo Praise in Cuba.* Berkeley: University of California Press

Orozco, R., & Bolivar, N. (1998). *Cuba Santa: Comunistas, santeros y cristianos en la isla de Fidel Castro.* Madrid: Ediciones El Pais.

Palmié, S. (2002). *Wizards and scientists: Explorations in Afro-Cuban modernity and tradition.* Durham. NC: Duke University Press.

Román, R. (2007). *Governing spirits: Religion, miracles, and spectacles in Cuba and Puerto Rico, 1898-1956.* Chapel Hill: University of North Carolina Press.

Samuel, G. (2010). Possession and self-possession: towards an integrated mind-body perspective. In L. Huskinson and B. E. Schmidt (Eds.) *Spirit possession and trance: New interdisciplinary perspectives* (pp. 35-70). London, NY: Continuum

Schieffelin, E. L. (1985). Performance and the cultural construction of reality. *American Ethnologist 12* (4): 707-724

Sharp, L. L. 1999. Fighting for the afterlife: Spiritists, Catholics, and popular religion in nineteenth-century France. *The Journal of Religious History 23* (3): 282-295

Sharp, L. L. (2006). *Secular spirituality: Reincarnation and Spiritism in nineteenth-century France.* Lanham, MD and Plymouth: Lexington Books.

Stoller, P. (1989). *Fusion of the worlds. An ethnography of possession among the Songhay of Niger.* Chicago: University of Chicago Press

Taussig, M. (1993). *Mimesis and alterity: A particular history of the senses.* New York and London: Routledge

Washington, P. (1995) [1993]. *Madame Blavatsky's baboon: A history of the mystics, mediums, and misfits who brought Spiritualism to America.* New York: Schocken Books

Willis, R. (1999). *Some spirits heal, others only dance. A journey into human selfhood in an African village.* Oxford: Berg

Wirtz, K. (2007). *Ritual, discourse, and religious community in Cuban Santería: Speaking a sacred world.* Gainesville: The University Press of Florida

A medium incorporating Ogun during a Candomblé ceremony in Brazil. Photo by Bettina Schmidt.

MEDIUMSHIP IN BRAZIL: THE HOLY WAR AGAINST SPIRITS AND AFRICAN GODS

BETTINA E. SCHMIDT

Question: A drunkard walks in the middle of the rush hour over a busy highway and is not hit by a car despite swinging back and forth. Why?
Answer: The drunkard is protected by several disincarnated spirits who also like alcohol and want to be provided with alcohol by this drunkard a bit longer.

This joke is, as I was told in Brazil, quite popular among Brazilian Kardecists, but not only among them. It highlights aspects of the spiritual world and the Kardecist doctrine (whenever you see someone drunkenly staggering across the road you will now think of Brazilian spirits who like alcohol). In addition the joke also shows that speaking about spirits is quite normal in Brazil as Fátima Regina Machado (2009) confirms in her PhD thesis. She investigated the presence of experiences with so-called abnormal[1] phenomena in everyday Brazil. Though her study is not representative of Brazilian society at large, it does indicate some interesting aspects, such as the extent of the phenomena: from the overall sample (M = 306), 82.7% (N =

306) mentioned in their questionnaire responses they had one or more psi experiences (ESP and/or PK); 74,2% mentioned they had at least one extrasensory experience (ESP), and 55.9% had an extramotor experience (PK). (Machado, 2009).

In a pre-study Machado had found that 89.5% of students spoke openly about having a psi experience, while in a similar US survey only 55% reported them. She concludes that Brazilian culture and society can be characterized by an enormous openness towards paranormal experiences and a distinct willingness to speak about them (2009).

Looking back to my recent experience during fieldwork in São Paulo I can confirm her portrayal. I arrived in Brazil in February 2010 with the idea to study (generally speaking) spirit possession in Brazil. Though I had visited Brazil twice before, this was my first research project in Brazil. My former projects had brought me to the Caribbean, New York and its Caribbean Diaspora, as well as to several places in Hispano America. Initially, whenever I started new empirical research, I had problems finding someone who would speak openly about religious experiences outside the mainstream religion (as soon as one is accepted by the leader of a religious community, contacts quickly become easier to establish). People usually shy away from telling an outsider, in particular a foreigner, about supernatural experiences with spirits of the deceased or deities.

However, I had fewer problems establishing first contact in São Paulo.[2] When I left Brazil at the end of June, I had attended ceremonies at various afro-Brazilian religious communities, spiritist centres, and Pentecostal churches and had interviewed several priests and priestesses, as well as other members of religious communities, and discussed with them their religious experiences with the supernatural. Though some parts of the rituals remained secret, I was able to attend an initiation ritual into Candomblé, a highly regarded afro-Brazilian religion. Even when I visited evangelical church services I usually encountered someone speaking openly about experiences with the divine. Religions offer a vital coping strategy for unusual experience, particularly religions centred on mediumistic ability.

Mediumship is so common in Brazilian religions that Brígida Carla Malandrino (2006) speaks of a *continuum mediúnico* (medium continuum) of Umbanda, Kardecism and Candomblé, the three main religious traditions in which mediumship plays a central role. Though these religions differ in many aspects, the term *Espiritismo* is sometimes used as an umbrella for religions utilising mediumship. Therefore, when Machado writes that both Brazilian 'espiritistas' and 'evangelicals' see religion as an instrument to cope with abnormal experiences (Machado, 2009), it is somewhat unclear whether she refers only to Kardecism or to the range of religions in the 'medium continuum,' because Umbanda and Candomblé perform similar functions. Crucially for the focus of this chapter, Machado's statement joins two usually opposite poles of Brazilian religious traditions, the 'evangelicals' and the 'espiritistas'. Among a vast number of Brazilian evangelical churches is an increasingly influential group that have declared a Holy War against the Brazilian espiritistas and their spirits. The largest in this group of 'neo-Pentecostalism' (Mariano, 1995) is the Universal Church of the Kingdom of God (Igreja Universal do Reino de Deus); though it is neither the only one nor the oldest, it is the most visible. Before I go deeper into this religious war between the Holy Spirit and the spirits and deities of the medium religions in Brazil, I need to introduce the main traditions.

The Range of Medium Religions in Brazil

I have already mentioned the main religious traditions employing mediumship in Brazil (Kardecism, Umbanda and Candomblé), though they are not the only ones. It is impossible to give an adequate overview of all religious traditions with mediumship currently active in Brazil, even if one could fill the pages of a book instead of a single book chapter. The problem increases when one considers the various local names, sub-groups and developments. Umbanda alone changes so fast that it is difficult to keep track of all the new practices and beings. It might be better to speak – as Malandrino (2006) and others do – of a continuum of religious practices with Kardecism on one end and the African derived traditions, such as Candomblé, on the other. However, even this is problematic because of the many variations within each tradition. Some Afro-Brazilian *terreiros*[3] could be situated more towards Kardecism while others are clearly on the African end of the continuum. While Malandrino (2006) emphasizes the African elements of Umbanda and categorizes it as an Afro-Brazilian religion, *mães* and *pais de santo*[4] of Candomblé usually reject the notion that Umbanda belongs to the group of Afro-Brazilian religions.

Candomblé represents a conglomerate of African traditions that were transformed into Brazilian ones. Vagner Gonçalves da Silva (1994) even goes so far as to describe Candomblé as the reinvention of Africa in Brazil. Based on the customs of the enslaved Africans who were transported to Brazil, Candomblé started as a 'culto africano' (African cult) in a relatively unorganized way. During the nineteenth century the first 'casas de Candomblé' (Candomblé houses) were founded, which became the birthplace of the traditions we combine today under the term Candomblé or, better, Candomblés. The tradition that became most famous, following many academic and non-academic publications, is the Bahian version of Candomblé, which emphasizes the Nago nation (derived from the West African ethnic language group of Yoruba). Other versions of Candomblé are based on Jéje (derived from the Ewe-Fon), and Angola (usually regarded as Bantu). Reginaldo Prandi (2005) categorizes Candomblé and the other Afro-Brazilian religions as ethnic religions and states that the *orixás*[5] occupy the core of the Brazilian soul.

All these ethnic religions were developed in certain areas of Brazil, for instance, Tambor de Mina in the state of Maranhão, Batuque in Rio Grande do Sul and in the Amazonian region, Macumba in Rio de Janeiro, and Xangô in Recife (Harding, 2005).[6] Due to internal migration these religions and others can now be found in São Paulo. The belief system of these religions is based around the worship of African deities who can incorporate a human being. The incorporation, or possession, is the core of the religious practice and is crucial to most rituals. If it occurs outside the close community of the terreiro, it is regarded as a sign that the person needs to become initiated and to join the community. Equally important is the consultation of one's fate through oracle reading by the priest (jogo de búzios), and the sacrifices to the orixás. The devotion of the orixás comprises lifelong obligations and the fulfilment of extensive rituals.

On the other side of the spectrum is Kardecism, also called Espiritismo. Kardecism is based on the writings of the French schoolteacher Leon Hypolite Denizard Rivail (1804–1869). Under the pseudonym Allan Kardec he described, in his many publications, the world of the spirits of the dead and the way to communicate with them. Shortly after publication his teaching reached Brazil where it gained much attention. For people at the end of the nineteenth and the beginning of the twentieth century it offered an alternative spirituality that lacked the negative images of the Afro-Brazilian religions. While the practice of Afro-Brazilian religions was regarded as black magic, and legally restricted until the 1970s (see Maggie, 1986), Kardecism and its numerous variations, under the label Espiritismo, were tolerated.

Mediumship is the core of Kardecism. Kardecists believe that everyone has some kind of mediumship ability, though often undiscovered or underdeveloped. Importance is given to the training of mediums to further their ability. In Kardecism, the term mediumship embraces a wide range of abilities. It can mean that someone can feel the presence of spirits, or see them, or hear them, or that someone has premonitions of things that are yet to happen. It can also mean that someone automatically writes messages from the spiritual world without controlling the arm and hand, or that someone incorporates a discarnate spirit for a while so that this spirit can deliver a message to the world of the living. The aim is to help the living and the dead, whether by delivering messages from the dead to the living or by healing. Mediums usually have to follow strict rules of behaviour: acting non-aggressively, always being polite towards other people, and abstaining from alcohol and other drugs.

In the middle of these two poles lies Umbanda, which includes certain African traditions and beliefs (such as the orixás), but also has a strong Kardecist influence, as the incorporation of belief in reincarnation signifies. Umbanda first emerged in the 1920s and 1930s in urban Brazil, predominately amongst middle-class Kardecists (Silva, 1994). However, for a long time their intention to avoid the oppression of other more visibly 'African' religions failed. With reference to police reports from the 1940s, Maria Helena Villas Boas Concone and Lísias Negrão (1985) describe how Umbanda became the target of political oppression in São Paulo. Umbanda was stigmatized as black magic until umbandistas increased the institutionalization of the religion by founding, for instance, a federation (in 1953) and continuing the series of national congresses that had begun in 1941 (in Rio de Janeiro).

Through their efforts Umbanda finally became visible as a nationally wide-spread, though still mainly urban, religion. Through the federations, umbandistas operated the Brazilian form of clientelism[7] and developed political influence (Concone & Negrão, 1985). It did not last long, however. Though some scholars still describe Umbanda as the true Brazilian religion, Umbanda is declining in political influence and membership numbers. Nonetheless, Umbanda still presents a very interesting religious development, in particular because of its wide range of variations. Despite all differences a central aspect is always the incorporation of supernatural beings, though the type of these *guías* (guides) varies. Usually the Umbanda cosmos embraces seven or eight types of entities, such as the *caboclos* (indigenous spirits), *pretos velhos* (spirits of old black slaves), *boiadeiros* (spirits of cowboys), *ciganos* (spirits of gypsies), *marinheiros* (spirits of sailers), and *exús* (seen as a messenger or trickster spirit as well as an orixá) and *pomba giras*, the female counterpart of the male exús in Umbanda.

The Candomblé orixás are also part of the Umbanda cosmology, although the umbandistas do not ordinarily incorporate deities. Interestingly, however, umbandistas will occasionally incorporate the spirits of the orixás, because they are supposed to have been derived from living beings, hence also having spirits themselves. In one terreiro I have seen an altar for extraterrestrials next to one for North American Native Americans, as well as symbols for Celtic deities, all typical of the symbolic and ritual diversity of Umbanda and its constant transformation. As in Kardecism, the aim of the incorporation of all types of entities is to help people, though it is not unheard of a spirit to incorporate a person purely for entertainment.

The three Brazilian religious traditions I have just introduced – Espiritism, Umbanda and Candomblé – have also developed a range of combinations (such as Umbandomblé, Umbanda Esoterico, and Espiritismo Encruzilhada), though in most cases the mães and pais de santo who practise more than one tradition are quite strict to practise them on separate days, sometimes even in separate weeks or months. Individuals are less strict and move back and forth from one tradition to the other whenever they want. For instance, Malandrino (2006) states that 42.10% of Umbanda priests have Kardecist backgrounds. Most of the mães and pais de santo in Umbanda that I spoke with were also initiated in Candomblé, and some of the espiritistas also practised Umbanda. It seems usual in Brazil to move through various religious traditions during a life time, and sometimes they are even practised at the same time, but for different purposes. Confronted with the inability to separate or categorize the religious traditions of Brazil, André Droogers (1987) – following Carlos Brandão's (1978) proposal of 'a grand symbolic matrix of common usage' – outlines the Minimal Brazilian Religiosity (religiosidade minimal brasileira) that manifests itself publicly in secular contexts and constitutes the Brazilian culture. Though his approach to religion (and to culture) is basically essentialist (see Dickie's, 2007 critique), he highlights an aspect that is also important in the following discussion of mediumship religions in Brazil. The Minimal Brazilian Religiosity is product as well as producer; it establishes unity and construes cultural identity (Droogers, 1987).

The New Religious Composition of Brazil and the Rise of the UCKG

Since the 1970s the number of members has declined for all but one of the religions mentioned above: only Espiritismo was shown to have gained members in the 2000 census, while the Afro-Brazilian religions declined (Malandrino, 2006). It might be that this statistical increase can be explained by people using the term 'Espiritismo' as an umbrella category for all kinds of Afro-Brazilian traditions in order to prevent the negative perception of 'black magic.' Another reason, according to Prandi, is that Afro-Brazilian religions have failed to establish proper institutions and efficient structures that could attract new members (Prandi, 2005, quoted in Malandrino, 2006). The biggest impact on the Brazilian religious world, however, has come from the success of neo-Pentecostalism.

Brazil is in the middle of an incredible religious transformation that has the power to reshape society. Usually described as a Roman Catholic country, academics speculate about the outcome of the new census and the predicted shift in religious commitment. Already the figures of the last census in 2000 confirmed a demographic shift from Roman Catholicism to Evangelical, and in particular Pentecostal, churches.[8] Though the number of people indicating that they belonged to Roman Catholicism was the large majority (73.8%), the figures for Evangelical churches continued to rise (15.4%). People who have practised Umbanda are now joining the Pentecostal churches in great numbers, in particular the Universal Church of the Kingdom of God (UCKG).[9]

Gedeon Alencar (2005) includes the UCKG in his overview of Brazilian forms of Protestantism. He distinguishes between different stages: Protestantism of the immigrants, Protestantism of the missionaries, Pentecostalism brought to Brazil by foreigners, and contemporary Protestantism, led and founded by Brazilians. In the latter he includes neo-Pentecostalism but also non-Pentecostal forms of Protestantism. André Corten, Jean-Pierre Dozer and Ari Oro (2003) even compare the significance of Pentecostalism to the Protestant Reformation, and state that Pentecostalism affects the history of the southern hemisphere as the Reformation did the West. To highlight the fundamental differences between 'traditional' Pentecostalism and the 'modern' form, Ricardo Mariano (1995) successfully coined the term 'neo-Pentecostalism'. This term is used today to describe the Brazilian form of Pentecostalism, which is quite different from the one introduced early in the twentieth century by mostly North American missionaries. The Assembly of God, for instance, one of the 'traditional' Pentecostal movements, rejects any comparison between Umbanda and Pentecostalism in general (Alencar, 2005).

The UCKG was founded in Rio de Janeiro in 1977 by Edir Macedo Bezerra, who still leads the church as bishop in a quite authoritarian manner. Macedo, born into a Catholic family, attended Umbanda rituals until he converted to the New Life

Pentecostal Church in the 1960s. For ten years he worked with Walter Robert McAlister, the Canadian founder of the church, in Rio de Janeiro until he decided to found his own church: the Universal Church of the Kingdom of God. In just a few years the UCKG outnumbered the New Life Pentecostal Church in membership and national significance. Currently, in Brazil, the UCKG owns TV and radio stations, several newspapers and journals, and has more than three million members in Brazil alone (Oliva, 1995). After it entered Brazilian politics in 1986 it soon managed to get several delegates elected to the Federal Congress, the Constituent National Assembly, and other legislative assemblies at national and local levels (see Oro, 2005). Some even say that President Lula won his election only with the support of the UCKG. However, it is now no longer just a Brazilian phenomenon and is present in more than thirty countries. The UCKG is probably the largest and most important new church in the so-called developing world (Corten, Dozer & Oro, 2003).

At the centre of the UCKG theology is demonic possession, with the liberation ceremony on Fridays as the core function. Satan and the demons are regarded as inferior spirits (Oliva, 1995), who constantly disturb 'the mental, physical and spiritual order,' according to Macedo, and are the main problem (Oliveira, 1998). They are responsible for all the misery and evil in the world. It is the responsibility of everyone to intervene and to 'liberate' the world – and oneself – from demons. The other religions – and in particular the Afro-Brazilian religions – are guilty of bringing demons into the world, while the UCKG frees the world of demons.

For the UCKG Satan and the demons exist as personified beings, and not only in a symbolic manner. Demons were created by Satan, who is their leader, while Satan was created by God, but was expelled from heaven. Demons can manifest themselves as spirits without body or heart and bring evil into the world. Salvation can bring only God's word. Fernando da Silva Pimentel (2005) interprets the figure of Satan in the UCKG as the result of syncretism between the perception of Satan in US-Pentecostalism and aspects of Afro-Brazilian traditions, in particular Umbanda in Rio de Janeiro. However, the demons also include the gods of the Ancient Greeks, Romans, Mesopotamia, Egypt, other African cosmologies, Asian religions and so on.

The UCKG distinguishes sharply between divine inspiration by the Holy Spirit – since the end of the nineteenth century a central aspect of the Pentecostal movement – and demonic possession, and rejects any attempt to compare both. According to UCKG theology, demons cannot really incorporate a body, or possess the soul, as both make a substantial unity and so cannot be controlled by demons. 'Demonic possession is characterized as paralysing the will and distracting the conscience by a play of fantasy, or, in other words, by the demon' (Oliva, 1995).[10] José Sorafim da Silva (1998) lists ten symptoms of demonic possession as described in UCKG leaflets, among them nervousness, headaches, insomnia, suicidal tendencies, depression, vision, and hearing voices. The first step towards healing is to discover the identity of the demon. The first question is, therefore, always 'What is your name?' – a crucial moment of the exorcism in the UCKG (Almeida, 2003).

The exorcism itself is initiated by shouting repeatedly 'In the name of Jesus, in the name of Jesus, in the name of Jesus' (Silva, 1998). I also heard the constant shouting of 'Go away! Go away! Go away!,' though the final salvation can bring only God's word so that all members of the congregation are encouraged to join the loud screams 'In the name of Jesus!' until the possessed person collapses. I have also seen pastors and their assistants supporting the verbal attack by pressing their hands on or above the head of the possessed person, and in this manner they pass their own positive energy to that person. Members of the congregation are asked to support this effort by stretching their arms and hands towards the front where the exorcism takes place.

However, in order to conduct an exorcism it is essential that the demon manifests first in a human person. Spirit possession is, therefore, part of the exorcism process according to UCKG theology (Birman, 1996), and this role belongs to women, as Pimentel explains. The UCKG has a high number of women among its members, though the positions inside the church hierarchy are filled by men, with the exception of assistants. According to the founder of the UCKG, Bishop Macedo, women are housewives and mothers and should be quiet (Pimentel, 2005). As mothers and housewives women are also responsible for keeping evil away from the family and for exorcising evil if necessary. Thus, it is the duty of women to protect their families and to fight the demons. In order to do this, women must first be exorcised of their own demons so that (second step) the troublesome demons will manifest in their bodies. The third step is to exorcise the demons from the women's bodies (Pimentel, 2005), which allows them to accommodate the Holy Spirit.

Pimentel, who interviewed several women of the UCKG after being exorcised, writes that by providing their body for this ritual women gain a new significance within their families and for their lives. She interprets the exorcism as empowerment for women: 'In other words, the demon takes from the devotee the blame for her/his actions, but not the responsibility of an individual to confront and liberate. Responsibility is placed on the shoulders of women' (Pimentel, 2005).[11] In the theological discourse of the UCKG individuals can be possessed by demons only when they are empty of the Holy Spirit, so in order to be filled by the Holy Spirit the demons have to be exorcised. In the terminology of the UCKG the ceremony is known as 'despossession' (despossessão). In this way spirit possession is allowed only when conducted in the temple (the church building of the UCKG), according to strict rules, in services known as 'sessão de descarrego' (session of discharge or unload), during which the spirit possession is initiated by pastors who will not experience it themselves. Pimentel argues that the rituals of spirit possession and exorcism have a therapeutic function for the women and – as I add – for the community. The

UCKG reorganizes the symbolic universe and brings order into chaos, unfortunately it does this by demonizing every religious manifestation that does not fit into the UCKG doctrine and lies outside the symbolic order of the UCKG.

The Holy War – Brazilian Style

The relationship between Pentecostalism and the Afro-Brazilian religions and Espiritismo was never going to be a good one, especially when one considers the classification of the African deities, Umbanda guías and spirits of the dead as demons within Pentecostal theology. Walter Robert McAlister of the New Life Pentecostal Church in Rio de Janeiro published, in 1968, a hugely popular manifesto with a verbal attack on the Afro-Brazilian religions, *Mãe de Santo*. In this book he recounts the life story of a Candomblé priestess (mãe de santo), Georgina Aragão dos Santos, and her conversion to Pentecostalism. This biography outlines McAlister's strategies in the spiritual battle against Afro-Brazilian demons that later inspired Macedo and others to follow him on this path.

In the 1980s the aggression of neo-Pentecostalism towards the Afro-Brazilian religions increased slowly until, in the 1990s, open hostility finally broke out (Mariano, 1995). Following McAlister's example, Macedo, too, published a book in which he attacked the Afro-Brazilian religious experience in such a way that legal actions were taken against the book and later editions had to be revised. In *Orixás, caboclos & guías: deuses ou demônios?* (1988), Macedo outlines his doctrine and states that anyone who attends terreiros or spiritist centros is an 'easy target' for demonic attacks. Even family members or friends can become targets of these demons, as he explains with several testimonies of converts who have attended Afro-Brazilian ceremonies before converting to the UCKG. However, the book's biggest impact came from the many photos of Afro-Brazilian rituals, in particular the ones showing blood sacrifice, the 'Achilles heel' of Afro-Brazilian religions (Silva, 2007). Taken out of context they confirm the prejudices against Afro-Brazilian religions and their common perception as being 'bloody' and 'primitive.' And not only animals are sacrificed but also humans, as Macedo writes in his book.[12]

Then, in 1994/1995, the UCKG declared the Holy War against Macumba, and later against all Afro-Brazilian religions, including Espiritismo. Despite religious freedom and an increasing visibility of Afro-Brazilian culture,[13] the UCKD, with increasing aggressiveness, attacked aspects of the religious practice of Afro-Brazilian religions. In particular, incorporation and spirit mediumship became the target of neo-Pentecostal pastors who demonized, and even ridiculed, the practice on national TV. It also became customary to encourage congregations to confront the members of terreiros in their neighbourhood. These 'confrontations' often had (and still have) a violent character, as Vagner Gonçalves da Silva reports. From newspaper articles he collected numerous reports of neo-Pentecostals invading terreiros with the intent of destroying altars and other religious symbols, and exorcizing everyone they encountered. He even found cases where members of a UCKG attacked umbandistas with stones, and where they kidnapped a woman in order to convert her (Silva, 2007). More common, however, is the organization of marches around a terreiro or the broadcasting of hymns via loudspeakers. The aim is to intimidate the visitors of a terreiro and prevent them from entering, or to disturb rituals inside, the terreiro. Silva (2007) also mentions distributing leaflets and preaching (with loudspeaker) during public ceremonies, such as at the festival for Iemanjá[14] in Rio de Janeiro.

Almeida (2003) calls this attack against the wide range of 'catholic-afro-Kardecist' religions the 'war of the possessions.' Roman Catholicism and some aspects of popular Catholicism, such as the worship of saints, were also targeted by the UCKG, which sees a demon behind every image of a saint (Oliva, 1995; Pimentel, 2005). But the UCKG had to learn that certain Catholic icons are too powerful. In 1996 a pastor dared to kick the statue of the National Patron of Brazil, Nossa Senhora Aparecida, in a service that was broadcast on TV. This (infamous) 'kicking the saint'-incident rebounded and the UCKG, including Macedo himself, had to apologize – in public – for this attack against the Virgin Mary (Almeida, 2003; Birman & Lehmann, 1999)

Unfortunately, the attacks against the Afro-Brazilian religions continue, as I observed in São Paulo in 2010. Though the late pai Francelino won a court case against the UCKG that would have forced them to broadcast daily for a week a one-hour documentary with a statement from Afro-Brazilian religious leaders on the UCKG TV station (nationwide), the decision was overruled before the first broadcast (personal information in May 2010 in São Paulo). This action, however, has demonstrated the power of legal resistance and encouraged other mães and pais de santo to pursue Pentecostal pastors in court (Silva, 2007). But there are more ways to show resistance, for instance, by organizing a peaceful march around the neighbourhood to show their commitment and solidarity.

In March 2010 mãe Marcia in São Paulo organized a procession in her neighbourhood that led from a terreiro nearby to her terreiro where she conducted, together with the pai de santo of the other terreiro, a public ceremony to celebrate the beginning of the new ritual year. Another way to resist the constant attacks is to wear demonstratively 'African' dresses and colours, even when going to the supermarket. Pai Francisco (during an interview on 21 May 2010 in São Paulo), told me that it is not enough to dress in special African-style dresses during festivals; it is more important to show in everyday situations one's commitment to an Afro-Brazilian religion. Another contribution to this struggle is the growing number of African cultural centres and initiatives against religious intolerance. At the inauguration of a Centro Cultural Africana in Barra Funda, São Paulo, several of the speakers mentioned the significance of the mães and pais de santo to Afro-Brazilian heritage, and specially prepared certificates were handed out to some of the priests and priestesses (on 18 May 2010).

The Holy War against Espiritismo, Umbanda and the other Afro-Brazilian religions is incomprehensible when one considers the many similarities between the UCKG and the Afro-Brazilian religions. Ari Oro (2006) even describes the UCKG as 'macumbeiro,' shaped by Macumba. As explained above, the UCKG cultivates spirit possession – in order to exorcize the demons publicly. One can say, therefore, that the UCKG also belongs to the group of Brazilian mediumship religions, but with the opposite theological designation of the supernatural entities that incorporate people – demons instead of deities and spirits. Nonetheless, it is still mediumship, following Charles Emmons's (2000) definition as 'the transfer of information from discarnate beings or souls to the living through another living human who is sensitive to such information'. Even the function of the practice is, in the end, therapeutic in both cases, though, again, the theological perception is contrary. The UCKG initiates the possession by spirits (called demons) in some people – usually women – with the aim of exorcism as the only solution to many problems. Whereas the mediums in Umbanda and Espiritismo look for the incorporation, or other forms of mediumship, in order to receive information to assist others, in Candomblé the possession itself has therapeutic effect (see Birman, 1985).

Why, then, is the UCKG so aggressively against the group of mediumship religions? Looking at the national census it is obvious that the UCKG and the other neo-Pentecostal churches vastly outnumber the mediumship religions. Why attack a group that is – nationwide – nearly invisible, with a following of just 3%? Looking at the statistical shift from Umbanda to the UCKG documented in the national census, one could assume that the reason behind the attack on Afro-Brazilian religions is a campaign to attract new members. However, Vagner Gonçalves da Silva (2007) argues that it is not a strategy against the lower social classes from which the UCKG and other neo-Pentecostal movements recruit their members. Instead, he connects the attack to the role of spirit possession within the UCKG. Neo-Pentecostalism offers its congregation an experience of religious renewal that can be experienced inside the body and not just on a symbolic level. The bodily experiences have been, as Vagner Gonçalves da Silva writes, a monopoly of Afro-Brazilian religions and Kardecism. By targeting these religions, and demonizing their spiritual entities, neo-Pentecostalism aims to attract those looking for an ecstatic experience but without the negative image of 'black magic.' Pentecostalism has, as Silva (2007) highlights, the advantage of the social legitimacy of Christianity. It is, therefore, not (only) a strategy to recruit converts from the Afro-Brazilian religions and Espiritismo, but a way to attract converts from the wide range of Brazilian society who, as stated at the beginning of this chapter, can be characterized by an enormous openness towards paranormal experiences. It is indeed a 'fight of the possessions' as Almeida writes.

Conclusion

I excluded from my discussion one religious tradition that is competing with neo-Pentecostalism for members, the Renovação Carismática Católica (the Charismatic Catholic Revival). Introduced to Brazil in 1968 this charismatic movement clashed immediately with the Roman Catholic Church, with the Comunidaded Eclesias de Base (grass-roots churches), as well as outside the Church with Pentecostalism (Prandi, 1998), in both cases successfully: Antônio Flávio Pierucci and Reginaldo Prandi (1998) attest to a growth of the Charismatic Revival, while the grass-roots movement declines in importance. They attribute this increase to the fact that the charismatic movement uses similar techniques to Pentecostalism, such as the reintroduction of miracles and ecstatic experiences of individuals (Prandi, 1998).

However, the ecstatic experience of the Charismatic movement is connected to the Holy Spirit and has a different quality. People experience divine inspiration and ecstasy, but this experience – though also combined with an altered state of consciousness – cannot be described as mediumship if we continue with Emmons' definition of a transfer of information (quoted above). But, if divine inspiration by the Holy Spirit is to be excluded, why is the possession of orixás included? Pais and mães de santo make a strict distinction between the incorporation of guias and spirits in Umbanda and possession by the African deities of nature, the orixás. Pai Zezinho explained to me that the spirits and caboclos enter the body of the medium as external entities that will leave after the possession episode. Part of the orixá remains, however. Pai Zezinho explained that an orixá rises from the heart up to the head when it takes over the control of the body. An orixás is a force of nature and as such is not limited like a spirit of a deceased human being (on 23 April). Following this definition one could indeed compare the orixá possession with the divine inspiration. But, as demonstrated above, the opposite is in-fact the case. Ecstatic experiences, such as those associated with mediumship, are still categorized according to the social stature of the religion, as well as the social background of its adherents.

Notes

1. The term 'abnormal' does not necessary indicate that one has to categorize the experience as pathological. Referring to Cardeña and Krippner, 'abnormal' is defined as irregular or uncommon (quoted in Machado 2009).

2. The study leave was funded by the Santander Mobility Grant and Bangor University. In São Paulo, colleagues at the Department of Postgraduate Studies in Study of Religions at the Pontifícia Universidade Católica (PUC)

have helped to initiate the contacts with religious communities. I want to express my deepest gratitude to Frank Usarski and his colleagues.

3. Brazilian term for the location of a religious community, originally in rural areas where a terreiro includes, apart from one or more buildings, outdoor space for rituals. However, a terreiro can also be in an urban area such as São Paulo, composed only of a building.

4. Brazilian terms for female and male priests usually used in all Afro-Brazilian traditions including umbanda though recently the terms ialorixá and babalorixá have become popular.

5. Brazilian term for Afro-Brazilian deities based on Yoruba tradition. In tambor de minha the term voduns is used for the deities based on the Dahomian tradition.

6. In addition to these Brazilian versions the recent spread of a Yoruba tradition (sometimes also called 'culto afro') is notable in Brazil, usually with a Nigerian priest as founder of the community. Despite the declared purpose to (re)introduce the 'correct' Yoruba tradition and in particular the cult of ifá, the priests are by and large babalorixás and not babalowas, hence not ifá-priests.

7. See da Matta's excellent description of Brazilian society and culture and its form of clientelism (da Matta, 1991).

8. See Pierucci (2004) for the decline of traditional religions in the 2000 census.

9. I will use the English short form though in Brazilian publications the name is usually shortened as IURD for Igreja Universal do Reino de Deus.

10. 'A possessão diabólica se caracteriza pela paralização da vontade e divisão da consciémcia sob o jugo da fantasia, ou seja, do demônio.'

11. 'Ou seja, o demônio retira do fiel a culpa sobre seus atos, mas não tira a responsabilidade que a indivíduo tem de enfrenta-lo e libertar-se. Responsabilidade essa que é duplamente assumida pela mulher.'

12. This strategy of expanding blood sacrifice from animals to human beings is quite common as I explained with regard to Haitian vodou in an earlier publication, see Schmidt (2001).

13. For instance, see Vagner Gonçalves da Silva (2007) on the change of textbooks.

14. African water goddess, also regarded as mother of the orixás.

References

Alencar, G. (2005). *Protestantismo Tupiniquim: Hipótese sobre a (não)contribuição evangélica à cultura brasileira*. São Paulo: Arte Editorial.

Almeida, R., de (2003). A guerra dos possessões. In A. P. Oro, A. Corten and J.-P. Dozon (Eds.), *Igreja Universal do Reino de Deus: Os novos conquestadores da fé* (pp.321-342). São Paulo: Paulinas.

Birman, P. (1985). *O que é Umbanda*. São Paulo: Abril Cultural.

Birman, P. (1996). Cultos de possessão e pentecostalismo na Brasil: Passagens. *Religião e Sociedade*, 17(1-2), 90-109.

Birman, P., & Lehmann, D. (1999). Religion and the media in a battle for ideological hegemony: The Universal Church of the Kingdom of God and TV Globo in Brazil. *Bulletin Latin American Research, 18*(2), 145-164.

Brandão, C. R. (1978). O número dos eleitos; Religião e ideologia em uma sociedade de economia agrária no Estado de São Paulo. *Religião e Sociedade, 3*, 53-93.

Concone, M. H. V. B., & Negrão, L. (1985). Umbanda: Da representação à cooptação. O envolvimento político partidário da Umbanda Paulista. In D. Brown *et al.* (Eds.), *Umbanda e Política* (pp.43-79). Rio de Janeiro: Ed. Marco Zao.

Corten, A., Dozer, J-P., & Oro, A. P. (2003). Introdução. In A. P. Oro, A. Corten and J-P. Dozon (Eds.), *Igreja Universal do Reino de Deus: Os novos conquestadores da fé* (pp.13-45). São Paulo: Paulinas.

da Matta, R. (1991). *Carnivals, rogues, and heroes: An interpretation of the Brazilian dilemma*. Notre Dame: University of Notre Dame Press.

Dickie, M. A. S. (2007). Religious experience and culture: Testing possibilities. *Antropologia em Primeira Mão, 98*, 5-18.

Droogers, A. (1987). A religiosidade minima Brasileira. *Religião e Sociedade, 14* (2), 62-86.

Emmons, C. F. (2000). On becoming a spirit medium in a 'rational society'. *Anthropology of Consciousness, 12* (1-2), 71-82.

Harding, R. E. (2005). Afro-Brazilian religions. In L. Jones (Ed.), *Encyclopedia of religion (2nd ed.; Vol. 1)* (pp.119-125). Farmington Hills: Thomson Gale.

Macedo, E. (1996). *Orixás, caboclos y guías: Deuses ou demônios?* Rio de Janeiro: Ed. Universal.

Machado, F. R. (2009). *Experiências anômales na vida cotidiana: Experiências extra-senório-motorras e sua associação com crenças, atitudes e em-estar subjetivo*. Unpublished PhD thesis, University of São Paulo.

Maggie, Y. (1986). O medo do feitico: Verdades e mentiras sobre a repressao as religioes mediunicas. *Religiao e Sociedade*, 13(1), 72-86.

Malandrino, B. C. (2006). *Umbanda: mudanças e permanencies. Uma análise simbólica*. São Paulo: Ed. PUC-SP.

Mariano, R. (1995). *Neo Pentecostalismo: Os pentecostais estão mudando*. Unpublished MPhil thesis, University of São Paulo. (later published under the title *Neopentecostais: sociologia do novo pentecostalismo no Brasil*. São Paulo: Ed. Loyola, 1999)

McAlister, R. (1983). *Mãe de Santo*. Rio de Janeiro: Ed. Carisma.

Oliva, M. M. C. (1995). *Ação diabólica e exorcismo: Na Igreja Universal do Reino de Deus*. Unpublished MPhil thesis, Pontifícia Universidade Católica, São Paulo.

Oliveira, I. X., de (1998). *A ação pastoral da Igreja Universal do Reino de Deus: Uma Evangelizacão inculturada?* Unpublished MPhil thesis, Pontifícia Universidade Católica, São Paulo.

Oro, A. P. (2003). A Política da Igreja Universal e Seus Reflexos nos Campos Religioso e Político Brasileiros. *Revista Brasileira de Ciências Sociais, 18* (53), 53-69.

Oro, A. P. (2006) O neopentecostalismo 'macumbeiro'. In A. C. Isaia (Ed.). *Orixás e Espíritos: O debate interdisciplina na pesuqisa contemporânea* (pp.115-128). Uberlândia: EDUFU.

Pierucci, A. F. (2004). "Bye bye, Brasil": O declínio das religiões tradicionais no Censo 2000. *Estudos Avançados, 18* (52), 17-28.

Pierucci, A. F., & Prandi, R. (1998). Introdução: As religiões na Brasil contemporáneo. In R. Prandi (Ed.), *Um sopro do Espírito: a renovação conservadora do Catolicismo carismático* (pp13-26). São Paulo: Ed. University of São Paulo.

Pimentel, F., da S. (2005). *Quando ssiquê se liberta do demônio: Um estudo sobre a relação entre exorcismo e cura psíquica em mulheres na Igreja Universal do Reino de Deus.* Unpublished MPhil thesis, Pontifícia Universidade Católica, São Paulo.

Prandi, R. (1998). *Um sopro do Espírito: A renovação conservadora do Catolicismo carismático.* São Paulo: Ed. University of São Paulo.

Prandi, R. (2005). *Segredos Guardados: Orixás na alma brasileira.* São Paulo: Companhia dass Letras.

Schmidt, B. E. (2001). The interpretation of violent worldviews: Cannibalism and other violent images of the Caribbean. In B. E. Schmidt and I. W. Schröder (Eds.), *Anthropology of violence and conflict,* (pp.76-96). London: Routledge.

Silva, J. S., da (1998). *Caçadores de demônios: Demonização e exorcismo com método de evangelização no neopentecostalismo.* Unpublished MPhil, Pontifícia Universidade Católica, São Paulo.

Silva, V. G., da (1994). *Candomblé e Umbanda: Caminhos da devoção brasileira.* São Paulo: Ed. Ática.

Silva, V. G., da (2007). Neopentecostalismo e religiões Afro-Brasileiras: Significados do ataque aos símbolos da herança religiosa Africana no Brasil contemporâneo. *Mana, 13* (1), 207-236.

A Candomblé medium incorporates the Orixá Oxum, Salvador, Bahia.

PSYCHEDELIC POSSESSION: THE GROWING INCORPORATION OF INCORPORATION INTO AYAHUASCA USE

DAVID LUKE

Sometimes an astonishing discovery can be simultaneously eclipsed by the realisation of something even more astonishing – in this case it was the fact that the discovery was astonishing in the first place. A few years ago, whilst researching the use of the highly psychoactive Amazonian jungle decoction called ayahuasca and its magico-religious use in Brazil I was informed that incorporation rituals had been adopted for use in recent years within the practices of the Sainto Daime church, a syncretic Christian ayahuasca-using group widespread in Brazil. Brazil is, of course, home to numerous new syncretic Christian Afro-Brazilian religions, such as Umbanda, which combines elements of European, indigenous Brazilian and African diaspora religious influence. One of the core features of Umbanda is the utilisation of trance 'incorporation' – a term preferred by practitioners (e.g., Marques, 2007) and some researchers (e.g., Groisman, 2013) for what has elsewhere been called voluntary possession (e.g., Oesterreich, 1966), or trance or spirit possession (e.g., Bourguignon, 1976; Klass, 2003; Lewis, 1978), although some contemporary writers continue to use the terms interchangeably (e.g., Dawson, 2010, 2011, 2012), whereas others discuss the inherent difficulty in defining such a cross-culturally nuanced phenomenon as possession (e.g., Cohen, 2008).

Slowly, over the last few decades, there has been a growing fusion of these two techniques of magico-religious practice (Dawson, 2011, 2012), with individuals within Santo Daime church combining both incorporation and the ingestion of psychedelic potions within the same ritual, a combination that is appropriately termed *Umbandaime*. On first hearing about this I was astonished because psychedelic possession or incorporation is so rarely discussed in the literature, but, then, the more I thought about it, I became increasingly astonished at this fact in itself. The question arose as to why there is an apparent absence of incorporation with traditional plant psychedelic use, when so many other ostensibly paranormal or parapsychological practices abound with these substances; be it divination, psychic diagnosis, shamanic healing, mediumship and communication with other spirits, out-of-body experiences and travelling clairvoyance, and so on (e.g., see Luke, 2010, 2012). This lead to further questions, such as how incorporation became incorporated into ritual ayahuasca use, and what this in itself signifies. Before proceeding, however, a note here is required to indicate that this essay does not explore the ontology of the experiences here described, be it entity encounters or possession, as detailed discussion of the relevant arguments can be found elsewhere (for possession see, e.g., Bourguignon, 1976; Klass, 2003; Lewis, 1978; for psychedelic entity encounters see Luke, 2011a). Indeed, Lewis (1978, p.26) notes that, "the majority of anthropological writers on possession have been...absorbed in often quite pointless debates as to the genuineness or otherwise of particular trance states."

The Growing Incorporation of Incorporation into Ayahuasca Use

While conducting research amongst ayahuasca groups in northern Brazil a few years ago I was surprised to come across a branch of

Santo Daime that utilised incorporation in its ceremonies, and so I conducted an interview with one of the mediums. Having previously trained in Harner Foundation (non-psychedelic) shamanic counselling in the US, the medium already had a native American spirit guide prior to joining the CEFLURIS Santo Daime church at Mapiá, in the Amazon, in the 1990s. Curiously enough, the native spirit guide was somebody who had been friends with the medium before they had died. Working alongside Santo Daime mediums already utilising the Umbanda spirits at Mapiá he trained in Umbandaime but continued to use his native American guide as his main incorporating spirit under the influence of ayahuasca – even working on one of the lead mediums at Mapiá and becoming accepted into the circle of practicing mediums, consisting only of women. The medium eventually left Mapiá and continued working in northern Brazil, where we met, and he informed me about the relatively unknown combination of ayahuasca and incorporation.

Despite the relative obscurity of Umbandaime outside of Brazilian Spiritist circles, some English language texts are available that plot the history and contemporary practice of Umbandaime (e.g., Dawson, 2010, 2011, 2012; Marques, 2007; Polari, 1999), and can be consulted for a more comprehensive account than that given here. Starting with Umbanda, as the oldest branch, its history is somewhat hazy, but it undoubtedly has its origins in the fusion of Afro-Brazilian religious influences and Kardecist Spiritism – a system of belief similar to the Spiritualism of Victorian Britain but which is based on the teachings of the Nineteenth century French spiritual philosopher Allan Kardec. Perhaps the earliest agreed progenitor of Umbanda is a young navy cadet officer called Zélio de Moraes who, in 1920 in the city of São Gonçalo, across the bay from Rio de Janeiro, defied the usual Kardecist Spiritist practices of the time during a séance when he incorporated both indigenous (caboclo) and African slave (preto velho) spirits of the dead, rather than the usual Caucasian ones

(Brown, 1994). Sometime later in the 1920s Moraes set up the first Umbanda 'centro' in Niteroi, which then moved to central Rio where it flourished. Combining Catholicism, Spiritism and Afro-Brazilian influences – especially the incorporation of Orixás (deities, typically of Yoruba origin), pretos velhos and caboclos – and the use of mediumship, Umbanda is also porous to other religious and esoteric influences and fast became popular among the middle classes and the poorer communities alike. It spread widely during the 1970s and 1980s and had 17,000 registered centros by 1990 (Brown, 1994) but numbers gradually declined after that.

It was shortly after the formation of Umbanda in the urban sprawls of eastern Brazil that Santo Daime emerged from the jungles of Acre in western Brazil in the 1930s. As a rubber tapper in the forest, the healer Raimundo Irineu Serra (Mestre Irineu) encountered indigenes using ayahuasca in a shamanic manner and developed its use as a sacrament in a Christian-based religion – albeit one without recourse to scripture, and where some importance was given to interaction with nature spirits, though not spirits of the dead (Dawson, 2011, 2012). This first Santo Daime community was called Alto Santo and fractured in the 1970s, following Mestre Irineu's death, when Padrinho Sebastião Mota de Melo broke away and founded the Centro Ecléctico da Fluente Luz Universal Raimundo Irineu Serra (CEFLURIS) branch, which ultimately situated itself in Céu do Mapiá, Amazonas, deep in the jungle.

Other non-Santo Daime churches also appeared in the early years, the two largest surviving ones of which we know being the Barquinha and the União do Vegetal (UDV). Having also practiced with Mestre Irineu in Rio Branco, Acre, the ex-sailor Daniel Pereira de Mattos (Frei Daniel) established the Barquinha (little boat) religious community there in 1945, and it never spread much beyond the state of Acre (Labate, 2006). The last of the three ayahuasca religions to be formed, the UDV, began its lineage independently of the Santo Daime and was officially established in Porto Velho (state of Rondônia) in 1965 by the rubber tapper José Gabriel da Costa (Mestre Gabriel), although it was also reputedly founded in 1961 at the Sunta rubber camp on the Bolivian-Brazilian border (Goulert, 2006).

To varying degrees, each of the three groups have clear tri-continental spiritual inspirations. There are European influences, such as Catholicism and Kardecist Spiritism in all three, and even Masonry in the case of UDV. Afro-Brazilian influences from the Umbanda cult, for example, are also apparent in all of them, with elements of the African Casa das Minas and other traditions as well in the UDV (Luke, 2011b). Finally, each group is ultimately defined by its utilisation of Brazilian indigenous practices through the utilisation of ayahuasca itself.

Each of these continental influences provides its own methodology for approaching the divine: prayer in the case of Catholicism, visionary experience from the indigenes, and incorporation from the African traditions (Araújo, 2006), although it should be noted that the French Spiritist influence also champions incorporation too. Additionally, each technique also offers a different relationship to the spirit world: prayer facilitates faith in, and a reverence for spirit, visions mediate a direct experience of spirit, and incorporation enables a becoming of, or merging with spirit (Luke, 2011b).

In accordance with the doctrinal influences at play in each of the three ayahuasca groups we see varying degrees of recourse to these three spiritual technologies, particularly with regard to incorporation. Despite Mestre Gabriel's prior Kardecist spirit guide incorporations and although heavily influenced by Afro-Brazilian religion, the UDV do not incorporate (Goulart, 2006), whereas the Barquinha do (Araújo, 2006; Groisman, 2013), and probably did so before Santo Daime. Nevertheless, the Barquinha refer to their incorporation mediumship as a less complete embodiment of spirits with the term 'irradiation', in that the spirit radiates through them rather than fully incorporating (Frenopoulo, 2006). Finally, within the Santo Daime – the oldest, largest and most widespread of the three religions – a growing 'Umbandaization' (Dawson, 2012) of the religious practice is evident within the widespread CEFLURIS branch.

The Prepossessing Power of Possession

This synthesised practice initially began in 1977 when Padrinho Sebastião, a Spiritist medium prior to joining the Santo Daime in the mid-1960s, began incorporation of several spirits while suffering an illness that lasted three years, following the murder by daimistas of an apparent Quimbanda practitioner at Padrinho Sebastião's centre in Rio Branco (Marques, 2007). By the time CEFLURIS Santo Daime (hereafter just called Santo Daime) arrived at Mapiá in 1983 the Padrinho and his followers, who now included growing numbers of counter-culture itinerants from across Brazil and beyond, had developed a number of rituals utilising incorporation, though their use was limited.

In the early 1980s Santo Daime expanded and two churches opened in Rio de Janeiro, bringing in a further surge of white middle-class followers, and with them came elements of Umbanda, which was extremely popular at that time in Rio. The urban daimistas in turn increasingly reached Mapiá, and by 1990, when Padrinho Sebastião died, the third generation of Santo Daime leadership saw the widespread use of incorporation, which by the late 1990s had become part of their cultic calendar (Dawson, 2011). Currently, according to Dawson (2011, 2012) Umbandaime is continuing to grow in popularity, with increasing numbers of both followers and incorporation rituals and styles within Santo Daime. Curiously, however, the use of ayahuasca, or Santo Daime, is apparently not being adopted in return by Umbanda centros, although some Umbanda followers are joining the Santo Diame churches. Indeed, there is now a church in São Paulo that calls itself a temple of Umbandaime (see www.umbandaime.com.br) and the cult even has its own active Facebook group.

Psychedelic Possession Outside of Umbandaime and Barquinha

In many ways both psychedelic plant practice and mediumship – be it through incorporation or through clairaudience – most likely have their roots in what modern researchers loosely call shamanism. Shamanism, strictly speaking, comes from the Tungusic word šaman and, according to Eliade (1972), it is pre-eminently a religious phenomenon of Siberia whereby the ecstatic state is considered the religious experience par excellence and so, in its simplest sense, shamanism is the mastery of techniques of ecstasy. The term shaman has since been applied by researchers from various fields to those in other cultures who perform similar functions. Shamanism also utilises religious, magical, spiritual, healing and trance aspects but is not essentially just any one of these things (Eliade, 1972), and alternatively has been described as comprising "a group of techniques by which practitioners deliberately alter or heighten their conscious awareness to enter the so-called 'spirit-world', accessing material that they use to help and to heal members of the social group that has acknowledged their shamanic status" (Krippner, 2000, p.98). Typical magico-religious techniques for altering consciousness include what may be called 'magical flight' or 'soul flight' and possession (i.e., incorporation), as well as auditory driving techniques (e.g., chanting, singing and drumming), fasting, drugs, austerities, isolation, sleep deprivation, seizures, etc. (Winkelman, 1990).

Thought of by many as the primary magico-religious activity of humans, predating all religions (e.g., Eliade, 1972; Winkelman,

1990), the origins of the practice of both mediumship and psychedelic plant usage are thought to stem from shamanism. However, not all shamanism utilises psychedelic plants, nor incorporation, so neither practice should define shamanism, indeed a survey by Peters and Price-Williams (1980) of 42 different shamanic-like groups across the globe found a variety of ways in which trance was utilised. Spirit possession, defined as "any altered state of consciousness (ASC) indigenously interpreted in terms of the influence of an alien spirit", was found to be practiced solely by 43% of the groups investigated, whereas 24% practiced only magical flight, defined as an ASC "interpreted as soul journey to heaven, other worlds, underground, or horizontally" (Peters & Price-Williams, 1980, p.408). A further 26% practiced both types of trance, whereas only 7% practiced neither, so it can be seen that spirit possession, or incorporation, is widely practiced across different cultures, indeed in the majority of those (69%) studied in this survey.

Unfortunately, no evaluation is made by Peters and Price-Williams of the relative number of different ethnic groups practicing shamanism that combine both incorporation and the use of plant psychedelics. However, some simple exploration of the 42 groups in the survey reveals that only 7% of the groups are particularly renowned for making use of psychoactive plants in their typical practices (14% if you include the use of tobacco), and of these only the tobacco-using Akawaio and the *Amanita muscaria* mushroom-using Chukchi engage in spirit possession, accounting for only 7% of those groups using spirit possession.

Lending some support to this supposed capacity of *A. muscaria*, the pioneering psychedelic mushroom researchers Wasson and Wasson (1957) note that while most 'mycophobic' (fungus fearing) nationals, such as the English, traditionally ascribe poisonous qualities to this mushroom, the French historically refereed to it as causing demonic possession. Nevertheless, it is clear from these two cases in Peters and Price-Williams' (1980) survey that the combination of both incorporation and use of psychedelics within shamanism is not common. Indeed, the identified incorporation may not even be typically mediumistic, as with the Akawaio whose incorporation occurs on an ongoing basis with multiple spirits, so that the shaman's body can house his own spirit and numerous others, which stay with him all the time (Butt, Wavell & Epton, 1966) in what Lewis (1978) describes as a constant state of latent possession.

There are also geographical trends in the distribution of indigenous groups utilising plant psychedelics or engaging in incorporation. In a survey of what she called 488 different indigenous 'societies' distributed around the globe, Bourguignon (1976) found that 52% engaged in what she termed possession trance, but that it was far more prevalent in sub-Saharan Africa (66%) than in the Americas, especially among North American indigenous groups (25%). Conversely, the traditional indigenous use of plant psychedelics is far more prevalent in the so-called New World (the Americas), than elsewhere, particularly Africa and Europe (see Schultes & Hofmann, 1992). For example, Luna (1986) indicates that at least 72 indigenous groups in the Western Amazon region alone make use of ayahuasca, and this is only one of many ethnobotanical psychedelics in the Americas.

Taking a similar approach to Peters and Price-Williams, by surveying 47 different magico-religious healing practitioner groups, Winkelman (1990) aimed to determine a taxonomy of the different spiritual technicians occurring in the sample. Extracting over 200 phenomenological variables, and reducing and clustering these using various analytic techniques, a number of distinct practitioner clusters emerged. Only those termed shamans or shaman-healers made use of psychedelic plants and magical flight, whereas those termed mediums did not make use of psychedelics and (all but one) engaged in 'possession trance' (incorporation). Different socioeconomic conditions prevailed for these different groups too, with shamans occurring only among nomadic and hunter-gatherer people, shaman-healers among agricultural subsistence people, and mediums typically occurring among more politically integrated and sedentary cultures. Additionally, whereas shamans and shaman-healers were typically selected by illness, involuntary visions, dreams or vision quests, the mediums were selected on the basis of their spontaneous possession experiences (Winkelman, 1990).

Applying Winkelman's (1990) grouping to the shamanic cultures selected in the Peters and Price-Williams (1980) survey would surely lead to a reclassification of many of the purely spirit possession shamanic groups to the status of mediums, rather than shamans. Perhaps most importantly, what we find from Winkelman's research is that the use of psychedelics and incorporation tend to occur separately in distinct magico-religious practitioner categories, as largely supported by the statistics above that emerged post hoc when exploring Peters and Price-Williams' survey data, and to some extent by global geographical trends too.

Of course, there are some examples of indigenous groups who utilise psychedelic plant shamanism in conjunction with incorporation, but these seem to be the exception rather than the rule. Reference to such pharmacologically aided incorporation is occasionally made in texts on possession (e.g., Bourguignon, 1976; Klass, 2003; Sargant, 1973), but typically without recourse to good evidence, authoritative references or even identification of the substances or peoples involved. It would take a thorough and massive research undertaking to make a comprehensive analysis, but based on a preliminary review of a good number of relevant texts it proved difficult to discover much reference to both practices among the same people. Two exceptions, besides those mentioned above, are the Yanomami of Venezuela (e.g., Jokic, 2008b) who utilise 'epena' or 'yopo' snuff (usually derived from *Anadenanthera peregrina* seeds), and incorporate various hekura spirits. The other is the Mitsogho people of Gabon who utilise both iboga (*Tabernanthe iboga*) and incorporation in their rituals

(Maas & Strubelt, 2003), although this is apparently reserved for female Ombwiri (or Ombudi) trance possession initiates only, who may use the iboga to assist in their vision of the healing genies (Goutarel, Gollnhofer, & Sillans, 1993).

Any Body for Anybody:
Shape Sharing or Shape Shifting?

Despite identifying their incorporation, Jokic (2008b) notes that the Yanomami retain both consciousness and control over their actions during hekura spirit incorporation, and relates it to the state of shamanic transformation, metamorphosis or shapeshifting into a spirit animal, which is prevalent among psychedelic plant shamanic groups. Indeed the experience of shapeshifting into an animal under the influence of psychedelic substances is relatively well known, particularly the transformation into large felines, as has been reported by more than one anthropologist experimenting with large doses of LSD (Masters & Houston, 1966; Rätsch, 2004), a psychologist experimenting with ayahuasca (Shanon, 2002) and a psychotherapist experimenting with harmaline (a typical chemical constituent of ayahuasca) (Naranjo, 1973), and which is also a known myth or experience of indigenous ayahuasca shamanism, such as among the Cashinahua (Lagrou, 2000), the Sharanahua (Siskind, 1973), and the Conibo-Shipibo (Harner, 1973a) of Brazil and Peru, and the Tukano of Colombia (Reichel-Dolmatoff, 1975). Indeed, Stone (2011) notes that shamanic transformation into a jaguar is still a widespread belief in the Amazon. However, it has been noted that, unlike mediumistic incorporation per se, shamanic incorporation – if that is what it is – of animals is not of a specific deceased animal but of the spirit of the "tiger-in-general" (Gauld, 1983, p.17).

In his assessment of psychedelics in European witchcraft, Harner (1973b) presents evidence that the solanaceous plants (such as mandrake, henbane, belladonna and datura), were supposedly favoured by witches for shapeshifting activities and were the source of reports of lycanthropy, which were in truth only lycanthropy experiences rather than actual objective shapeshifting phenomena. Additionally, Harner (1973b) notes from his anthropological fieldwork in Ecuador among the Shuar (inappropriately termed the Jivaro), that they use both solanaceous and non-solanaceous psychedelics in their shamanic practices, but they only use the solanaceous datura privately for vision quests because it is so strong as to prevent the shaman from performing their normal (e.g., under the influence of ayahuasca) ritual activities.

In regards to shapeshifting then, Yanomami incorporation by hekura spirits does not map directly to the mediumistic incorporation by personified Orixás or the spirits of slaves as found in Umbanda, but seems to be more of a general animal spirit transformation or incorporation. However, beside the jaguar spirit noted by Jocik (2008b) examples of some of the hundreds, or perhaps thousands (Chagnon, 1992) of hekura that exist include the moon spirit, the darkness spirit, the spirit of the whirlpool, and the Milky Way spirit (Lizot, 1991), so such incorporation is neither standard mediumship nor all shapeshifting it would seem. Furthermore, it's a moot point whether a line can be drawn between incorporation by the spirits of the deceased and the spirits of nature.

One further thing to consider is that, with the incorporation of hekura spirits, the shaman sings the spirits - which are between a few millimetres and a couple of inches in size - into their chests where they can be commanded, either to be sent to harm one's enemies, or to help cure sick kinsman (Chagnon, 1992). Perhaps the difference between this and typical shamanic control of spirits, as opposed to mediumistic incorporation, is that the Yanomami shaman keeps his numerous spirits under control in his chest, instead of externally as with other shamans – though the notions of things internal and external to one's body is somewhat arbitrary with the concept of magical flight, where the body remains where it is but one's consciousness 'travels'. In any case it is the issue of control and command that is crucial here, as Lewis (1978) notes, although they are also possessed by the spirits, the Tungus shamans say that they themselves possess the spirits in return.

With the possible exception of the Yanomami then, and perhaps the Chukchi and the Mitsogho (and neighbouring Fang), and the Akewaio – if you include tobacco as a psychedelic, which it can be with high enough doses of nicotine – there are few apparent shamanic groups that mix plant psychedelics with incorporation, with the spirits of deceased humans at least. The question remains why this is so. Psychedelic explorer and bard Terence McKenna offers an insight into this by suggesting that shamanism transcends mediumistic incorporation as it aims to command rather than merely communicate with spirits:

> The essential and defining element of shamanism is ecstasy. The shaman is a specialist in the sacred, able to abandon his body and undertake cosmic journeys "in the spirit" (in trance). "Possession" by spirits, although documented in a great many shamanisms, does not seem to have been a primary and essential element. Rather, it suggests a phenomenon of degeneration; for the supreme goal of the shaman is to abandon his body and rise to heaven or descend into hell – not to let himself be "possessed" by his assisting spirits, by demons or the souls of the dead; the shaman's ideal is to master these spirits, not to let himself be "occupied" by them (McKenna, 1992, p.58).

Indeed, Eliade (1972) earlier asserted this position by stating that the primary phenomenon of shamanism is magical flight to the heavens or the underworld, not incorporation and even though this latter phenomenon is universally distributed in its use by shamans it does not necessarily belong to shamanism – although others disagree (for a discussion see Lewis, 1978; Peters & Price-Williams, 1980). One instance of possible support for Eliade's position comes from Jocik's (2008a) research with Buriat shamans. Following years of suppression under Soviet anti-religious ideology, traditional Buriat shamanism all but died out but is now being revived, except that shamans now practice a kind of amnesic incorporated mediumship, and indicate that they have not yet developed the skills required to attain the amnesic-less trance magical flight state of their forebears. Jocik argues that the lack of shamanic flight and memory is a side effect of the lack of inherited initiation into shamanic practice and represents an impoverished form of shamanism. In any event, whether incorporation is separate to shamanism or not, psychedelic incorporation, in particular, seems very much the exception rather than rule given that the two practices are seldom elsewhere combined but, independently, are both globally widespread.

Psychedelic Possession Outside of Shamanism, and Inside Ordinary People

Outside of the anthropological literature there are a few isolated cases of psychedelic-induced incorporation or possession, of course, but 'few' is very much the operative term here. For example, the original discoverer/inventor of LSD, the chemist Albert Hofmann, describes the initial stages of his first accidental LSD trip thus:

> All my efforts of will seemed in vain; I could not stop the disintegration of the exterior world and the dissolution of my ego. A demon had invaded me and taken possession of my body, my senses, and my soul. A terrible fear that I had lost my mind grabbed me. I had entered another

world, a different dimension, a different time (Hagenbach
& Wertmüller, 2013, p.43).

However, as the first person ever to take LSD, nay, to be spiked
unwittingly with LSD, Hofmann was perhaps scratching around
and seized the notion of possession as a trope within which
to couch his experience, for certainly there was no wealth of
well-voyaged psychonautic log books or psychedelic language
available upon which to draw in 1943 when Hofmann's surprise
trip occurred. Undisputedly, though, he had no control of the
experience and, at times, of his body, and while he looked on as his
ego dissolved he felt he had become possessed, and yet the kind of
demonic possession to which Hofmann refers is rarely reported,
and indeed Hofmann's trip ended somewhat less fearfully and
he returned to normal. It is possible that Hofmann was speaking
metaphorically, or that he feared he had been possessed, for bad
trips had no cultural context at that time, and he reports none
of the behaviour of possession, only the lack of ordinary control,
though nothing else, demonic or otherwise, compelled him in
lieu of his own volition.

Nevertheless, in the course of my research into psychedelics and
ostensible paranormal phenomena (Luke 2012) I have received
two first-hand accounts of supposed spontaneous (involuntary)
incorporation with MDMA, both benign, and a further
second-hand account where a witness believed a person under
the influence of LSD was possessed, and which involved some
violence and self harming. However, these isolated cases come
from encounters with many hundreds of people who have taken
psychedelics, with many having done so thousands of times, so
the incidence of this phenomenon would seem very low. Indeed,
even for those who are experienced in incorporation the use of
psychedelics is not an incorporation trigger, at least in the case of
the Voodoo mambo that anthropologist Francis Huxley (1966)
gave LSD to, as she ended up having a conversation with one of

her loa rather than being incorporated by them. As such, though without much evidence, possession researcher Bourguignon, is of the opinion that, "possession trance is not induced by drugs, alcohol or other biological or biochemical factors" (Bourguignon, 1976, p.41).

While Huxley's mambo is an isolated case it points to something extraordinary about the use of psychedelics, and that is that encounters with supernatural entities are relatively common, or at least they may be relatively common with the right set, setting and substance. In some cases, however, only the substance in the right dosage is necessary. Giving the endogenous psychedelic compound N,N-dimethyltryptamine (DMT) to research volunteers, psychiatric researcher Strassman (2008) reported that over half of the high dose participants had at least one entity encounter experience, though possession was not reported. Survey data from non-clinical users and non-users of psychedelics also supports this (Luke & Kittenis, 2005) with 32% of those using psychedelics reporting entity encounter experiences occurring under the influence of psychedelics, compared to 2% of those under the influence of non-psychedelic psychoactive drugs (e.g., alcohol, prescription drugs). In the same survey, encounters with divine beings under the influence of psychedelics was reported by 28% of illicit drug users, compared to 0% of non psychedelic-users while under the influence of non-psychedelic psychoactive drugs.

And yet despite these relatively high rates of supernatural entity encounter experiences with the non-indigenous non-clinical use of psychedelics, reports of possession are scarce – in fact practically the only references to psychedelic drug possession in the literature relate to the legalities of having a psychedelic substance in one's possession. So, to add to Eliade's (1972), McKenna's (1992) and Winkelman's (1990) assessment that, in the encounter of spiritual entities, shamanism primarily entails magical flight and not trance possession – psychedelics themselves tend to lead those using them towards entity encounter experiences rather than entity incorporation experiences, and so traditionally psychedelics best serve a possession-less shamanic spirit encounter, as in magical flight, rather than a full blown possession experience. Among occultists this distinction reflects the difference between evocation and invocation, and the use of drugs is generally only advised for the former (e.g., Carroll, 1987), although some modern occult psychonauts, presumably previously practiced in spirit invocation, do occasionally attempt intentional incorporation (i.e., invocation) under the influence of psychedelics (e.g., Xeper, 2005), though such accounts are rare and come with a disclaimer.

So Why is Umbandaime on the Rise?

Buried within this question lies its opposite, why isn't traditional psychedelic shamanism particularly engaged in incorporation? Could it be that the Yanomami, Chuckchee, Akawaio, Fang and Mitsogho shamans are playing a dangerous game by utilising both powerful mind altering substances and somewhat risky spirit possession? Perhaps - though both paths separately have their own challenges and dangers, but relative risk assessments are not meaningful or possible within the scope of this essay. One thing to note is that the incorporation is conducted by specialist mediums in the case of the Fang and Mitsogho, and with the Yanomami and the Akawaio it often involves the control of multiple spirits simultaneously rather than the simple 'one host one spirit' typical of ritual incorporation practices, so such psychedelic possession is apparently not straightforward even when it is practiced.

So, too, Santo Daime and the derivative Umbandaime are practices likewise not typically shamanic, but instead somewhat divorced from the shamanic ayahuasca practice from which they were themselves derived. It is not clear which indigenous group was first encountered by Mestre Irineu in the jungles of Acre that then lead to his discovery of ayahuasca and the formation of the Santo Daime church – perhaps it was the Kashinawa – but typically among Amazonian tribes, non-shamans may drink ayahuasca within a ritual or healing context, but, traditionally, it is not taken in a regimented religious manner at is with Santo Daime.

Drawing upon Winkelman's (1990) taxonomy of magico-religious practitioners, it is apparent that the use of ayahuasca was adapted from hunter-gatherers, most likely, and slowly reinvented for the sedentary politically integrated people of Brazil. Initially these people were the poor, racially mixed working classes of the sparscly populated state of Acre, but increasingly these became predominantly more the white middle class professionals of the Brazilian mega-cities (Dawson, 2011, 2012). And as the religion's demographic shifted this way so too did its attitude towards mediumship, increasingly conforming to Winkelman's classification of mediumistic, not shamanic, practice. Nevertheless, besides the drinking of ayahuasca itself, Sainto Daime still retains some shamanic elements, such as soul flight, at least for those few daimistas who perceive it that way (Dawson, 2012).

As a consequence of this apparent 'religionising' of a shamanic practice, the somewhat distinct role of shaman has become diluted. For despite having a padrino in the Santo Daime *works* (ceremonies), there is no one person who takes the sole shaman role and many within the work adopt the role of shaman-healer, ultimately leading to the addition of 'trance possession' to the practice as the system evolves in the manner in which Winkelman (1990) envisages that shamanism changes with increased socioeconomic development. Indeed, with all of the established congregation having a role – a vast increase in the number of roles available within the Umbandaime setting relative to the traditional shamanic use of ayahuasca – the whole evolutionary chain of Winkelman's magico-religious practitioner taxonomy is represented in one sitting, with everything from shamanism to incorporation being performed.

A good example, from elsewhere, of this possible evolution of shamanism towards mediumship via modernisation comes from Harner's (1972) fieldwork with the Shuar. Harner is informed by Shuar shamans that the Canelos shamans upriver, who are more integrated with foreign missionaries than the Shuar, are said to possess the "white man's" tsensak (spirit) and can perform feats not possible for other shamans in the region, such as the ability to become possessed with the souls of the dead and to act as oral mediums. Similarly, some researchers (e.g., Dobkin de Rios & Rumrrill, 2008) consider that the influx of "Western" ayahausca tourists in Peru is likewise breaking down the traditional craft of psychedelic shamanism, so that ayahuasca shamanism is becoming commercialised in Peru as much as Santo Daime has partially religionised ayahuasca shamanism in Brazil and beyond. Indeed, evidence of this religionisation is apparent from some Amazonian Brazilian indigenous groups of Kashinawa and Apuriná who have recently been converting to Santo Daime (Labate, 2006).

Nevertheless, numerous researchers assert that Santo Daime practices remains shamanic (for a review see Labate, 2006), though many of these researchers were writing before the period in which Umbandaime began flourishing. Alternatively Cemin (1998) views shamanism as only involving 'ex-corporation' (i.e., magical flight) and so the incorporation practices of CELFURIS render this branch of Santo Daime not shamanic, whereas the original Alto Santo branch remains shamanic, though Labate (2006) suggests this is more an artefact of Cemin's theoretical model than an empirical fact. Ultimately, however, whether Santo Daime retains shamanic elements within its practices or not, it is de facto an organised religion with a large body of followers and includes many non-shamanic, mediumistic and religious elements – rather than being the magico-religious practice of an individual working alone for the benefit of their community.

Shamanic… or Individualistic, Pluralistic, Consumerist and Technologized?

In the view of Dawson (2011, 2012) the specific type of incorporation that is becoming most popular reveals a great deal about the cultural direction in which the religion is being pulled. Accordingly, Dawson, somewhat functionalistically, posits that the use of incorporation in Umbandaime takes three forms; private possession and expressive possession – both of which are types of individual possession – and interactive possession. Private possession is the incorporation of spirits in such a way as to not distract others during the work, and provides an opportunity for daimistas to exert their ability to remain disciplined, firm and focused in the face of the challenging circumstances of being under the influence of ayahuasca, and in praying with the less evolved spirit that they are hosting.

Expressive possession involves the incorporation of the classic Umbanda spirits, such as the coboclos and pretos velhos, and despite a traditional resistance to incorporation by Orixás these too are also now increasingly appearing in daimista trances (Dawson, 2012, 2012). This rather more theatrical kind of possession, according to Dawson (2011, p.155), "appears to have no obvious ritual function other than the dramatic externalisation of the incorporating spirit's presence."

Finally, interactive possession is utilised only by trained mediums who incorporate suffering spirits of the dead in order to help them, usually through the assistance of other mediums – who sometimes incorporate higher spirits to help them. This kind of possession is a work of charity, and allows mediums to distribute healing energy to others and to act in an oracular manner to advise others in the group. This latter type of possession is performed almost entirely by women.

In categorising the different types of Umbandaime possession Dawson notes that expressive possession is the type that is becoming most popular amongst the growing urban-professional daimistas. Available to all Umbandaimistas, not just trained mediums, the theatrical expressive possession meets the demands of the "self assertive and expressive preoccupations of the late-modern individual" (Dawson, 2011, p.160), and characterises the 'new era spectrum' urban professional, who typically embody an individualistic, pluralistic, consumerist and technologized worldview. In the view of Dawson, the Umbandization of Santo Daime, in effect, is a direct consequence of modernisation, urbanisation and gentrification, thereby somewhat indirectly supporting the mapping of Winkelman's (1990) evolution of magico-religious practitioners, as outlined earlier.

Synthesis and Analysis

Incorporation as a practice is no stranger to shamanism, and is fairly common in various indigenous groups across the globe, particularly in Africa. However, some researchers argue that magical flight, as opposed to incorporation, is the defining mode of spirit contact in shamanism, and according to Winkelman's data-driven classification of magico-religious practitioners, shamans and incorporating mediums belong in distinct categories and generally have different lifestyle modes and exist in different socio-economic strata. The use of psychedelic plants for spirit contact is also fairly widespread within global shamanism, and is especially prevalent in the Americas, where shamanic incorporation is less apparent.

Even though there remains a possibility that psychedelic possession is relatively common – but for some reason goes largely unreported – there is good reason to accept that the use of psychedelic plants combined with incorporation is uncommon within shamanism, particularly in public healing rituals. Furthermore, although supernatural entity encounters are fairly widespread among non-indigenous, non-clinical, psychedelic users there remains an apparent lack of reports of spontaneous possession, or even intentional incorporation with these substances, somewhat matching the trends in the shamanic use of psychedelics. It would seem, then, that psychedelics are better suited to magical flight than incorporation.

One theory put forward for the apparent preference for magical flight over incorporation among shamans is that shamanism is not about relinquishing control to the spirits but about controlling them so they can do one's bidding. Possible gender explanations probably deserve exploration in this regard too, as mediumistic incorporation is typically performed by woman (Kehoe & Giletti, 1981) whereas shamans, who engage in the ex-corporation of ecstatic magical flight, are typically men, as many tribes prevent or restrict female shamans, such as the Yanomami (Chagnon, 1992), whereas it appears that the reverse is true in far fewer tribes, such as the Mapuche of Chile. However, the apparent gender difference between mediumship and shamanism deserves further research, is outside the scope of this paper, and is debatable.

Given the apparent divergence of practice of psychedelic use and incorporation within shamanism, the report of a growing utilisation of these techniques in concert within the ayahuasca-using Santo Daime church warrants explanation. To this end a number of factors seem feasible, such as: the explicit eclectic nature of the CEFLURIS lineage and the latent mediumistic heritage of its leaders; the changing demographic of the followers and their changing needs towards a more expressive religious practice; the modernisation, urbanisation and gentrification of the religion; and, ultimately, the religionising of the shamanic practice of ayahuasca use along the dimension, delineated by Winkelman, that occurs as shamanism moves from nomadic and hunter-gatherer groups towards sedentary politically integrated 'mega-citizens.' Given that population growth and urbanisation are increasingly increasing, the question arises as to whether Umbandaime is the prototype supersyncretic suburban shamanism of the future? Only time will tell.

Acknowledgements

With thanks to Fabio Eduardo da Silva, Michael Winkelman, Michael Baillot, Natalie Godward, Sarah Poland, Danny Diskin, Anna Hope, Greg Taylor and Jack Hunter for help with research and the preparation of this manuscript.

References

Araújo, W. S. (2006). The Barquinha: Symbolic space of cosmology in the making. *Fieldwork in Religion, 2* (3), 350-362.

Bourguignon, E. (1976). *Possession*. San Francisco, CA: Chandler & Sharp.

Brown, D., DeG., (1994). *Umbanda: Religion and politics in urban Brazil*. New York: Columbia University Press.

Butt, A., Wavell, S., & Epton, N. (1966). *Trances*. London: George Allen & Unwin.

Carroll, P. J. (1987). *Liber null and psychonaut: An introduction to chaos magic*. York Beach, ME: Samuel Weiser.

Cemin, A. (1998). *Ordem, xamanismo e dádiva: o poder do Santo Daime*. Unpublished PhD thesis, Department of Anthropology, University of São Paulo.

Chagnon, N. A. (1992). *Case Studies in cultural anthropology: Yąnomamö*. Fort Worth, TX: Harcourt Brace Jovanovich.

Cohen, E. (2008). What is spirit possession? Defining, comparing and explaining two possession forms. *Ethnos, 73* (1), 101-126.

Dawson, A. (2010). Taking possession of Santo Daime: The growth of Umbanda within a Brazilian new religion. In B. Schmidt and L. Huskinson (Eds.), *Spirit possession and trance: new interdisciplinary perspectives* (pp.134-150). London: Continuum

Dawson, A. (2011). Spirit, self, society in the Brazilian new religion of Santo Daime. In A. Dawson (Ed.), *Summoning the spirits: Possession and invocation in contemporary religion* (pp.143-161). London: I. B. Taurus & Co.

Dawson, A. (2012). Spirit possession in a new religious context: The Umbandaization of Santo Daime. *Nova Religio: The Journal of Alternative and Emergent Religions, 15* (4), 60-84.

Dobkin de Rios, M., & Rumrrill, R. (2008). *A hallucinogenic tea, laced with controversy: Ayahuasca in the Amazon and the United States*. Westport, CT: Greenwood Press.

Eliade, M. (1972). *Shamanism: Archaic techniques of ecstasy*. Princeton, NJ: Princeton University Press. (Originally published in French in 1951).

Frenopoulo, C. (2006). Healing in the Barquinha religion. *Fieldwork in Religion, 2* (3), 363-392.

Gauld, A. (1983). *Mediumship and survival: A century of investigations.* London: Paladin.

Goulart, S. L. (2006). Religious matrices of the União do Vegetal. *Fieldwork in Religion, 2* (3), 286-318.

Goutarel, R., Gollnhofer, O., & Sillans, R. (1993). Pharmacodynamics and therapeutic applications of iboga and ibogaine. *Psychedelic Monographs & Essays, 6,* 70-111.

Groisman, A. (2013). *Ayahuasca religions, mediumship and religious agency: Health and the fluency of social relations.* Paper presented at Breaking Convention: The 2nd Multidisciplinary Conference on Psychedelic Consciousness, University of Greenwich, London, 12-14 July.

Hagenbach, D., & Wertmüller, L. (2013). *Mystic chemist: The life of Albert Hofmann and his discovery of LSD.* Santa Fe, NM: Synergetic Press.

Harner, M. (1972). *The Jivaro: People of the sacred waterfalls.* Berkeley, CA: University of California Press.

Harner, M. J. (1973a). Common themes in South American Indian yagé experiences. In M. J. Harner (Ed.), *Hallucinogens and shamanism* (pp.155-175). New York: Oxford University Press.

Harner, M. J. (1973b). The role of hallucinogenic plants in European witchcraft. In M. J. Harner (Ed.), *Hallucinogens and shamanism* (pp.125-150). New York: Oxford University Press.

Huxley, F. (1966). *The invisibles: Voodoo gods in Haiti.* New York: McGraw-Hill.

Jocik, Z. (2008a). The wrath of the forgotton Ongons: Shamanic sickness, spirit embodiment and fragmentary trancescape in contemporary Buriat shamanism. *Sibirica, 7* (1), 23-50.

Jokic, Z. (2008b). Yanomami shamanic initiation: The meaning of death and postmortem consciousness in transformation. *Anthropology of Consciousness, 19* (1), 33-59.

Kehoe, A. B., & Giletti, D. H. (1981). Women's preponderance in possession cults: The calcium deficiency hypothesis extended. *American Anthropologist New Series, 83* (3), 549-561

Klass, M. (2003). *Mind over mind: The anthropology and psychology of spirit possession.* Lanham, MD: Rowman & Littlefield.

Krippner, S. (2000). The epistemology and technologies of shamanic states of consciousness. *Journal of Consciousness Studies, 7* (11-12), 93-118.

Labate, B. C. (2006). Brazilian literature on ayahuasca religions. *Fieldwork in Religion, 2* (3), 200-234.

Lagrou, E. (2000). Two ayahuasca myths from the Cashinahua of northwestern Brazil. In L. E. Luna. and S. F. White (Eds.) *Ayahuasca reader. Encounters with the Amazon's sacred vine* (pp.31-35). Santa Fe, NM: Synergetic Press.

Lewis, I. M. (1978). *Ecstatic religion: An anthropological study of spirit possession and shamanism* (2nd ed.). Harmondsworth, Middlesex, UK: Penguin.

Lizot, J. (1991). *Tales of the Yanomami: Daily life in the Venezuelan forest.* Cambridge: Cambridge University Press. (trans. E. Simon).

Luke, D. (2010). Anthropology and parapsychology: Still hostile sisters in science? *Time & Mind: The Journal of Archaeology, Consciousness and Culture, 3* (3), 245-266.

Luke, D. (2011a). Discarnate entities and dimethyltryptamine (DMT): Psychopharmacology, phenomenology and ontology. *Journal of the Society for Psychical Research, 75*, 26-42.

Luke, D. (2011b). The light from the forest: The ritual use of ayahuasca in Brazil: Special issue of *Fieldwork in Religion 2* (3), by B.C. Labate & E. MacRae [book review]. *Time & Mind: The Journal of Archaeology, Consciousness & Culture 4*(3), 361-364.

Luke, D. (2012). Psychoactive substances and paranormal phenomena: A comprehensive review. *International Journal of Transpersonal Studies, 31*, 97-156.

Luke, D. P., & Kittenis, M. (2005). A preliminary survey of paranormal experiences with psychoactive drugs. *Journal of Parapsychology, 69* (2), 305-327.

Luna, L. E. (1986). *Vegetalismo: Shamanism among the Mestizo population of the Peruvian Amazon.* Stockholm: Almquist & Wiksell International.

McKenna, T. (1992). *Food of the gods: The search for the original tree of knowledge - A radical history of plants, drugs, and human evolution.* New York: Bantum.

Maas, U., & Strubelt, S. (2003). Music in the Iboga initiation ceremony in Gabon: Polyrhythms supporting a pharmacotherapy. *Music Therapy Today (online), 4* (3), available at http://musictherapyworld.net

Marques, A. A., Jnr. (2007). *The incorporation of Umbanda by Santo Daime.* Unpublished article extracted (trans. D. Thornton) from "Tambores pará a Rainha da Floresta: a inserção da Umbanda nenhuma Santo Daime" [Drums for the Queen of the Forest: the insertion of Umbanda in Santo Daime], unpublished masters thesis, Pontifícia Universidade Católica de São Paulo, Brazil.

Masters, R. E. L., & Houston, J. (1966). *The varieties of psychedelic experience.* London: Turnstone.

Naranjo, C. (1973). Psychological aspects of the yagé experience in an experimental setting. In M. J. (Ed.), *Hallucinogens and shamanism* (pp.176-190). New York: Oxford University Press.

Oesterreich, T. K. (1966). *Possession, demoniacal and other, among primitive races, in antiquity, the Middle Ages, and modern times.* New Hyde Park, NY: University Books. (Trans. D. Ibberson. Originally published in German, 1921).

Peters, L., & Price-Williams, D. (1980). Toward an experiential analysis of shamanism. *American Ethnologist, 7,* 397-418.

Polari de Alverga, A. (1999). *Forest of visions: Ayahuasca, Amazonian spirituality and the Santo Daime tradition.* Rochester, VT: Park Street Press.

Rätsch, C. (2004, June). *Psychedelics and enlightenment.* (Audio CDR). Paper presented at the international conference Exploring Consciousness: With What Intent?, Bath Spa University, UK.

Reichel-Dolmatoff, G. (1975). *The shaman and the jaguar: A study of narcotic drugs among the Indians of Colombia.* Philadelphia, PA: Temple University Press.

Sargant, W. (1973). *The mind possessed: A physiology of possession, mysticism and faith healing.* London: Heinemann.

Schultes, R. E., & Hofmann, A. (1992). *Plants of the gods: Their sacred, healing, and hallucinogenic powers.* Rochester, VT: Healing Arts Press.

Shanon, B. (2002). *The antipodes of the mind: Charting the phenomenology of the ayahuasca experience.* Oxford: Oxford University Press.

Siskind, J. (1973). Visions and cures among the Sharanahua. In M. J. Harner (Ed.), *Hallucinogens and shamanism* (pp.28-39). New York: Oxford University Press.

Stone, R. E. (2011). *The jaguar within: Shamanic trance in ancient Central and South American art.* Austin, TX: University of Texas Press.

Strassman, R. (2008). The varieties of the DMT experience. In R. Strassman, S. Wojtowicz, L.E. Luna and E. Frecska (Eds.), *Inner paths to outer space: Journeys to alien worlds through psychedelics and other spiritual technologies* (pp.51-80). Rochester, VT: Park Street Press.

Wasson, R. G., & Wasson, V. P. (1957). *Mushrooms, Russia, and history* (2 Vols.). New York, NY: Pantheon.

Winkelman, M. (1990). Shamans and other "magico-religious" healers: A cross-cultural study of their origins, nature and social transformations. *Ethos, 18* (3), 308-352.

Xeper (2005). DXM and entity contact. *Silver Star: A Journal of New Magick (online), 4,* 20.

Preto-Velho (old slave) spirits puff on their characteristic pipes before an Umbanda session in Rio de Janeiro. Photography by Diana Espírito Santo.

Anomalous Mental and Physical Phenomena of Brazilian Mediums: A Review of the Scientific Literature

Everton de Oliveira Maraldi
Wellington Zangari
Fatima Regina Machado
Stanley Krippner

Mediumship can be simply defined as the supposed ability of an individual to be in regular contact with the deceased, or to serve as an instrument of communication and action for the spirits or other supernatural beings. Brazilian mediumistic religions (that is, religions in which mediumship is a central component of doctrine and ritual practices) were developed along elaborate historical and cultural trajectories. One of the main roots of mediumistic practices in Brazil dates back to the time of slavery, when African slaves and their descendants tried to protect and preserve their traditions by fusing them with Catholic tradition, because Catholicism was hegemonic in Brazil, and African rituals were condemned by the Church. Of all mediumistic movements in Brazil, Candomblé (in its varied forms in different parts of the country) is the one that most closely resembles the original religions of Africa, retaining the original names and worship of many West African 'Orixás' – the so-called primordial forces of nature (Bastide, 1960). In its turn, in Umbanda - a typically Brazilian religion – syncretism is much more evident in the mixing of Indigenous, Christian and African heritages, also including elements of Kardecist Spiritism (Zangari, 2003). Umbanda ceremonies ('giras') are generally practiced in spiritual settings like temples, called 'terreiros.' Each 'terreiro' is led by an individual who acts as a spiritual advisor (called 'Pai de Santo'/'Mãe de Santo') for the Umbanda adepts. The 'giras' are commonly used for healing, giving advice, and providing magical spells, and are filled with percussive music and dancing. Umbanda rituals are thought to stimulate reported alterations in consciousness more often than Kardecist séances do, although Frigerio (1989) has suggested that 'giras' may cover different levels of possession trance.[1]

The dissemination of Kardecist Spiritism in Brazil is much more significant than in its own country of origin, France, the home of Allan Kardec (1804-1869), whose writings triggered the development of the movement (Lewgoy, 2008). Moreover, unlike the philosophical and scientific doctrine originally promoted by Kardec, the Brazilian version of Spiritism has come to acquire a far more religious character as a result of both its initial assimilation by the lower social classes, and of the established syncretism between popular Catholicism and mediumistic practices (Stoll, 2002). Another Brazilian religious movement that incorporated elements from Umbanda and Kardecism in its services is the Santo Daime, whose rituals are based on the use of a psychoactive tea, ayahuasca, as a sacrament (Krippner & Sulla, 2000; Luke, this volume).

The ethnic make-up of these religious groups has historically reflected a continuum, with Candomblé appealing mainly to Afro-Brazilians of poorer segments of society, Kardecism appealing to people with middle and upper social conditions, and Umbanda appealing to a more varied mixture of ethnicities primarily from the lower classes. However, descriptions of recent changes in demographic data related to ethnicity and social conditions in each religious group defy any rigid categorization along these lines and testify to the transformation of the 'religious landscape' in Brazil (Brown, 1994; Weiss & Nunes, 2005). Kardecism and Umbanda were recently influenced by the *new-age* movement, and many Umbanda temples are now integrating elements from different esoteric and shamanic-like traditions, thus also appealing to people of middle and upper social conditions (Isaia & Manoel, 2012; Magnani, 2005). Either way, along a spiritual continuum, these three groupings represent a commonality of belief in a spiritual world, the power and efficacy of spirit agents, and the ability of humans (more or less developed in each individual) to interact with and embody these presumed agents through different techniques – most of them apparently involving some form of dissociative state.[2]

It is often said that Brazil is a *warehouse* of anomalous/paranormal experiences (see, for example, Playfair, 2011). A recent survey (Machado, 2010) investigated the prevalence of psi[3] related anomalous experiences and found that 253 (82.7%) of the 306 participants (undergraduate students and/or workers, aged 18-66, in São Paulo City), reported having had at least one psi experience (from the general sample, 74.2% stated having experienced ESP and 55.9% stated having experienced PK). No significant difference as to religiosity was observed between psi 'experiencers' (EXPs) and 'non-experiencers' (NEXPs). Nevertheless, EXPs believed significantly more in reincarnation than NEXPs, while the latter considered the survival of the soul or spirit significantly more impossible. EXPs believed significantly more in the power of crystals, pendulums, and astrology than NEXPs, and also EXPs reported attending tarot card readers, fortunetellers and mediums or psychics significantly more than the NEXPs. Similar results were obtained in a previous survey (Zangari & Machado, 1996) in which 89.5% of the respondents (from a sample of 181 undergraduate students), reported at least one anomalous experience in a questionnaire that included not only ESP and PK experiences, but also out-of-body experiences, apparitions and memories of previous lives.

Curiously, however, there are only a few studies which have scientifically assessed the possible existence of paranormal abilities among Brazilian mediums or other research participants. In the first part of the Twentieth century, mediumistic practices (especially the therapeutic ones) were considered illegal in Brazil, and they were invariably described as either symptoms of psychopathology or evidence of charlatanism (Augras, 1983; Hess, 1991). It was only years later that sociologists such as Bastide (1960, 1971) and Herskvovits (1967) started to develop sociological and psychological interpretations for mediumistic experiences that would not stigmatize mediums as mental patients or charlatans. Contemporary clinical and psychosocial studies have also suggested that mediums are, as a group, at least as healthy as their cultural referent groups (Moreira-Almeida, Lotufo Neto, & Cardeña, 2008), and that mediumistic practices may indeed have therapeutic and social (supportive) functions (Leão & Lotufo Neto, 2007; Maraldi & Zangari, 2012; Moreira-Almeida & Koss-Chioino, 2009).

In spite of their importance in the development of a more fruitful and non-stigmatizing approach to the study of mediumship, the aforementioned investigations have not specifically addressed the occurrence of anomalous[4] mental or physical phenomena among mediums. Mediums and psychics are frequently said to possess privileged or private information about the living or the deceased that could not be obtained by normal means, sometimes concerning future events. Some mediums are apparently able to reproduce the same writing or painting style of famous deceased writers or painters, allegedly without previous knowledge of art and having had little access to formal education. Some mediums are also said to 'materialize' or move objects without physical contact. Both Kardecist and Umbanda mediums are trained to enter altered states of consciousness, and these alterations are considered by some to be psi-conducive (Stanford, 1978). Is it possible to regard some of the experiences reported during mediumistic sessions as evidences of extra-sensory or psychokinetic abilities? Are there more than just normal cognitive, psychosocial or psychodynamic processes taking place in these contexts? Although the academic literature in this respect is particularly scarce, there are some interesting contributions that point to mixed results, sometimes in favor of an anomalous or paranormal interpretation, and sometimes not.

The aim of this chapter is to summarize the most important Brazilian evidence in this regard, focusing on experimental and quasi-experimental investigations, as well as relatively controlled case studies that were published in scientific journals, masters theses and doctoral dissertations. We emphasize, however, that there is a great deal of anecdotal evidence in the Brazilian non-scientific literature concerning these phenomena that deserves careful evaluation. References to this literature will be made throughout the chapter where appropriate. Our intention, nonetheless, was to include a detailed description only of those investigations that were submitted to a peer-review process. There are also many other quantitative and qualitative studies concerned with the psychopathological and psychosocial aspects of these experiences that would be valuable for a broader discussion of the data presented here, though they will not be analyzed in this paper (see, for example, Maraldi, 2013; Maraldi, Machado & Zangari, 2010; Moreira-Almeida, Lotufo Neto & Cardeña, 2008; Maraldi & Zangari, 2012; Negro, Palladino-Negro & Louzá, 2002; Zangari, 2003).

Firstly, we will review a series of studies that were conducted with samples of Umbanda mediums in Brazil, assessing the possibility of ESP or PK phenomena among those subjects. Secondly, we will consider the results from case studies with mediums of different modalities (physical mediumship, mediumistic surgery, mediumistic painting and writing) assessing physiological, psychological, geomagnetic and observational variables possibly related to these phenomena. Finally, we will evaluate the limitations of the studies reviewed, their main contributions and implications, and then, based on the previous steps, we will propose some guidelines for future investigations.

Investigations of Psi Abilities of Mediums in Brazil

The first empirical study of psi with mediums in Brazil was carried out by Adelaide Petters Lessa in 1972. Her work had a double merit: (1) it was the first experimental research in Brazil that had mediums as participants; and (2) it was the first parapsychological research conducted in order to obtain a doctorate degree in the country, as far as we know. Lessa earned her doctorate in Psychology from the Institute of Psychology of the University of São Paulo with a dissertation on precognition (Lessa, 1975). During her doctorate course, she was an intern for a period at the former Foundation for Research on the Nature of Man (today Rhine Research Center), in Durham, NC, having Dr. J.B. Rhine as her advisor. There she got a REG (random event generator) for use in her study. The equipment was loaned to her by Dr. Helmut Schmidt. Besides the presentation of the literature review of studies on precognition to the academic Brazilian community, the aim of her dissertation was verifying experimentally the performance of different groups of people in a precognition task. The participants were asked to try to guess which one of two bulbs (one yellow and one blue) of Schmidt's equipment would be illuminated. The participant should press a button corresponding to his/her choice and only then would the machine randomly make one of the bulbs turn on. The participants were divided in three groups: (a) a group, which she called 'logical,' consisted of university students from courses like Theology, Psychology, Communication and Arts, Law, Sociology, Biology, Geography and History, among others, as well as elementary school and high school teachers and teachers from the University of São Paulo; (b) a group of blind people; (c) a group she called 'esoteric' that was formed by Buddhists, Hatha Yoga practitioners and Spiritists – 37 of them were Kardecist mediums. A total of 275 people participated in Lessa's experiment, being 126 men and 149 women, aged from 13 to 73 years old. They did 48,000 trials with 24,318 hits with a positive deviation of 318, critical ratio = 2.90 and p = 0.0018. In spite of the general score for hits being statistically significant, Lessa considered the results had been inflated by the significant results produced by the esoteric group, notably the scores obtained by the Spiritists (p = 0.000007) and by the Hatha Yoga practitioners (p = 0.0004). Lessa considered that the number of Spiritists (37) may have interfered with the results for the general performance of the groups. She lamented the fact that she could not analyze more thoroughly the performance of the mediums and expressed her desire that other researchers in future studies could examine them more closely (Lessa, 1975, p. 293).

Thirteen years after Lessa's doctoral dissertation presentation, three other studies with Umbandist mediums were conducted by Patric V. Giesler. Giesler presented his first study in two articles published in *Parapsychological Review* (Giesler, 1985a, 1985b). In the first article, the author presents ethnographic aspects of Umbanda, its historical aspects and the function of possession trance as a central element in that religion. Giesler describes Umbanda rituals, called 'sessões' or 'giras,' as:

> divination consultation and its closely associated healing rites, many [individuals] turn to Umbanda for assistance with spiritual development or defense against black magic, for counseling regarding personal and/or Family conflicts or for healing. (Giesler, 1985a, p. 6)

Giesler went through consultations with mediums incorporated by their guide spirits. He asked for information about friends of his friends or their relatives. The mediums incorporated by their spirit guides gave him some answers, but they were very generic and were within expectations. Besides that, they seemed to tergiversate by talking about the researcher's life, referring especially to future events. Giesler also decided to consult the incorporated spirits about the location of lost or stolen objects, since such information could be better suited to testing objectively the parapsychological hypothesis. The events seemed to fit the classical cases of spontaneous psi. In general, the cases that seemed least explainable by chance were not those when the spirit guides said precisely where the objects were, rather the cases apparently least explainable by chance were those in which the spirit guides performed or taught certain rituals that would supposedly help the consultant find the lost or stolen objects. Eventually, Giesler conducted three pilot studies in which these rituals were followed in the same way as they had been taught by the mediums, but with the application of additional controls. The task consisted of trying to choose the picture corresponding to an object hidden in a pool of four pictures (a target and three decoys). According to the researcher:

> For two of the trials, the client's sketch and comments were evaluated against photos of four different sites by four untrained, independent judges. The target photos were awarded the highest averaged ratings! On the other trial, judging was not done; I had served as client and tried just 'following' my impressions, as is done by the typical client, rather than sketching and writing comments. By this means I went directly to the packet of target-site pictures hidden by my co-experimenter! (Giesler, 1985a, p. 7)

Giesler's hypothesis is that the spirit guides do not use their psi directly, but they help the consultants (or clients) to use theirs, similar to what British researcher Kenneth Batcheldor (1968, 1979, 1982) proposed in order to explain PK-conducive situations. According to Batcheldor, the context (psychodynamics of the sessions) is more important than the presence of an agent or epicenter for the occurrence of PK events. The fundamental principle was the 'total belief' in PK (an incremented belief in the possibility of a PK occurrence) by means of suggestion or 'artifact induction' (artificial production of phenomena). It diminishes the participants' resistance in the sessions and improves their belief in PK so that it would propitiate the production of a PK event. The same idea could explain the use of ESP by Umbanda clients. By using the same model to analyze Umbanda consultations, Giesler concluded that psi experiences reported by the participants serve as a 'witness inhibition' because such experiences are interpreted among adepts of Umbanda as spiritual facts. Besides that, in Umbanda there is a neutralization of 'ownership resistance' inhibition because the client is led to believe that the spirits are in charge of psi and not them. Finally, Giesler proposes that by the 'total belief' the objective of sessions has the same characteristics as Batcheldor's sessions, although the content is different (advice for personal problems – in the case of Umbanda – and movement of objects by PK – in the case of Batcheldor's work).

In his second article, Giesler (1985b) explores how and why the same psychodynamics proposed by Batcheldor would be induced in Umbanda's consultations and would propitiate ESP occurrences. Firstly, he examines the Batcheldorian features in the training of mediums and in their relationship with the clients. Then, he examines the role of the mediums as facilitators for the clients' psi.

The training to become an Umbandist medium is gradual. The candidate often assists incorporated mediums and learns how the mediumistic activity is performed. The aspirants start to be trained in private sessions during which they experience alterations of consciousness induced by the sounds of drums and chanting. They are convinced that they are possessed or incorporated by spirits when they feel they automatically assume certain behaviors typical of incorporation. They are conscious of what is happening around them but they say they have only partial control of their muscle actions. Mediums' convictions about their own incorporation by spirits is important to induce the clients' confidence in mediums' powers in order to attenuate their ownership resistance. This, in turn, reinforces the widespread belief among Umbandists that mediums frequently have special abilities or gifts to perform their mediumistic function. Such gifts or special abilities would permit that mediums receive messages from the spiritual world, which means they have more spontaneous paranormal experiences. However, in Giesler's words:

> ...[probably only few] mediums may be gifted psychics and may indeed rely on their abilities in the consultation. Since I do not have documented evidence of this, I would suggest that at best gifted psychics are as rare in Brazil (whether associated with Umbanda or not) as in America or Europe. What Umbanda gives them is a socioculturally acceptable context in which to be psychic. (Giesler, 1985b, p. 13)

In short, the context would be as fundamental for triggering psi as the 'total belief' is in Batcheldor's system. It stimulates the use of the extrasensory perception of the client himself/herself, fed by an intense feedback of paranormal-type narratives. Giesler finishes defending the importance of considering anthropological aspects in the understanding of psi functioning and in the methodology of psi research.

In a second investigation, Giesler (1985c) conducted three experimental studies on psychokinesis (PK). Each experiment was done with adepts of one of the Afro-Brazilian religions (that Giesler qualifies as 'shamanic' in his article): Candomblé (described as the purest African religious group), Caboclo (described as a relatively syncretic group), and Umbanda (the most highly syncretic religion). From the analysis of the differences among these groups in terms of the claims and beliefs of their practitioners, Giesler raised three hypotheses: (1) the cult shamans[5] or mediums were using a mixture of PK and various forms of suggestion in their healing ceremonies; (2) their PK abilities had been developed through the cult initiatory and mediumistic training procedures; and (3) that Candomblé cultists would demonstrate more psi than members of the Caboclo cults, and the Caboclo cultists would demonstrate more psi than the Umbanda practitioners. In each study, 10 cultists and 10 non-cult controls were tested with a Schmidt random-event generator under two target conditions: with and without a trance-significant symbol (a figure of a cult possession deity). In the 'trance-significant symbol' situation participants could choose a figure of a cult possession deity statue that would be put on the light bulbs (on one of them or on both of them) that would light randomly in the equipment loaned by Helmut Schmidt.

In the situation 'without a trance-significant symbol' the bulbs had no statues on them. Each participant participated in both experimental situations, 20 trial in each condition, 40 trials per subject. In each situation, the participant had to choose one of the bulbs that would light seconds later (in the 'trance-significant symbol' situation, the statue was put on the bulb he/she had chosen in advance). The overall average of the studies combined (including the control group), was significant to PK ($z = 2.67$; $p = 0.008$, two-tailed). The same was found when only the cult practitioners were considered: the score deviated significantly from mean chance expectation ($z = 2.22$, $p = 0.022$, one-tailed).

Cult practitioners scored better with the deity target than without it. The hypothesis for the differences among the three religions was not supported: Candomblé cultists scored lowest of all, and Caboclo and Umbanda groups scored equally well.

Giesler presents two interpretations of the significant statistical findings that point to evidence of PK: (1) probably the religions Candomblé, Caboclo and Umbanda use PK in their healing processes; (2) the researcher could have been using his own PK to confirm his expectancies.

A year later, Giesler (1986) published a new article in which he presents a report of three ESP studies with the same religious groups of his previous study (Candomblé, Caboclo and Umbanda). In each study, 10 cultists (five shamans and five initiates) and five non-cult controls were tested on a free-response (remote viewing) and on a forced-choice (ritual-object targets) GESP (general extrasensory perception) task. In the 'ritual-object' task, the subject was asked to guess which of three ritual objects (placed before the subject) was being selected and concentrated on by an agent in another location for a 10-second period. This process was repeated 30 times per participant.

Giesler's hypothesis was that the cultists would perform better than the non-cultists. However, the findings showed that non-cultists performed better than the cultists in the remote viewing tasks in two of the three studies. Giesler's analysis of the findings considers some interesting psychosocial aspects. According to Giesler, the cultists had a refusal reaction to the experimental procedure, considering it something apart of their normal context:

> They then refused to participate, saying they were not schooled for this kind of thing, but their particular shaman leaders insisted that they go ahead with it since I had made all the arrangements. I could not counter the shamans. My argument that the subjects needed to be willing and relaxed was irrelevant to them. From their view, what the tasks were, how they were to be done, or their 'results' pertained to my different world of books, and thus didn't mean anything to them. What was meaningful to them was to 'help' me with my project by just doing a trial, and – never mind the

details! As a consequence of cultists having these sorts of attitudes going into the tests, there arose several problems administering them (Giesler, 1986, p. 145)

As in previous articles, Giesler presents important methodological recommendations to researchers interested in conducting studies in the contexts he investigated.

Another interesting study with Umbandist mediums was conducted by Radin, Machado, and Zangari (2000). It was a double-blind experiment with the aim of exploring the effects of healing intention directed towards a distant person (in the United States), but also included a retrocognitive element (the person that received the distant healing intention from the mediums participated in the experiment two months before). The distant person's respiration, heart rate, fingertip blood volume, and spontaneous electrodermal activity were continuously monitored during 20 randomly counterbalanced one minute 'treatment' and control sessions. The experiment studied the effects of female Umbandist mediums who directed their healing intentions from Sao Paulo, Brazil towards volunteers who were monitored two months earlier in Las Vegas, Nevada. The task of the mediums in São Paulo City was looking at a computer screen taken to a 'terreiro.' In each 20-minute trial, the computer chose continuously and randomly between the image of a patient in Las Vegas and a neutral image. A drawing of Omulu, (an Orixá) was displayed on the screen in the interval between each random choice of images. The experiment was conducted in a 'terreiro' in São Paulo. Each medium was 'responsible' for influencing one of the participant patients. Each medium had to look at the computer screen and only in the moments when the picture of the patient was displayed, she had to try to influence his/her body in some way. The patients were monitored two months before the mediums tried to influence them and the mediums were told that they should try to influence the patients in the past, when they had been monitored for a 20-minute period two months before.

The findings showed that despite a separation of 6,000 miles in space and two months in time, the mediums' healing intention was associated with an increase in fingertip blood volume (p = 0.013, two-tail) and an increase in electrodermal activity (p = 0.031, two-tail) in the distant volunteers.

Another experimental study with mediums was conducted by Zangari (2007). It was carried out as part of his post-doctoral research in the Social Psychology Graduate Program of the University of São Paulo. The aim of his study was to test claims of precognitive abilities in Umbanda mediums. The study tackled two aspects: the phenomenological and the ontological. The phenomenological aspect considered the experience from the medium's point of view, his/her cultural significations and psychosocial functions. The ontological perspective considered the claims from an objective point of view, aiming to verify the existence of anomalous processes (precognitive phenomena) and possible psychological variables involved in their production. The ontological analysis was carried out by means of the application of the experimental procedure of 'precognitive habituation' developed by Daryl J. Bem (2003) with 52 Umbandist mediums from three different 'terreiros' in São Paulo City.

In the experimental procedure of 'precognitive habituation,' three types of images are classified as neutral (images of nature), stimulating (erotic images) and aversive (disgusting images, such as decomposing bodies, for example). During the experiment, two images (always pairs of the same type of images) are randomly shown to the participant. The participant has to choose the image he/she prefers between the two images shown on the monitor screen. After his/her choice is registered, the computer, automatically and independently from the participant's choice, randomly chooses one of the images presented to the participant and presents it to him/her in a subliminally. Experimentally, it is expected that: (1) when a pair of aversive images is presented, the participant will tend to prefer (to choose) the image the computer will present subliminally in the future because such images will seem less aversive to the participant due to the familiarity deriving from the precognitive contact he/she will have with it; (2) when a pair of stimulating images is presented, the participant will tend to choose the image that the computer will not show in the future. According to Bem, these experimental expectations on directions of effect are based on the familiarity effect, that is, the more contact someone has with a stimulus, its attractive effect is lower. Such an effect permits predicting the direction of effect when the stimuli are of a different type (erotic, aversive or neutral). In the mentioned study, the 52 Umbandist mediums were invited to participate in the procedure. A computer with the program developed by Bem and translated into Portuguese by the researcher was taken to the 'terreiros' of which the mediums were members.

The group of mediums as a whole did not score significantly for the main item evaluated (NE% = mean of scores of hits related to aversive/negative stimuli and to erotic/positive stimuli, 50.3%, z = 0.20, p = 0.421). In short, Zangari's study failed to replicate Bem's findings (2003), and it did not find any correlation between the performance of the subjects and the cognitive variables assessed. Zangari discusses his findings in the light of Social Psychology, emphasizing the meaning and cultural importance of the mediums' paranormal beliefs in the context of the religious symbolism of Umbanda.

While the aforementioned studies considered the possibility that certain mediums present specific psi abilities such as ESP or PK, a pilot study conducted by Hirukawa *et al.* (2006) – see also Kokubo (2006) for a review – studied what parapsychologists call 'field consciousness,' that is the idea that mind-matter interactions may occur when a large number of people share similar emotions and thoughts, forming a unified state of consciousness. Unlike previous investigations, this 'fieldREG' study was less concerned with individual performances than with the group's shared interactions in a given context, and its possible implications for the occurrence of anomalous phenomena.

With this aim in mind, the authors measured the fluctuations of data from devices called REGs or RNGs (Random Events Generators or Random Number Generators) during different religious rituals and other group meetings in Paraná, Brazil: Candomblé and Umbanda healing rituals; Guarani ceremonies (rituals of an indigenous ritualistic group); a Santo Daime service; a session of turning tables at FIES (*Faculdades Integradas 'Espírita'*); a session promoted by a Spiritist group called 'Samaritano,' devoted to offering Spiritist passes and 'magnetic therapy'; a Yoga class at FIES; and a live concert of Djavan, a famous Brazilian composer and singer. The main hypotheses were: (1) anomalous deviations of data generated by the REG would be obtained during the group events; (2) the effect sizes of the deviations would decrease proportionally the further the distance between the events and the REGs; and (3) the effect sizes of the anomalous deviations would depend on the number of participants attending the events. In some cases, more than two REGs were used in order to check consistency of devices and the effect of distance (one REG was set in a distant place to serve as a control for distance).

Analysis of 26 datasets (13 events) showed significant anomalies of the output Z^2 that occurred frequently and was significant (6 of 26 datasets were significant, p = 0.0015, direct probability, one tail). Moreover, there were significant negative correlations between the Z values of the RNG and the measuring time, the event time, and its distance from the center of the city. The hypothesis related to the number of participants was not confirmed. It is important to note that these results in themselves do not legitimize or deny the efficiency of each ritual and ceremony, nor do they validate particular spiritual and religious beliefs.

Mediumistic Surgery
(Anomalous Healing Experiences)

From the first half of the Twentieth century to the present day, spiritual healing has been an important part of Brazil's cultural and religious heritage. Initially, it was seen as a marginal movement, mainly attractive to people of lower social conditions and/or patients disillusioned with orthodox medical treatments; but now it is seen as a form of complementary, alternative or integrative medicine, even having the approval and recommendation of certain physicians, especially those that share some of the spiritistic beliefs and values (Greenfield, 1987; Hess, 1991; Lewgoy, 2006). In fact, many of the spiritual treatments are promulgated and practiced by Brazilian spiritists, ranging from the most widespread ones such as passes and laying on of hands (fluidic or magnetic therapy), to what has been called 'mediumistic surgery,' a more controversial form of spiritual healing, as described by Moreira-Almeida, Almeida, Gollner, & Krippner (2009, p. 4):

> During this procedure, healers claim to be under the influence of spiritual entities and appear to use knives or other sharp instruments to make incisions in patient's bodies, extract tissues, scrape eyeballs or perform other unconventional and disconcerting maneuvers. Usually these "surgeries" are performed in circumstances that expose the patients to many sources of infection: surgeries are performed in open areas or in dirty rooms with hundreds of people closely observing. Many times, mediumistic surgeons do not wear gloves, do not wash their hands before or between surgeries in rapid turnovers, do not clean the skin to prepare for the surgery, and use dirty or rusted tools. Many observers claim that

these procedures are performed with no anesthestic or antiseptic procedures yet result in no pain or infection.

One of the most popularly attended mediumistic surgeons of Brazil was José Pedro de Freitas (1921-1971), known as 'Zé Arigó.' Arigó gained worldwide fame for treating hundreds of patients per day. Many of his patients came from different Brazilian regions, and also from other countries. Reports concerning Arigó's successful surgeries include extraordinary reports of cancers being cured, the blind seeing, the lame walking, and tumors being removed without blood or pain (Arigó was said to control the discharge of blood only by firmly ordering the patient to do so). But despite the supposed spectacular cures attributed to Arigó (and, more specifically, to his guide or 'spiritual mentor,' allegedly the spirit of a German physician called 'Dr. Fritz'), apparently no controlled investigation was designed to test or verify, in some way, his paranormal abilities, except for a few unsystematic attempts to accompany the surgeries more carefully (Fuller, 1974; Pires, 1966/2008).

Another well-known mediumistic surgeon, who is still alive and currently working in Abadiânia, a city located in Goiás (a Brazilian state in the center of the country), is João Teixeira de Faria, known as "João de Deus" (John of God) or "João de Abadiânia" (John from Abadiânia) (Bragdon, 2002; Cumming & Leffler, 2007). In a preliminary investigation (Moreira-Almeida, Almeida, Gollner, & Krippner, 2009) with the main purpose of examining the claims of individuals submitted to mediumistic surgery to its curative powers and authenticity, thirty surgeries were observed and videotaped, and tissues from 10 patients were removed and analyzed. Right after the procedure, while patients rested in a recovery room, an anamnesis and a physical examination of the surgical wounds were performed by two physicians on six of the ten patients (the other ones left the room before the researchers had arrived). Other aspects such as antisepsis and analgesia were also investigated, including a second physical examination of the patients three days later. Follow-up questionnaires were sent to patients whose tissues had been submitted to histocytopathological examination. Patients' medical problems ranged from chronic degenerative disorders to cancer, breast nodules, heartburn, chronic pain, visual disorders, goiter and vertigo. Surgeries occurred in a large, non-sterilized and open room, but the instruments used were clean. Incisions were made with sterilized scalpels or kitchen knives. On the other hand, João de Deus did not wear appropriate gloves nor did he wash his hands. There was no use of antiseptic or anesthetic procedures, and only one of the six patients interviewed reported pain.

For six months, follow-up information was obtained from four of the six patients. Two subjects reported significant improvement, and two reported no change in their medical conditions. No sign of infection was observed in the surgical wounds during the three days of observation. The histocytopathological analysis revealed that the tissues were indeed from the patients' bodies (and not from animals or other persons, as would be expected if the medium was cheating). The most interesting finding was that the extracted tissues did not show specificity to a given pathology, and incisions were superficial. The tissues analyzed in the study could not explain the reported cure, because there was no direct relation between them and the ailments.

Some of the limitations of the study included:

- The sample was small and the follow-up examination of surgical wounds did not cover all of the potential period for the emergence of infections of surgical sites, and infections may have developed after the end of the investigation.
- The medium's suggestive behaviour (sometimes theatrical, charismatic and enthusiastic); the overall religious atmosphere; the strong emotional involvement of patients, and many other psychophysiological and group factors

could account for the absence of pain and the subsequent reports of improvement (especially in cases of non-specific or possible psychosomatic diseases, for example chronic pain), although an explanation in terms of placebo effects would not be entirely feasible considering the long period (six months) during which the follow-up questionnaires were obtained.

- It should also be noted that there is no way of gauging if the reported recoveries were spontaneous or due to other factors unrelated to the visit to the medium. Also self-reports in medical improvement may not be accurate.
- Although there was no evidence of fraud, matching blood type and tissue histocompatibility would be a recommended procedure for future studies.

If the mediumistic surgeries of Arigó and João de Deus seem too aggressive or even dangerous for some, there are other forms of spiritual healing practices in Brazil that do not make use of scalpels or knives, but are said to involve only spiritual phenomena, and the beneficial or therapeutic effects of which are accessible through scientific observation. In a study by Leão and Lotufo Neto (2007) the impact of spiritual practices in the clinical and behavioral evolution of inpatients with mental disabilities was evaluated in a Brazilian health institution. The institution, Centro Espírita Nosso Lar Casas André Luiz (henceforth called CENCAL), provides multidisciplinary attendance to 650 interned patients with mental and multiple disabilities (according to ICD-10). As CENCAL follows the Spiritist philosophy, the patients also receive spiritual assistance in the form of prayers and 'mediumistic communications' (spiritists believe that the patients, even though not deceased, are able to temporarily leave their bodies to use the body of a medium, and then express their suffering verbally).

Two groups were compared, each one with 20 patients: the experimental group (submitted to spiritual practices) and the control group. In order to obtain clinical and behavioral data, the Interactive Observation Scale for Psychiatric Inpatients (IOSPI) was employed. Patients did not know whether they were selected for the experimental group or not, and the study staff did not know which patients were supposed to communicate. In fact, the experimental group of 20 patients was determined on the basis of identification criteria during mediumistic sessions (contacted inpatients were identified by their names, or when the alleged spiritual communications revealed personal, behavioral and clinical characteristics that helped to identify them). The experimental group was derived from 650 patients in the hospital. There were 58 alleged communications during the research, of which only 20 filled the appropriate identification criteria. According to the authors: 'the comparison of control group (n = 20) with the experimental group (n = 20) verified the difference of variation between the groups (p = 0.045)' (Leão & Lotufo Neto, 2007, p. 23). Further statistical analysis showed the occurrence of a positive correlation, demonstrating the 'possible benefits of such intervention" (p. 23).

Although the evidence suggests a possible beneficial effect arising from these spiritual practices, it does not demonstrate that inpatients had really left their bodies or communicated their suffering through the mediums, or that their mental health improvement was due exclusively to the spiritual practice. As the sampling criteria was based on the obtained 'mediumistic communications,' and given the fact that the researchers did not offer specific examples or more detailed illustrations of the analysis of the 58 'communications,' unknown factors other than spiritual phenomena could be involved in the results. In fact, it is not possible to evaluate, in face of the data presented, complex matters such as the mind-body problem or the spiritualistic hypothesis (as the authors intend to do in the discussion section), since the research was unable to adequately access the paranormal phenomena supposedly underlying the sessions, but only the patient's observed improvement. Thus, the authors' suggestion that 'this spiritual practice offers a communication opportunity for the individuals who are unable to communicate through conventional ways of communication' (p. 26) seems untenable based on the available data. In turn, even if we consider that something paranormal really was taking place during those séances, how could we differentiate (in terms of experimental control) between a spiritualistic interpretation and the super-psi hypothesis (telepathy, for example)? Furthermore, how could it be possible for a mentally retarded individual to communicate *normally* through a medium? These fundamental questions have to be answered before any speculation regarding the mind-body problem, and the explanations need to be empirically oriented, rather than based on prior metaphysical or religious definitions.

Physical Mediumship
(Anomalous Physical Phenomena)

Brazil has many interesting examples of physical mediumship, such as the famous medium Carmine Mirabelli (1889-1951), whose alleged phenomena ranged from materializations of spirits to levitation and movement of objects without contact (Dingwall, 1961; Goes, 1937). Although some believe that Mirabelli presented striking paranormal abilities (Palhano, 1994), it is known that he sometimes employed certain techniques of sleight of hand (Correio Paulistano, 1916). Other illustrative instances of physical mediumship can be found in the cases of Anna Prado (Faria, 1921; Magalhães, 2012), Francisco Peixoto Lins, known as 'Peixotinho' (Beloff & Playfair, 1993; Ranieri, 2003), and Otília Diogo (Rocha, 2011). In general, these studies have many significant problems, such as the lack of appropriate controls against fraud (for example, naïve acceptance of the conditions imposed by the medium or his/her 'spiritual guides'), overconfidence in the presumed suitability and honesty of the medium, and unsystematic, biased and/or enthusiastic observation (for example, descriptions of events are usually mingled with religious/spiritistic teachings and beliefs).

However, a more systematic and impartial investigation was conducted by Krippner, Winkler, Amiden, Crema, Kelson, Arora, & Weil (1996) concerning apparent anomalous physical phenomena in the presence of a Brazilian medium called Amyr Amiden, who lives in Brasília, the capital of Brazil. A man in his fifties at the time of this investigation, Amyr was a workers' union secretary (he is now retired and devotes himself to healing sick people). Of Syrian descent, Amyr was raised in the Muslim faith but claims to find inspiration in all religions. He told the researchers that 'green people' visited him when he was a child and that he was 'transported' to their planet. He also used to dream of them.

An interdisciplinary team of researchers observed Amyr for 20 sessions over eight days in order to record the unusual phenomena that frequently occurred in his presence, including the appearance of jewelry and polished stones from nowhere that seemed to fall nearby, and the stigmata-like appearance of a blood-like substance on Amyr's forehead, palms, and on the back of his hands. On one occasion Dr. Krippner asked him if he felt that the phenomena happened by the work of some spiritual force or entity that was operating in him, and the name 'Christ' was mentioned in the dialogue. Instantly, Amyr began to 'bleed' from his palms and the back of his hands, and a dark red mark also appeared on his forehead. These phenomena were rated in a 5-point scale by three members of the research team at each moment, and those that obtained a mean rating of 2.1 or higher were termed 'apparent anomalous phenomena.' (Even though the researchers realized that the ratings only utilized integers, they used 2.1 in anticipation of variance among the judges). The scores obtained were used for comparative purposes regarding the other variables of the study – a detailed description of each observation with means and individual ratings can be found in the original paper (Krippner *et al.*, 1995). Whenever there was a lull in the conversation, and when Amyr felt that an unusual event was about to occur, readings were taken of his pulse, blood pressure, and saliva pH. Reports of ostensible psychokinetic phenomena had been previously linked with solar flares and electrical storms, as measured by magnetometers (Persinger & Cameron, 1986). Thus, the researchers also registered geomagnetic fluctuations in the Brasilia area, where the sessions took place, to see if there would be any correlation between the geomagnetic readings and the observed anomalies. The setting for the research was the International Holistic University in Brasília.

Amyr refused any remuneration for his collaboration. The medium remarked that he rarely has volitional control over the phenomena, but that there are 'signs' that they will occur, for example, the taste of acid in his saliva, the loss of his color vision, the appearance of sweat on his hands. He drank a great deal of water during the sessions, believing that it serves as a 'conductor' for the unusual phenomena. On no occasion did Amyr enter the places where the sessions were held before the rest of the group, and one of the researchers (Stanley Krippncr) inspected those places each morning to be sure that it contained no unusual objects which could later be labeled 'materializations.' Krippner also had Amyr under close observation at all times, paying attention to any unusual or rapid body movements. No evidence of deception was found by the researchers.

Of the 97 unusual events observed and recorded by the research group, 91 received a mean rating above 2.1, thus being labeled as 'apparent anomalies' (the term 'apparent' was employed to indicate that their ratings did not necessarily involve an explanation of the phenomena in terms of paranormal processes). Each physiological and geomagnetic measurement was pared with the scores in the anomalous rating scale, immediately preceding the observed events and immediately after their occurrence. The diastolic blood pressure readings that followed the apparent anomalous events were significantly correlated with the anomaly ratings (r = 0.71, p = 0.01, 2-tailed, 1df), possibly suggesting that Amyr had an 'adrenaline rush' shortly after an anomalous occurrence. Blood pressure readings, as a whole, were somewhat elevated, and were indicative of hypertension. To measure geomagnetic activity, a magnetometer, on loan from the University of Brasilia, was placed in an outdoor shed where it was used to monitor local geomagnetic activity. The geomagnetic readings preceded by anomalous events were significantly correlated with the anomaly ratings (r = 0.64, p = 0.01, 2-tailed, 15df). The range of the magnetometer readings was largest on the day in which the ratio of events rated as 'apparently anomalous' was 1 anomaly every 13.71 minutes. When each ratio of possible anomalous events per day was paired with the National Geographic Data Center's index for the Southern Hemisphere for the five days on which formal sessions were held with Amyr, a high and significant correlation was found (r = 0.93, p = 0.02, df = 3). When the index for South America was used for these five days, the correlation was still elevated but non-significant (r = 0.83, p = 0.09, df = 3).[6]

Some of the limitations of this study included:

• Physiological recordings and the geomagnetic data were taken in such an irregular fashion that there may have been misleading artifacts in the derived statistics.
• Some of the means used for this study were based on the scores of two raters, and occasionally only one person was present during an allegedly anomalous event.
• The services of a magician skilled in sleight-of-hand were not employed, although this could be of great importance to clarify the source of the phenomena. The presence of a magician would be important because the gemstones that appeared are fairly common in Brazil; another reason is that Amiden worked in the export-import trade and

would have had access to most of the other artifacts that appeared. The red blood that appeared on Amyr's body could have been beet juice, but this hypothesis could not be checked. Krippner (2002) was also able to explain Amyr's stigmata by non -paranormal means. Video and audio recordings of each session were not obtained. Prior to and after each research session, the experimental setting should be photographed for later analysis.

- It would be useful if the 'materialized' objects could be dusted for fingerprints as soon as they appear.
- A follow-up session that could check if those phenomena were repeatable was not conducted.

Unfortunately, Amiden's physician observed the increase in Amiden's cardiovascular and gastrointestinal problems following the researchers' visit in 1994, and insisted that plans for future researches were cancelled, and it was done.

Artistic Mediumship
(Anomalous Creative Experiences)

Chico Xavier (1910-2002) was probably the most famous and important Spiritist medium of Brazil. He was considered very gifted in automatic or mediumistic writing ('psicografia' in Portuguese), and produced over 400 books on a wide range of subjects, having sold several millions of copies, with all copyright earnings donated to charity. Xavier's talent for writing poetry and reproducing (or 'intermediating') the style of great literary writers could not be easily attributed to mere pastiche (Rocha, 2001; 2008). Many Spiritists believe that he presented reliable evidence of anomalous phenomena. Among other things, Xavier claimed to receive automatic messages from the deceased in response to requests from their families. The available studies in this respect are scarce, but the evidence include very specific information provided about the deceased that was sometimes not accessible to the family, but was later confirmed to be true (Severino *et al.*, 1994), as well as similarities between a signature reproduced by the medium and the signature of the deceased person (Perandréa, 1991). Although such evidences have been recently questioned (Maraldi, 2013; Visoni, 2012), there is no doubt that Xavier's case is very intriguing and defiant, and certainly deserves further research. In this sense, it is astonishing and disappointing to discover the lack of references about him in different scientific databases. Even the parapsychological literature contains very little information about him (see, for example, Playfair, 2010).

There are also many other instances of artistic mediumship in Brazil that have not yet been subjected to scientific investigation, as is the case with the so-called painter mediums. Practiced by Brazilians, such as the famous Luiz Antonio Gasparetto (Gasparetto, 2009, 2013a, 2013b), mediumistic painting is characterized by the supposed ability of an individual to serve as an instrument for deceased artists continuing to produce their works of art. The justifications raised for such a return of illustrious or unknown painters are varied; they are often based on the belief that the artists are trying to demonstrate their survival after death, thus leaving a message of hope and consolation to those who still inhabit this world. Like automatic writing, mediumistic paintings try to reproduce the same style employed by the deceased painters, in order to allow their identity to be verified *post mortem*.

Is it possible to consider these mediumistic productions as representative of the deceased artists to whom they are attributed? This is a very difficult question to resolve in scientific terms, considering the subjectivity involved in the analysis of artwork. However, there are some qualitative criteria on which we can rely to construct such an analysis – the stylistic movement to which the deceased artist belonged, the technical and formal characteristics of his paintings, his signature, the themes or subjects of his productions, the conceptual proposal of the author regarding his works, and so on. We are convinced that it is not possible to reach a *definitive* conclusion – as in many other areas of science – but, considering the greater or lesser weight of the data, the mediumistic paintings could, perhaps, be admitted as *suggestive* evidence of paranormal processes, especially in cases in which the medium had little access to formal education, and very limited or no previous knowledge of art.

Following this path of analysis, Maraldi & Krippner (2013) conducted a series of investigations into the painting activities of Jaques Andrade. Born in 1945, Jaques Andrade, who has been active in the Brazilian Kardecist movement for many years, has dedicated most of his religious life to mediumistic painting at his center, the Leonardo da Vinci Salon of Mediumistic Art (Lima, 1998; Lins, 1999). Data about the medium were collected on several different occasions, from 1998 to 2013, and include psychophysiological measures (hand temperature, heart rate, bilateral skin conductance, muscle tension, and electrical brain activity), psychological measures (Dissociative Experiences Scale – DES, Tellegen Absorption Scale – TAS, Revised Transliminality Scale – RTS, and Childhood Trauma Questionnaire – CTQ), artistic material, observational data (photographs of paintings, observations of the medium in action), and some basic socio-demographic and biographical information. Andrade was very cooperative and accommodating in all of the various encounters with him, and no evidence of deception or bad intent could be found.

Andrade's social profile reveals a 67-year-old man, single, with low income, retired, who attended only elementary school. Besides his poor social conditions, Andrade was a victim of significant social discrimination and trauma due to his auditory impairment. Whereas his mediumship 'developed' only in adulthood, in a Kardecist temple, Andrade believes that he had out-of-body experiences when he was a child. Andrade's aspiration for drawing dates back to early childhood (it was first noticed by his mother), a long time before he initiated his work as a medium. Andrade claims not to have taken any sort of painting course prior to the manifestation of his mediumistic experiences. However, a Brazilian Spiritistic blog (Intermédium, 2012) has recently published an interview with Andrade in which it was mentioned that in his childhood he took a few classes in a School of Fine Arts. Those classes were said to be a preparation for his future work as a medium.

Andrade's scores for the DES fit him in the highly dissociative category (>30 cut-off score). Depersonalization/derealization experiences obtained the highest mean in comparison to the other subscales (amnesia and absorption) of the Dissociative Experiences Scale (the subscales were measured according to Carlson *et al.*, 1991).

His scores obtained in the Tellegen Absorption Scale and the Revised Transliminality Scale were also elevated. Some interesting items scored as 'true' by Andrade included: sense of presence, fantasy proneness, and absorption in nature and in art. Although he said to one of us that he remains in a conscious/waking state during the mediumistic activity, Andrade is usually not able to fully control his movements or ideas while he is painting.

Concerning the evalutation of his painting technique and style the researchers considered basically: (a) the general aspects of the painting technique employed by Andrade; (b) the main features and style of his pictorial productions; and (c) the behaviors displayed by the medium during the activity. The analysis of the painting technique and style served as a qualitative measure of creativity, and also as an impressionistic form of analysis concerning possible paranormal processes. Following this script, Krippner and Maraldi came to a few conclusions about the mediumistic painting activity performed by Andrade. A detailed description of the results can be found in Maraldi & Krippner (2013), but we can summarize the main findings as follows:

1. *The technique used to elaborate the paintings is, except in a few cases, the same for all 'spiritual' painters:* in general, the medium starts by spreading small amounts of paint on canvas or paper, at specific points, and then he moves his hands, with greater or lesser intensity and speed, mixing paints and outlining the contours that result in the final image. Although these performances are apparently improvised, during sessions open to the public, without the possibility of correction or improvement, they provide little evidence on the painters to whom they are attributed. (More recently, we have been informed that Andrade is currently employing the paint-brush instead of his hands, apparently because of skin irritation).

2. *Painting themes are always similar, and are not consistent with the themes usually explored by the artists to whom they are attributed to. These paintings also manifest an evident lack of depth and symbolic richness that was the hallmark of the works of many artists who allegedly signed such mediumistic productions.*

3. *Regardless of greater or lesser authenticity of signatures, one cannot be sure whether their reproduction was previously practiced by the medium, or whether there were intervenient factors of an unconscious nature.* At a first glance, the obtained signatures seem to be different from the originals. However, this kind of analysis would preferably require the evaluation of an expert, which the authors are not. Other methodological and conceptual problems should be considered, such as latent capabilities (Braude, 2000, 2002, 2003).

4. *The production time of each painting is extremely rapid, which tends to impress the observer by the medium's dexterity. However, this speed usually contrasts with the time that many artists took to finish some of their most important artworks.*

5. *While doing the paintings, Andrade does not provide other evidence of something effectively paranormal in his behavior. His actions are always the same and invariably ritualistic.* If during his performances the medium behaved in a way that expressed traits or behavioral characteristics of the deceased painters, it could be considered suggestive evidence of something paranormal (especially if such behaviors were known only by family members or people very close to the artist, rather than attitudes widely known or expected by the general public). Andrade typically adopts a ritualistic posture while he is painting. His movements, his gestures always suggest much more a creative urge than unique aspects of the personality of the deceased painters.

To the extent that Andrade attended only elementary school and lived his life under poor socioeconomic conditions, and was victimized by discrimination and trauma, his painting abilities and his precocious interest in art are indeed of a *creative* nature, in the sense of a creative coping strategy in opposition to suffering and low self-esteem. The dissociative and semi-automatic character of his work indicates that these talents and potentials were not entirely integrated into his ordinary stream of consciousness and self-concept, thus requiring a specific set of circumstances to evolve and develop, including a culturally validated form of expression (i.e., mediumship). However, Maraldi & Krippner (2013) do not reject entirely the possibility that paranormal processes are effectively underlying some of these experiences. But for now, they believe that there is still no sufficient evidence, particularly in the case of Andrade, to reach this conclusion.

In general, Andrade's psychophysiological data (see also Hageman *et al.*, 2010, and Hageman, Wickramasekera, & Krippner, 2011 for a detailed description of the results) revealed several incongruent findings: 1) there was a general reduction in skin conductance level across conditions. Since skin conductance is a measure of sympathetic activation or withdrawal, it is unusual to find it associated with constriction of the blood vessels and increased muscle tension during the imagination task, typically considered a relaxing condition – instead, both sets of data suggest increased sympathetic activation in these response systems. 2) The increase in muscle tension during the eyes-closed imagination condition and the associated increase in the percentage of alpha brain wave activity during imagination are also paradoxical – these two measures (muscle tension and alpha brain waves) are typically negatively associated, not positively associated. The former indicates tension, and the latter indicates relaxation.

In retrospect, there were specific incongruences or "disconnects" in the peripheral (or outer) and central (or inner) physiological response systems. These included deviations during Andrade's imagination condition that were discrepant from what is typically seen during an eyes-closed imagination condition. People with incongruences between Central Nervous System and Autonomous Nervous System can be described as periodically inhabiting two worlds, one in which they are rational, practical, and another in which their fantasy and emotional reactivity expand and deepen. These incongruences between verbal reports and physiological responses are essential to the discussion concerning dissociative processes, and deserve further investigation.

The neurophysiological research concerning mediumistic writing seems to suggest that dissociation could be trained until a point in which the individual becomes able to conduct certain tasks that usually require a great deal of concentration and effort (such as high quality writing), in a much more automatic way. In an investigation conducted by Peres *et al.* (2012) with beginners and advanced Spiritist mediums, all of them dedicated to the practice of automatic writing, the most experienced mediums evidenced a low activation of brain areas responsible for attention and planning while doing automatic writing, a result that not only justified their claims of dissociative state, but also seemed contradictory to the best textual productivity of these individuals during the task under dissociation compared to the same task when they were out of a dissociative state (the control condition). In other words, these individuals produced better writings in trance than in the control condition (according to an analysis of the quality of the writings by a specialist who was blind to the medium's degree of development and to which texts had been produced in the experimental condition). In less experienced mediums an inverse phenomenon was observed: the areas related to planning were more activated during the experimental condition, suggesting that they (consciously) were struggling to produce better writings when compared to the experienced mediums. Although experienced mediums reported being in a deeper trance, having little or no awareness of the content produced, the less expert mediums were in a less pronounced trance state, and usually reported they wrote phrases that had being dictated to them in their minds. For the mediums, these experiences were consistent with the idea that they were under the influence of spiritual entities.

In retrospect, these results seem to demonstrate that: 1) there is a measurable difference between beginners and experienced mediums, which suggests that dissociation may perhaps be trained or developed in some way, and 2) automatic productions cannot be entirely explained in terms of simulation or fraud. Although participants reported several dissociative and psychotic-like experiences, and also presented a pattern of cerebral activation that was similar to that of schizophrenic patients, they did not suffer from schizophrenia or other mental illness and were well-adjusted.

Limitations of the Studies
and Perspectives for Future Investigations

The studies reviewed are very mixed in terms of their methodological strength. Some of these investigations are well conducted and well controlled, but there are many pilot and exploratory investigations that would need further adjustments to keep up with a more rigorous and reliable methodology. It is not much to remember that extraordinary claims require extraordinary (or at least very good and well controlled) evidence. Some of the major difficulties that need to be overcome, especially concerning case studies are: 1) lack of high quality experimental controls; 2) inadequate instrumentation; and 3) inconsistent measurement of physiological variables. Once again, we have to say that these difficulties are not equally applicable to all aforementioned investigations, and to all aspects of the studies reviewed, but nonetheless they represent important challenges to be surmounted.

As many other studies in the area of psi research and anomalistic psychology, the outlined investigations offer intriguing and exciting perspectives for the future, but more studies are needed to establish the previous findings. As the reader could see, some of the available evidences are not positive for the existence of anomalous processes (for example, mediumistic painting). In other cases, the results are indicative of a possible mental or physical anomaly, although its origins and its nature are still unknown or merely hypothesized (as with studies with Umbandist mediums). Finally, there are other cases in which the evidence is suggestive, but is not easily interpretable, given certain methodological flaws, or a plethora of variables and explanations potentially involved (for example, anomalous healing experiences, physical mediumship). Good experimental research and well controlled case studies would demand adequate investment and funding.

Even though Brazilian researchers have initially faced the same funding issues that are common to foreign investigators in the area of parapsychology, it is now possible to foresee a better future in this respect, particularly considering that many undergraduate and graduate students in the University of São Paulo and in the Federal University of Juiz de Fora who are conducting research in the fields of Anomalistic Psychology and Spirituality and Mental health with financial aid from the universities, as well as from important scientific organizations in Brazil such as the FAPESP - Fundação de Amparo à pesquisa de São Paulo (Foundation for Research Support of São Paulo), the CNPq - Conselho Nacional de Desenvolvimento Científico e Tecnológico (National Council for Scientific and Technological Development) and the CAPES - Coordenação de Aperfeiçoamento de Pessoal de Nível Superior (Coordination of Improvement of Higher Education Personnel).

The studies outlined here may have implications for a more comprehensive understanding of the cultural aspects underlying anomalous experiences. In this sense, Giesler (1984) has called for a 'multi-method' approach that would: 1) focus more attention on the psi-relevant contexts in other cultures; 2) combine ethnographic and experimental methodologies so that the strengths of one offset the weaknesses of the other; 3) incorporate a 'psi-in-process' method into the field research design. 'With this approach, the researcher may study ostensible psi processes and their relationship with other variables in the contexts of cult rituals and practices such as divination, trance mediumship, and healing' (p. 315). This would allow for control of the conditions of a task, and the results could be evaluated with a minimum of interference of disturbance of the psi-related activity.

In a way very similar to Giesler's perspective, Roxburgh and Roe (2011) also argued for a mixed methods approach to combine qualitative and quantitative data in order to give a thorough account of the phenomenon of mediumship. Another interesting proposal, in complementariness to a psi-in-process approach, is the laboratory use of culture-specific techniques to promote alterations in consciousness. As an example, Rock, Storm, and Friedman (2012) have incorporated elements from shamanic-like journeying in a novel experimental protocol for the study of psi phenomena. Perhaps Umbanda rituals and other Brazilian religious practices could give us some insights on how we could elaborate innovative experimental protocols.

Finally, in keeping with a more culturally sensitive methodology, Maraldi & Zangari (2013) have defended the importance of investigating the social circumstances, religious beliefs, personality, economical condition, childhood, familiar and conjugal life of mediums and other research participants in these studies in order to obtain a better understanding of how their behaviour and their subjective experiences can influence, or even determine (or be determined by), their mediumistic manifestations. Carvalho (1994) and Carvalho and Amaral (1994) also emphasized the psychological, social and cultural factors involved in psi phenomena and mediumship, and developed interesting psychodynamic hypotheses that are still in need of further evaluation.

Final Considerations

The aim of this chapter was to review the scientific literature concerning anomalous mental and physical phenomena of Brazilian mediums from different religious groups. The review included experimental investigations and case studies with controls for certain variables. The results are sometimes suggestive of anomalous processes, and encourage future studies with a more rigorous methodology.

Reports of anomalous experiences seem to be very common in Brazil (see Machado, 2010; Playfair, 2011; Zangari & Machado, 1997). As a matter of fact, there are many other interesting scientific contributions that were not reviewed here, but that concern phenomena such as claimed past-life memories (Andrade, 1986), poltergeist cases (Machado, 2008), and alien abduction experiences (Martins & Zangari, 2012). We hope that the present paper will inspire additional investigations on mediumship, psi and related topics in the area of anomalistic psychology in Brazil.

Acknowledgements

The first author expresses his gratitude to FAPESP – Foundation for Research Support of São Paulo for funding his doctoral research. The last author would like to thank Saybrook University Chair for the Study of Consciousness. We also would like to thank Patric Giesler for all the material he kindly provided us for this chapter.

Notes

1. For our purposes here, we can define possession trance as "a temporary alteration of consciousness, identity, and / or behavior, attributed to possession by a spiritual force or another person, and evidenced by at least two of the following: 1) Single or episodic replacement of the usual sense of identity by that attributed to the possessing force; 2) Stereotyped and culturally determined behaviors or movements attributed to the possessing identity; 3) Full or partial amnesia for the event." (Cardeña, van Dujil, Weiner & Terhune, 2009, p. 173).
2. Dissociative experiences can be defined as "reported experiences and observed behaviours that seem to exist apart from, or appear to have been disconnected from, the mainstream, or flow, of one's conscious awareness, behavioural repertoire, and/or self-identity. Dissociation is a noun used to describe a person's involvement in these reported dissociative experiences or observed dissociative behaviours." (Krippner, 1997, p. 8)
3. Psi-related experiences or spontaneous psi "include reports of apparent telepathy (direct mind-to-mind communication), clairvoyance (anomalous knowledge of distant events), precognition (knowledge of the future) ..., or psychokinesis [PK] (mind over matter)" (Targ, Schlitz, & Irwin, 2000, p. 219). The term ESP (or extra-sensory perception) is "taken to signify a spontaneous [psi] experience which, in the opinion of the experient, entailed an anomalous transfer of information" (p. 223).

4. Cardeña, Lynn, and Krippner (2000, p. 4) define an anomalous experience "as an uncommon experience (e.g., synesthesia) or one that, although it may be experienced by a substantial amount of the population (e.g., experiences interpreted as telepathic), is believed to deviate from ordinary experience or from the usually accepted explanations of reality".'

5. Giesler (1985c) explains in the footnote 5, p.335: "I use the term *shaman*... to distinguish the sacerdotes of the highest level of mediumistic expertise from the aspirants of the first developmental levels (*initiates*), and I refer to those in between as *mediums* or *advanced mediums*. But of course, all initiates and shamans are mediums; the terms refer to the level of mediumistic expertise".

6. A non-parametric statistic was used since it was deemed unlikely that the data, especially the ratings on the Anomalies Rating Scale, were normally distributed. Presentation of the results of this data analysis use r to indicate the correlation, p to indicate the probability level (two-tailed for all correlations), and df to indicate degrees of freedom for each analysis.

References

Andrade, H.G. (1986). *Reencarnação no Brasil: Oito casos que sugerem renascimento.* São Paulo, Brazil: O Clarim.

Augras, M. (1983). *O Duplo e a Metamorfose.* Petrópolis, Brazil: Vozes.

Bastide, R. (1960). *Les religions Africaines au Brésil.* Paris, France: Presses Universitaires de France.

Bastide, R. (1971). *African civilizations in the New World.* New York, NY: Harper and Row.

Beloff, J., & Playfair, G.L. (1993). Peixotinho: A latter-day Brazilian Kluski? *Journal of the Society for Psychical Research, 59* (832), 204-206.

Batcheldor, K. J. (1979). PK in sitter groups. *Psychoenergetic Systems, 3,* 77-93.

Batcheldor, K.J. (1968). Macro-PK in group sittings: Theoretical and practical aspects. Unpublished manuscript, Exeter, England (amended 1981).

Batcheldor, K.J. (1982). Contributions to the theory of PK induction from sitter-group work. In The Batcheldor approach. Symposium presented at the meeting of the Parapsychological Association, Cambridge, England.

Bem, D.J. (2003). Precognitive habituation: Replicable evidence for a process of anomalous cognition. In S. Wilson (Chair), *Proceedings of Presented Papers of the Forty-sixth Annual Convention of the Parapsychological Association, 2003* (pp. 6-20), Vancouver, Canada.

Bragdon, E. (2002). *Spiritual alliances: Discovering the roots of health at the Casa de Dom Inácio.* Woodstock, VT: Lightening Up Press.

Braude, S. (2000). Dissociation and latent abilities: The strange case of Patience Worth. *Journal of Trauma and Dissociation, 1* (2), 13-48.

Braude, S. (2002). The creativity of dissociation. *Journal of Trauma and Dissociation, 3* (3), 6-25.

Braude, S. (2003). *Immortal remains: The evidence for life after death*. New York, NY: Rowman and Littlefield.

Brown, D. (1994). *Umbanda: Religion and politics in urban Brazil*. New York, NY: Columbia University Press.

Cardeña, E. Van Duijil, M., Weiner, L.A. & Terhune, D.B. (2009). Possession/trance phenomena. In P.F. Dell & J.A. O'Neil (Eds.), *Dissociation and the dissociative disorders: DSM-V and beyond* (pp. 171-184). New York: Routledge.

Cardeña, E., Lynn, S. J., & Krippner, S. (2000). Introduction. In E. Cardeña, S.J. Lynn, & S. Krippner (Ed.), *Varieties of anomalous experience: Examining the scientific evidence*. Washington, DC: American Psychological Association.

Carlson, E. B., Putnam, F. W., Ross, C.A., Anderson, G., Clark, P., Torem, M., Coons, P., Bowman, E., Chu, J. A., Dill, D., Lowenstein, R. J., & Braun, B. G. (1991). Factor analysis of the Dissociative Experiences Scale: A multicenter study. *American Journal of Psychiatry, 150*, 1030-1036.

Carvalho, A.P. (1994). Some socio-psychological aspects of psi. *Journal of the Society for Psychical Research, 59* (834), 364-366.

Carvalho, A.P., & Amaral, C.E.G. (1994). Mediumship, psychodynamics and ESP: The case of Cristina. *Journal of the Society for Psychical Research, 60* (836), 29-37.

Correio Paulistano. (1916). *No mundo das maravilhas: É mister que se faça luz na noite do mistério. O sr. Carlos Mirabelli, a nosso ver, não passa de um hábil prestidigitador.* (Várias edições de maio a 13 de Julho de 1916).

Cumming, H., & Leffler, K. (2007). *John of God: The Brazilian healer who touched the lives of millions*. New York, NY: Atria Books / Beyond Words Publishing.

Dingwall, E.J. (1961). Book review: Das Medium Carlos Mirabelli: eine Kritische Untersuchung. *Journal of the Society for Psychical Research, 41* (708), 80-82.

Faria, N. (1921). *O trabalho dos mortos (Livro do João)*. Rio de Janeiro: Federação Espírita Brasileira.

Frigerio, A. (1989). Level of possession awareness in Afro-Brazilian religions. *Association for the Anthropological Study of Consciousness Quarterly, 5* (2-3).

Fuller, J. G. (1974). *Arigó: surgeon of the rusty knife*. New York, NY: Thomas Y. Crowell.

Gasparetto, L.A. (2009). *Artiste Peintre Médium: Luiz Gasparetto*. Retrieved from http://www.youtube.com/watch?v=rtVKjbaSQfo

Gasparetto, L. A. (2013a). *Luiz Gasparetto – Pintura Mediúnica*. Retrieved from http://www.youtube.com/watch?v=KIQOKY3u7FQ

Gasparetto, L.A. (2013b). *Luiz Gasparetto–Pintura Mediúnica (Psicopictografia) 2/2 – 12/04/1981*. Retrieved from http://www.youtube.com/watch?v=QWzBfi3iRDE

Giesler, P. (1984). Parapsychological anthropology: I. Multi-method approaches to the study of *psi* in the field setting. *Journal of the American Society for Psychical Research, 78*, 289.

Giesler, P.V. (1985a). Batcheldorian psychodynamics in the Umbanda ritual trance consultation: Part I. *Parapsychology Review, 15* (6), 5-9.

Giesler, P.V. (1985b). Batcheldorian psychodynamics in the Umbanda ritual trance consultation: II. *Parapsychology Review, 16* (1), 11-14.

Giesler, P.V. (1985c). Differential micro-PK effects among Afro-Brazilian cultists: Three studies using trance-significant symbols as targets. *Journal of Parapsychology, 49* (4), 329-366.

Giesler, P.V. (1986). GESP testing of shamanic cultists: Three studies and an evaluation of dramatic upsets during testing. *Journal of Parapsychology, 50* (2), 123-153.

Goes, E. (1937). *Prodígios da Biopsychica obtidos com o médium Mirabelli: experiências com o famoso metergico e documentado estudo de psychismo fhenomenal.* São Paulo, Brazil: Typographia Cupolo.

Greenfield, S.M. (1987). The return of Dr. Fritz: Spiritist healing and patronage networks in urban, industrial Brazil. *Social Science and Medicine, 24* (12), 1095-1108.

Greenfield, S.M. (1994). A model explaining Brazilian Spiritist surgeries and other unusual, religious-based healings. *Subtle Energies and Energy Medicine Journal, 5*(2), 109-141.

Hageman, J.J., Peres, J.F.P., Moreira-Almeida, A., Caixeta, L., Wickramasekera, I., & Krippner, S. (2010). The neurobiology of trance and mediumship in Brazil. In S. Krippner & H. Friedman (Eds.), *Mysterious minds: The neurobiology of psychics, mediums, and other extraordinary people* (pp. 85-111). Santa Barbara, CA: Praeger.

Hageman, J.J., Wickramasekera II, I. & Krippner, S. (2011). Across cultural boundaries: Psychophysiological responses, absorption, and dissociation comparison between Brazilian Spiritists and advanced meditators. *Neuroquantology, 9* (1), 5-21.

Herskovits, M.J. (1967). *Les bases de l'anthropologie culturelle.* Paris, France: Payot.

Hess, D. (1991). *Spiritists and scientists: Ideology, spiritism, and Brazilian culture.* Pittsburgh: Pennsylvania State University Press.

Hirukawa, T., Hiraoka, R., Silva, F.E., Pilato, S., & Kokubo, H. (2006). Field REG experiments of religious rituals and other group events in Paraná, Brazil. In *3ʳᵈ Psi Meeting – Proceedings of Presented Papers.* Curitiba, Brazil (pp. 109-118).

Intermédium. (2012). A pintura mediúnica de Jacques Andrade. Retrieved from http://intermedium-gespe.blogspot.com.br/2012/04/pintura-mediunica-de-jacques-no.html

Isaia, A.C., & Manoel, I.A. (2012). *Espiritismo e religiões afro-brasileiras: história e ciências sociais.* São Paulo, Brazil: Unesp.

Krippner, S. (1997). Dissociation in many times and places. In S. Krippner & S.M. Powers (Eds.), *Broken images, broken selves: Dissociative narratives in clinical practice* (pp. 3-40). Washington, DC: Brunner/Mazel.

Krippner, S., Winkler, M., Amiden, A., Crema, R., Kelson, R., Lal Arora, H. & Weil, P. (1996). Physiological and geomagnetic correlates of apparent anomalous phenomena observed in the presence of a Brazilian sensitive. *Journal of Scientific Exploration, 18,* 281-298.

Krippner, S., & Sulla, J. (2000). Identifying spiritual content in reports from ayahuasca sessions. *International Journal of Transpersonal Studies, 19,* 59-76.

Krippner, S. (2002). Stigmatic phenomena: An alleged case in Brazil. *Journal of Scientific Exploration, 16* (2), 207-224.

Kokubo, H. (2006). International parapsychological studies in Japan and South American countries. *Journal of International Society of Life Information Science, 24* (2), 367-369.

Leão, F.C., & Lotufo Neto, F. (2007). Spiritual practices in an institution for mentally disabled. *Revista de Psiquiatria Clínica, 34* (1), 23-28.

Lessa, A. P. (1975). *Precognição.* São Paulo, Brazil: Duas Cidades.

Lewgoy, B. (2006). Representações de ciência e religião no Espiritismo Kardecista: Antigas e novas configurações. *Civitas – Revista de Ciências Sociais, 6* (2), 151-167.

Lewgoy, B. (2008). A transnacionalização do Espiritismo Kardecista Brasileiro: Uma discussão inicial. *Religião e Sociedade, 28* (1), 84-104.

Lima, I.W.R. (1998). Pesquisa de atividade psicopictográfica de Jacques Andrade [Research into the psychic paintings of Jacques Andrade]. *Proceedings of the 3rd Psi Meeting,* Curitiba, Brazil.

Lins, R.D. (1999). Psicopictografia: Uma nova abordagem conceitual e um estudo de caso. In *Teoria Parapsicológica Geral.* Recife, Brazil: Instituto Pernambucano de Pesquisas Psicobiofísicas.

Magalhães, S.N. (2012). *Anna Prado: A mulher que falava com os mortos.* Brasília, Brazil: Federação Espírita Brasileira.

Magnani, J.G.C. (2005). El neoesoterismo en Brasil. In M. Moravčíková (Ed.), *New age.* Bratislava.

Machado, F.R. (2008). A new look at haunting and poltergeist phenomena: Analyzing experiences from a semiotic perspective. In J. Houran & R. Lange (Eds.), *Hauntings and poltergeists: Multidisciplinary perspectives.* Jefferson, NC: McFarland.

Machado, F. R. (2010). Anomalous (extrasensorymotor) experiences in daily life and their association with beliefs, attitudes, and subjective well-being. *Boletim Academia Paulista de Psicologia, 30* (79), 462-483.

Maraldi, E.O. (2013). El caso del medium Chico Xavier: Una interpretación psicológica. *E-Boletín Psi – Boletín Electrônico del Instituto de Psicologia Paranormal, 8* (1).

Maraldi, E.O., Machado, F.R., & Zangari, W. (2010). Importance of a psychosocial approach for a comprehensive understanding of mediumship. *Journal of Scientific Exploration, 24* (2), 181-196.

Maraldi, E.O., & Zangari, W. (2012). Therapeutic and projective functions of dissociative practices in religious context. *Boletim Academia Paulista de Psicologia, 32*(83), 424-452.

Maraldi, E. O. & Krippner, S. (2013). A biopsychosocial approach to creative dissociation: remarks on a case of mediumistic painting. *Neuroquantology, 11* (4), 544-572.

Martins, L.B., & Zangari, W. (2012). Relations among typical contemporary anaomlous experiences, mental disorders and spiritual experiences. *Revista de Psiquiatria Clínica, 39*(6).

Moreira-Almeida, A., Lotufo Neto, F., & Cardeña, E. (2008). Comparison of Brazilian Spiritist mediumship and dissociative identity disorder. *The Journal of Nervous and Mental Disease, 196* (5), 420-424.

Moreira-Almeida, A., Almeida, T. M., Gollner, A. M., & Krippner, S. (2009). A study of the mediumistic surgery of John of God. *The Journal of Shamanic Practice, 2* (1), 21-31.

Moreira-Almeida, A., & Koss-Chioino, J. D. (2009). Recognition and treatment of psychotic symptoms: Spiritists compared to mental health professionals in Puerto Rico and Brazil. *Psychiatry, 72* (3).

Negro, P.J., Palladino-Negro, P., & Louzā, M.R. (2002). Do religious mediumship dissociative experiences conform to the sociocognitive theory of dissociation? *Journal of Trauma and Dissociation, 3* (1).

Palhano Jr., L. (1994). *Mirabelli – Um médium extraordinário.* Rio de Janeiro, Brazil: CELD.

Perandréa, C. A. (1991). *A psicografia à luz da grafoscopia.* São Paulo, Brazil: Fé.

Peres, J.F., Moreira-Almeida, A., Caixeta, L., Leão, F., & Newberg, A. (2012). Neuroimaging during trance state: A contribution to the study of dissociation. *PLOS ONE, 7* (11).

Persinger, M.A., & Cameron, R.A. (1986). Are earth faults at fault in some poltergeist-like episodes? *Journal of the American Society for Psychical Research, 80,* 49.

Pires, J.H. (1966/2008). *Arigó: Vida, mediunidade e martírio. 4° edição.* São Paulo, Brazil: Paidéia.

Playfair, G.L. (2010). *Chico Xavier: The medium of the century.* London, UK: Roundtable Publishing [International Spiritist Council].

Playfair, G.L. (2011). *The flying cow: Exploring the psychic world of Brazil.* Guildford, UK: White Crow Books.

Radin, D.I., Machado, F.R., & Zangari, W. (2000). Effects of distant healing intention through time and space: Two exploratory studies. *Subtle Energies and Energy Medicine Journal, 11* (3), 270-303.

Ranieri, R.A. (2003). *Materializações luminosas: depoimento de um delegado de polícia.* São Paulo, Brazil: LAKE.

Rocha, N.M. (2011). *O fotógrafo dos espíritos.* São Paulo, Brazil: EME.

Rocha, A.C. (2001). *A poesia transcendente de Parnaso de além túmulo (The transcendent poetry of Parnassus from beyond the grave).* Masters dissertation (Literary Theory). Institute for Studies of Language from the University of Campinas, Brazil.

Rocha, A.C. (2008). *The case of Humberto de Campos: Literary authorship and mediumship.* Doctoral thesis. Institute for Studies of Language from the University of Campinas, Brazil.

Rock, A.J., Storm, L., Friedman, H. L. (2012). Shamanic-like journeying and psi-signal detection: I. In search of the psi-conducive components of a novel experimental protocol. *Journal of Parapsychology, 76* (2), 321-326.

Roxburgh, C.E. & Roe, C.A. (2011). The future of mediumship research: A multimethods approach. In *54th Annual Convention of the Parapsychological Association – Abstracts of Presented Papers.* Curitiba, Brazil.

Severino, P.R. *et al.* (1994). *Life's triumph: Research on messages received by Chico Xavier.* São Paulo, Brazil: FE.

Stanford, R. (1978). Ganzfeld and hypnotic-induction procedures in ESP research: Toward understanding their success. In *Advances in Parapsychological Research, 5* (pp. 39-76). Jefferson, NC: McFarland.

Stoll, S.J. (2002). Religião, ciência ou auto-ajuda? Trajetos do Espiritismo no Brasil. *Revista de Antropologia, 45* (2).

Targ, R., Schlitz, M., & Irwin, H.J. (2000). Psi-related experiences. In E. Cardeña, S.J. Lynn, & S. Krippner (Eds.), *Varieties of anomalous experience: Examining the scientific evidence.* Washington, DC: American Psychological Association.

Visoni, V. M. (2012). Obras psicografadas (mediumistic writings). In: http://obraspsicografadas.org/

Weiss, R.A.A., & Nunes, M.J.R. (2005). New age and multi-religiosity in Brazil. In M. Moravčíková (Ed.), *New age.* Bratislava.

Zangari, W. (2003). *Incorporating spirits: A psychosocial analysis of the phenomena of mediumship among Brazilian mediums of Umbanda religion.* Doctoral thesis (Social Psychology). University of São Paulo, Brazil.

Zangari, W. (2007). Experiências Anômalas em Médiuns de Umbanda: Uma avaliação fenomenológica e ontológica. *Boletim Academia Paulista de Psicologia,* v. 2/07, p. 67-86.

Zangari, W., & Machado, F.R. (1996). Survey: Incidence and social relevance of Brazilian university students' psychic experiences. *European Journal of Parapsychology, 12,* 75-87

A medium trancing one of the Nine Emperor Gods in Singapore's Nine Emperor Gods festival at Choa Chu Keng Doumu Gong temple. Photograph by Fabian Graham.

SPIRIT MEDIUMS IN HONG KONG AND THE UNITED STATES

CHARLES F. EMMONS

The purpose of this chapter is to report on my investigations of spirit mediumship in two contexts: Hong Kong from 1980-1981, and the United States from 1993 to the present. This account necessarily includes a study of myself, because one of my methodologies was participatory science. In other words, after 1993 I became a spirit medium myself, partly for personal reasons following the death of my mother, and partly in order to do more involved participant observation.

In the Hong Kong research (Emmons, 1982) I performed in the roles of sociologist and anthropologist (having a PhD in the former and an MA in the latter). I also used some of the perspectives of parapsychology, comparing my data on ghosts (which are tied closely with spirit mediumship in Chinese culture) with apparition studies done primarily in the U.S. and the UK. By the time my wife (who is a spirit medium) and I published on our studies in the United States (Emmons & Emmons, 2003), I had become a Spiritualist as well.

I mention all of this in the interests of full disclosure, but also in order to clarify my use of multiple perspectives. Although my primary identity is that of a social scientist, I also claim (even as a sociologist) that exploring other ways of knowing helps to understand the phenomenon. Indeed, I argue for a 'phenomenological' approach as one useful way for sociologists to help make sense of anomalous experiences such as spirit mediumship. Simply put, when investigating unusual experiences, it just might help to ask the experiencers themselves what they think is going on. It might even help for the investigator to have the experience as well.

I am always alert to the need to balance my direct involvement with a skeptical sense of distance. Nevertheless, I do not expect any 'scientific' perspective on mediumship to be 'objective' either. Interestingly, it turns out that most spirit mediums in the United States (but not in Hong Kong) are rather skeptical themselves and usually need 'confirmations' that what they are doing is valid.

Another important point is that the normal scientific taboo against too great an involvement with the paranormal problematizes open inquiry into a category of experiences that are found in all societies and have evident social importance, whatever the 'reality' status they may or may not have. I argue for a completely open and multifaceted, multimethodological study of spirit mediumship, letting the results take us where they may.

Cultural Variation

In order to better understand the differences between Chinese and American spirit mediumship, it is important to look at the differing contexts in which they appear. To begin with, spirit mediumship is virtually universal in world cultures and overlaps shamanism (Emmons, 2003, p. 57), the former referring mainly to contacting the spirit world for information, the latter referring mainly to manipulating the spirit world to heal the sick.

In many societies spirit mediumship provides a mechanism for deprived groups, especially women, to gain spiritual political power (Lewis, 1966; Emmons and Emmons, 2003, pp. 70-71). However, in Zimbabwe for example (Lain, 1985; Emmons, 2003, p. 58), powerful political leaders have had access to spirit mediums that are considered more powerful than those available to lower-status individuals.

Elsewhere (Emmons, 2003; Emmons and Emmons, 2003) I have carried this cross-cultural analysis further, but the focus here is on the two cases of China (Hong Kong) and the U.S. The main differences between the two are that Chinese tend to take spirit mediums (and ghosts) for granted as a serious part of ancestor worship, whereas Americans have a variety of usually less serious understandings of mediums bordering on fortune telling and entertainment. Of course Spiritualists in the U.S. take spirit mediums seriously, but these mediums also serve clients who may not share their views.

Although the prehistory and history of spirit mediumship in China is complex and varied, ancestor worship seems to have trickled down from royalty and nobility to the masses over a long period of time. It has been more predominant among higher social classes that have a sizeable estate to protect within their lineage. Ancestor worship provides a basis for solidarity, keeping control over lineage (clan) interests by bringing together people with a common patrilineal ancestor. It has also tended to be more important in southern China where wet-rice cultivation traditionally required a large cooperative enterprise, giving greater incentive to use ancestor worship to preserve lineage solidarity among the work force (Emmons, 2003, p. 58).

Although wet-rice cultivation no longer exists in the urban part of Hong Kong of course, Hong Kong has preserved (at least through the time of my study, 1980-1981) much of the ancestor-worship culture of southern China, especially Kwantung Province. Nowadays the function of these practices is primarily to benefit the wealth and health of individuals and their extended family, or at least to relieve anxiety about wealth and health.

I know of at least three variations on the culture of spirit mediums in Hong Kong Chinese culture (Emmons, 1982, p. 187), of which the most relevant to ancestor worship is the *mun mai poh* ("ask-rice woman"). Traditionally one was supposed to bring some rice from the family kitchen to help the spirits recognize the client of the spirit medium. At the time of my study I observed people bringing a coin instead of the rice (money which was separate from the actual donation for the reading itself). Some mediums also ask for birth and death dates of the spirit, and for the location of the deceased's grave to help with identification. On the other hand, one of my informants told me that the family just brought some rice from home, said that the Laus (pseudonym) were looking for the Laus, and all the ancestors popped up at once.

Another potential obstacle to making contact with ancestral spirits, according to Chinese religious culture, which is extremely eclectic, is the possibility that the ancestors may have reincarnated already (a theme from Buddhism, an Indian import, that is in potential conflict with the older ancestor worship culture), meaning that there may be nobody home in the spirit world (Emmons, 1982, pp. 214-216). Some mediums don't want to try to contact spirits of people who have died more than two years ago, but the one medium I observed multiple times ignored this issue and went right on with it, in spite of using a Buddhist name and having Buddhist religious objects on her altar.

As noted above, traditional Chinese spirit mediumship is a tool for keeping in touch with ancestors, ideally up to four generations back (conceivably more than that in a clan shrine), which binds together all of their descendants in a kinship group. However, even when the extended family group breaks apart, the ideology of the ancestors watching over their descendants can be preserved. Thus, Chinese today can still worship their ancestors in exchange for return help from the ancestors in the daily lives of the living.

Here are examples of what one should do for one's ancestors, with the help of the spirit medium who conveys their needs by communicating their requests to the living clients (sitters). At least one should burn incense on the family ancestor worship altar, and often provide flowers and food (which is sometimes claimed to be symbolically eaten, or even to disappear, such as peanuts that are eaten without breaking the shell). But there may also be particular requests, for example for a car or town house, things that the ancestors need for the parallel life that exists in the other world (sometimes misleadingly translated as "hell"). These objects can be simulated in the form of effigies made from cheap materials like plastic. You can see objects like this, such as plastic jewelry sets, in American Chinatowns. One can also burn "hell bank notes" in grand denominations such as $50,000,000.

In return the living clients expect improvements in wealth and health. Sometimes requests are very specific. One person asked her ancestor to help her win the government housing lottery in Hong Kong (when there were insufficient public housing units available for everybody at once). She promised that if she won, she would worship his tablet (a piece of wood named for the spirit) on the altar, but if she didn't, she threatened to take his tablet off the altar.

This relates to the question of whether Chinese have been afraid of their ancestors (Emmons, 1982, pp. 21-23). Francis Hsu (1967, pp. 244-245) claimed that they were not, at least in the part of southwest China that he came from. However, I collected testimony, for example, from a woman who talked about how members of the family would get sick if they neglected to take care of their ancestors' tablets and graves. Also, spirits who have no one to worship them come back as dangerous ghosts during the Hungry Ghost Festival (Emmons, 1982, pp. 23-26). All of this reinforces the notion that spirit mediumship is seen as a serious, practical matter in traditional Chinese culture.

A good example that demonstrates this cultural expectation is the reaction people had to my participation with a spirit medium in Hong Kong (Emmons, 1982, pp. 204-205). Altogether I visited her five times as a client, sometimes waiting for hours in her crowded waiting room. Some of the locals began to recognize me from previous visits. Not realizing that I could understand Cantonese (the Hong Kong dialect of Chinese), somebody said, "If the Westerner keeps coming back, she must be good." But I was also being secretly rebuked, when an assistant of the medium said, "Here comes the Westerner again to chit-chat with his auntie." Chinese don't come to "chit chat" with their ancestors; they have serious business to conduct. Only somebody like me would use mediumship because I missed my relatives or was grieving or wanted friendly advice.

Switching now to the American context, spirit mediumship is much less integrated into the overall culture, which of course is extremely pluralistic and divided over religious issues. The most conspicuous use of spirit mediumship in the U.S. is associated with the Spiritualist Movement (Emmons, 2003, pp. 59-61). Spiritualists trace their origins to the young Fox Sisters in 1848 in Hydesville near Rochester, New York, and to the writings of Andrew Jackson Davis shortly thereafter. The mediumistic activities of the former were the phenomenon that spread the enthusiasm, and the intellectual work of the latter provided a kind of natural law doctrine. However, Spiritualists were generally opposed to forming established churches until the late nineteenth century.

Spiritualism was much more visible in the nineteenth century than it is today, not only because of the popularity of séances and public displays of both mental and physical mediumship (e.g., levitating tables and musical instruments), but also because Spiritualists were both religiously and politically radical in a turbulent time of industrial growth and social change (Emmons, 2003, pp. 59-61; Emmons and Emmons, 2003, pp. 269-271).

By now it has become partly incorporated into the New Age spiritual movement.

Just as the United States is very pluralistic culturally, so are the meanings and uses of spirit mediumship pluralistic, even those connected primarily to Spiritualism (Emmons and Emmons, 2003, pp. 141-177). Although the study that Penelope and I did was focused on mediums rather than their clients, it is evident both from our interviews with mediums and from observing public mediumship services that there is a partial disconnect between Spiritualist mediums and the frequently non-Spiritualist clientele that they serve.

Most people come to spirit mediums in Lily Dale and elsewhere looking for fortune telling. That is, they mostly want to know the future of their jobs, their love life, their health, finances, and so on. Often, however, they do want to connect with deceased loved ones in order to heal grief, which is closer to the purposes the mediums have in mind. It is common for the general public to confuse spirit mediums with "psychics" as well as "fortune tellers." Apparently for this reason many spirit mediums now bill themselves as "psychic mediums," trying to link more into a popular vocabulary.

In public platform mediumship services, or in regular church services, Spiritualist mediums usually try to bring in people's dead relatives and friends (especially in Lily Dale, which has rules about public services), in order to "prove the continuity of life." They may also mix in some homespun advice from the spirits. However, most mediums say that in private readings with individual clients, they give the clients what they want, which is mostly fortune telling, but also some contact with relatives both for grief reduction and for life advice. The mediums we interviewed also stressed that an important purpose of mediumship was spiritual growth, for both medium and sitter. And to sum it all up, most mediums would agree that it is supposed to be for healing of body, mind and spirit (Emmons and Emmons, 2003, pp. 141-177; Emmons, 2003, p. 61). I would say that it is very similar in function to counseling or life coaching.

Studying Mediumship: Hong Kong

As mentioned previously, my research on spirit mediumship in Hong Kong was embedded within a larger study: *Chinese Ghosts and ESP: A Study of Paranormal Beliefs and Experiences* (Emmons, 1982). Due to my background in anthropology, and to my interests in the sociology of knowledge, I think that it is always illuminating to reveal one's personal reasons for doing a piece of research. It helps to explain the frame being used and to alert readers to types of bias in the work. I had become involved in Hong Kong with the help of my former wife Chee Lee and her family, and I wanted to combine this opportunity with my longstanding interest in parapsychology from undergraduate days.

Although I had been trained as an anthropologist (MA, University of Illinois, 1966, specializing in the cultures of Southeast Asia), and as a sociologist (PhD, University of Illinois at Chicago, 1971, specializing in ethnicity), I also wanted to use these disciplines as ways of understanding issues in parapsychology. I had read a great deal about ghosts or apparitions in studies from the UK and the US, but had seen very little in parapsychology about other parts of the world. Indeed, even today my study is one of the very few cross-cultural studies of apparition experiences with a parapsychological component.

It finds, by the way, that apparition experiences in China and the Western world are very similar in core characteristics, in spite of cultural differences, arguing for a universal ghost (apparition) experience that is essentially mental rather than physical, although in many "evidential cases" still apparently "paranormal." This fits the "experiential source theory" more than the "cultural source theory" of anomalous experiences and beliefs (McClenon, 2002).

In other words, people in all societies have similar experiences with "wondrous events" (as McClenon calls them) that result in religious beliefs of various kinds to explain them, rather than the beliefs completely causing the experiences.

This work is already considered deviant according to unwritten rules in social science, because, to some extent, it truth-tests anomalous experiences (in the sense of identifying evidential cases), instead of merely looking for the social functions of people's beliefs about the paranormal. However, I was not yet interested in a spiritual or religious interpretation of ghosts and the spirit mediumship that connected them to ancestor worship. I *was* a deviant social scientist perhaps, but still only a scientist, not yet a Spiritualist. I thought that the amazing things I observed a spirit medium doing might well be explained as some kind of ESP. Today I still think that, but I am more open to the idea that she might really have been communicating with spirits.

Now, what were my methods exactly? I amassed a total of over 3,600 interviews, questionnaires, and observations in Hong Kong from June 1980 to January 1981. The best survey data came from a random telephone survey of 1501 people on Hong Kong Island, in which 50% said that they believed in ghosts (compared to 12% in the U.S. in 1978, which has increased to over 20% in recent decades), 24% in life after death (65% in the U.S. then), and 18% in spirit mediums (no data for U.S.).

These data really need some discussion. First of all, asking Chinese about religious beliefs is problematic, because traditionally they have been very eclectic and tolerant, in contrast to Americans who use belief more as a test of faith or loyalty. Next, it is odd that only 50% said that they believed in ghosts (although this is a high figure compared to the U.S. at that time), because 72% on the survey said that they practiced ancestor worship, which almost requires a belief in ghosts. One problem here is "social desirability response," in which people avoid unpleasant truths. In this case, Chinese often don't like thinking about ghosts. As one respondent said, "Ayaah! Why do you ask me about such unlucky things?" As another person said, the question in Hong Kong is not whether you "believe" in ghosts, but whether you are afraid of them.

Next, why is it that only 24% reported believing in "life after death"? I think that this is because the concept is often associated with Christianity (I found 21% Christian in my sample). Otherwise, again, why practice ancestor worship (72%) and worry about ghosts (50%) if there is no life after death? And finally, only 18% saying they believed in spirit mediums is odd, because 72% practiced ancestor worship, in which spirit mediumship plays an important part.

One insight into this apparent paradox may lie in the pattern I observed in which many people were critical of a certain medium, saying; "That didn't seem like grandpa she was bringing through." Or, in spite of lots of evidential information brought through, there were some details that didn't fit. It appeared that people generally believed that spirit mediumship was possible (more-so than in the United States, where it is more likely to be considered unscientific or phony). What they doubted in Hong Kong was not whether it could be done, but whether a particular spirit medium was good at it, or getting a particular case right (which is important if you want to give your ancestors what they're asking for).

Next let's go visit the spirit mediums. I am going to skip the Taoist automatic-writing medium I visited (Emmons, 1982, pp. 217-224) and concentrate on a mental medium (*mun mai poh*) whom I observed on five different occasions, in addition to interviewing someone who observed her once (Emmons, 1982, pp. 197-212). On my first visit to Sam Gu (pseudonym, meaning "Third Aunt," a name commonly taken by mediums after one of the names for the Chinese Buddhist goddess Kwan Yin), she told me that she had never contacted a spirit for a Western man before. Although I said some things in Cantonese, most communication was through a translator (my former wife Chee, a native of Hong Kong).

After hearing a brief identification of the spirit I was trying to contact (my mother's sister), Sam Gu rested her head on a little pillow on a table decorated with a red bulb, framed sacred writings, a statue of Sau ("Long Life"), incense, and offerings of fruit. There was also a pastry and a cup there, but an assistant told us that she ate very little all day after going into trance in the morning. This now makes me think of the ritual that most American mediums go through in terms of prayer and meditation before working, although they do very little work in more than a light trance in recent decades.

After raising her head, Sam Gu said, "Her husband died long ago; she was a widow for a long time. [Her husband did die about twenty-five years before she did.] She died of an illness, not just old age, died in a hospital. This woman had less than three children, a son and a daughter. She was pretty when she was young." [All correct.] That part was the identification process, aided by a genie (what parapsychologists would call a "control," and what Spiritualists would call a spirit guide), who had died when she was three. After this correct identification she said that she would ask the spirit to come up (Emmons, 1982, pp. 198-201).

Sam Gu's whole body shook, and her head rocked back and forth. These might seem like symptoms of spirit possession, but she never attempted (in any of her cases) to imitate voice or language. One exception to this is that on another occasion I did hear her speak briefly when her head was still on the pillow in a little girl voice (perhaps the voice of her genie). She did, however, speak in the first person as the spirit, making a gurgling noise, then sat up and said to Chee, "Hello, niece-in-law!" She did not appear to be in a trance state at that point and spoke normally. A great deal of fairly specific information followed, a high percentage of it correct (actually looking at the 1982 book now I think I may have been wrong about some of the parts that I had declared to be incorrect). What really startled me was the way she very specifically imitated my mother's way of scratching her itchy skin on her arms.

We also received a lot of information about one other spirit, much of it incorrect, but most of it correct and some of it intriguingly specific and unlikely (such as saying correctly that the spirit had two children, a woman who was a doctor, and a son who was an architect). My suggestion at the time (Emmons, 1982, p. 204), that I considered Sam Gu's performance more likely to be explained by ESP (telepathy between Sam Gu and me, or in some cases Chee) than by spirit contact, reveals the way I was thinking like a parapsychologist. Of course this is still a paranormal explanation. I remember being very curious about how she could seemingly know about things that had happened on the other side of the world that had been communicated in a language she didn't understand.

At the same time it is important to remember the social significance of this practice. I recall Sam Gu, speaking as my aunt, giving Chee's and my salary (overestimating 15 to 20%) with five kibitzers standing in the hallway watching and listening. Of course they were observing a bizarre cross-cultural contact experience, in which I was chit-chatting instead of asking serious ancestor worship questions, as I pointed out earlier. Nevertheless, the cultural universals, such as the medium going into an altered state at the beginning, and using a spirit guide or control, in spite of the differences in cultural functions, are worth noting as well.

To summarize briefly all five of my visits to Sam Gu (Emmons, 1982, pp. 204-213), the first three of ten spirit contacts seemed highly evidential, and nine of ten overall seemed better than guessing. However, she seemed to decline in accuracy over the twelve weeks I observed her, possibly because she was having health problems and working very long hours. I came to develop a friendly relationship with her and was disappointed when some Chinese people, who had come to her with me and with another individual I interviewed, criticized her work, especially during the time she was feeling unwell. They seemed to be very demanding that she get everything right and were not impressed at the good hits she had if she also made mistakes. In retrospect I am reminded of spirit mediums I have observed in the U.S. who report exhaustion and other health problems when they work too many hours.

There is one more thing I want to say about Sam Gu after the fact. I regret that I never told her that I was doing research. At the time it did not seem to me to be an ethical problem, because I did come to her genuinely as a client, and I did bring her a lot of business. I didn't tell her about my study because I did not want to create any artificial behavior, although coming to her as a Westerner was artificial enough. I did draw the line by not agreeing with the tactics of a Hong Kong filmmaker who was gathering information about spirit mediumship by taking a hidden tape recorder into Sam Gu's sessions. I never recorded, and I have preserved her confidentiality. Nevertheless, by the standards I have today, I would have asked for her informed consent. In later visits to Hong Kong, I was never able to locate her, and I wonder where she is today.

Studying Mediumship: The United States

There was a gap of twelve years between my Hong Kong study and the beginning of my research on spirit mediums in the United States. From a sociology of knowledge approach it is important to note that my involvement with the project, that culminated in *Guided by Spirit: A Journey into the Mind of the Medium* (Emmons and Emmons, 2003), began ten years before the publication of the book and a year before I started doing formal research on it.

After my mother died in 1993 I started to get the impression that she was communicating with me (Emmons and Emmons, 2003, pp. 101-107). At first I went through a process of skeptical testing of these notions, even though I could hear her voice in my left ear (not an "exterior voice," but the impression that the voice in my head was coming from the left). I noticed that I was getting evidential synchronicities, often in pairs. For example, when I was out running one day, I heard her voice say "Watch out" twice, about ten seconds apart, shortly after each of which a tricycle, then a bicycle did a u-turn right toward me. The scientist in me was beginning to think that not to see a pattern here was actually bad science.

I had a great many such experiences in those days, and I still think the communication occurs today, although I no longer hear a voice, I just get internal mental impressions. However, the experience that sealed the deal, both turning me into a Spiritualist and motivating me to study spirit mediumship in the U.S., occurred in 1994 (Emmons and Emmons, 2003, pp. 105-107).

Due to my research background studying ghosts, I used to get requests to participate in radio talk shows around Halloween (I tried to keep it serious). This happened in fall 1994 in Erie, Pennsylvania, my home town. A week or so before the broadcast the host told me on the phone that she suspected that a friend of hers was trying to communicate with her from the other side. One day as she arrived home in her car, she had begun to think about him and about some yearbook pictures they had been dealing with. She thought this peculiar because she hadn't thought of him for a long time. When she got into the house she opened the newspaper and saw in the obituaries that he had been in a car accident. I suggested, "Why don't you go get a reading from a spirit medium at the psychic fair at the Spiritualist Church on Saturday and see if you can contact him that way?" She declined on the grounds that she was a Catholic and thought that contacting a spirit medium was a mortal sin.

I had already planned to attend the psychic fair, and that Saturday I received a phenomenal (highly evidential) reading from Kitty Osborne, who ended up being one of my mediumship teachers in the church after I was inspired to join based on the fair. Everything in the reading seemed to apply very well to me, except for the very last thing she said, "I'm seeing something about a young man who died in a car accident, and it has to do with yearbook pictures." I replied, "That doesn't seem to fit for me, but I think I know who it's for." I was so stunned that I didn't have the presence of mind to ask her more questions about it, for which I have kicked myself ever since.

When I arrived home at my dad's house, with whom I was staying while on sabbatical leave, I got the notion that the man in the car accident was Bill (pseudonym for another common name) Ebersome. This was before I had taken any classes in how to do spirit mediumship. I checked the name out in the Erie phone book and could find no such surname. Nevertheless I called up the talk show host and told her about the reading. She accused me of making it up. Then I asked her sheepishly if the guy's name was Bill Ebersome. "Ebersome?" she replied, "Where did you get that?" OK, that was wrong. What was his first name? "Bill," she said.....OK, can I have half a point? It was enough to make me very curious. And I wondered if maybe "Ebersome" wasn't something like, "(I love you) ever so much."

Throughout the years I have done this research (I still can't help observing this process, even after the book was finished), I have had many evidential experiences involving mediumship performed by others, and even in my own mediumship. Keep in mind that from a parapsychological perspective I cannot rule out some kind of telepathy or clairvoyance in the following example, as opposed to spirit communication, but I find it highly evidential of some kind of paranormal communication.

One day in Lily Dale in 1996 I was about to go deliver messages as a "student medium" at an outdoor service at "The

Stump." Especially in my early days of doing mediumship, I used to doubt that I could get messages on the spot, so I would meditate beforehand and try to get messages for later. This time I got an image of a tall, thin man with a moustache and glasses standing in a particular spot by one of the benches at The Stump. In my mind I saw a gang of his spirit relatives cheering him, waving placards, and saying that he was a success, which he didn't want to accept. There were more details. I also received another message for "the youngest girl who is not a baby," although I got no visual image of her. I was supposed to tell her mother that she was very talented in music and very creative, but that her training should not be too restrictive, and so on. By the way, I wrote these down before leaving for The Stump.

When I arrived at The Stump I could easily identify the tall man out of the nearly 300 people there. It was also clear who the "youngest girl who is not a baby" was. Before I was called on to give messages (short readings in public platform style), another medium came to the same man and gave him quite precisely the message I had ready for him (about the crowd of relatives, his being a success but not accepting it, and all the rest). I was stunned. A little later a different medium went to the mother of the child and delivered the same message I was prepared to give her, except that she replaced "music" with "dance." Here was another double synchronicity for skeptical Charlie. I thought about the odds against identifying the right person out of 300, times doing it again (300 X 300 = 90,000), times whatever the odds are against giving such a detailed message times the odds against giving another one. The odds are astronomical. Yet I had not even given either message, and the proof status of this example in normal science is nil because it is "subjective." Nevertheless, this and many other such experiences have had the effect of making me treat the subject under investigation very seriously.

Such experiences have also impressed upon me the usefulness of both participatory science and phenomenological research methods. I was engaging in participatory science by putting myself in the role of spirit medium (like the mad scientist drinking his own potion). Asking spirit mediums (other ones, not just me), to describe their own experiences and interpret them from their own perspective is a phenomenological methodology. For other examples of phenomenological research on spirit mediums see the Gary Schwartz research team (Rock, Beischel and Schwartz, 2008), although they have also used laboratory methods in their work (Schwartz, 2002).

My wife Penelope and I used multiple research methodologies (another sound strategy) for *Guided by Spirit* (2003). In addition to the usual review of the literature, we interviewed 40 spirit mediums and collected biographies of 80 more (from the past century and a half), mostly from the two archives in the Spiritualist community of Lily Dale, New York. We also observed countless Spiritualist church services and public message services (such as at The Stump in Lily Dale), and did participant observation in the everyday life of Lily Dale among the mediums who are our friends and neighbors in the summertime. And, of course, we analyzed our own experiences. Penelope is a social worker, counselor and ordained Spiritualist minister and medium. She is much more completely immersed in mediumship than I am, and I have one foot in the phenomenon and one foot in social science.

Ideally we would have had a normal-science skeptic or debunker on our team as well for greater balance of perspective. However, we did analyze our data from several competing perspectives: social and behavioral science, scientific debunking, parapsychology, and some different spiritual perspectives (Emmons and Emmons, 2003, pp. 269-294).

Most importantly we let the spirit mediums tell their own stories (some of them through their autobiographies, written as early as the 1850s). This is the phenomenological approach. Nevertheless, we had a database of 120 mediums, which gave us a matrix of data that allowed for some statistical analysis as well. For example, in our sample, 59% of the nineteenth-century mediums were female, but only 27 % of spirit guides were female; 50% of mediums were female in the early twentieth century, and 26% of spirit guides were female; in the late twentieth century 74% of mediums were female, and 21% of guides were female (Emmons and Emmons, 2003, p. 234).

This shows that a high percentage of mediums have been female (even among the famous ones that were more likely to have biographies printed), but that they have supposedly been guided in the spirit world mainly by men (over 70%). This harks back to the 1850s when Spiritualist mediums were more radical than other feminists, daring to speak in public, whereas other feminists had men deliver their speeches before the 1860s. Nevertheless, the predominance of male spirit guides over the past century and a half somewhat moderates the claim that Spiritualism has been a beacon of gender equality in American religion.

Returning to a phenomenological perspective, I have never heard a single Spiritualist medium of either gender (not counting myself), talk about this issue of the gender of spirit guides, or heard much talk about feminism in general. But the fact is that Spiritualist Church services are usually about 80% female, both in overall attendance and in leadership, a figure that is also a good generalization for most New Age events I have attended in my study of the New Spirituality Movement (Emmons, 2010).

Most of our study, however, focused on how people become mediums and how they play their role and understand what they do as a mediums. All of this needs to be understood within the general pattern of how spirit mediumship is seen in American culture. In great contrast to the Chinese case, mediumship in the U.S. has no institutionalized position in the main religious traditions. Moreover, Western society has a strong scientific, rational bias, making the scientific claims of Spiritualism (that it provides evidence for the continuity of life), of questionable legitimacy (Garroutte, 1993).

Consequently, becoming a spirit medium in the U.S. is rather like being socialized to a deviant identity, that one usually achieves in spite of general lack of support from the wider community, and often family (Emmons and Emmons, 2003, pp. 171-209). By a process of differential association, some people have early childhood experiences (spirit guides, apparitions, near-death experiences, spontaneous mediumship), that propel them in the direction of this role, and they get enough support, especially in adult years, from kindred spirits and organized spiritual groups to take on the role of spirit medium.

For all that, spirit mediums have still been raised in the same skeptical culture (popular media about the paranormal notwithstanding), that either sensationalizes (and trivializes) psychic phenomena or considers their practitioners of dubious status and questionable authenticity. This results in most spirit mediums being skeptical of their own work. Eighty percent of our contemporary mediums considered "confirmations" (from clients or sitters that their readings were correct) to be important (51%), or very important (29%). I can really relate to this, due to my skeptical side and to my nervousness from time to time about whether I should even be studying this subject as a sociologist, which ironically just reinforces the importance of my participatory science approach.

One of my favorite confirmations comes from a medium in Lily Dale who once saw (clairvoyantly) a dog with a lit cigar in its mouth (Emmons and Emmons, 2003, pp. 38-39). When she reluctantly passed this information along to the woman who had come for a reading, the woman explained that she had lived at the end of a milk-truck delivery route. When the driver got to the end of his route, by her house, he would turn the truck around and toss his cigar out the window. Her dog would run over, pick the cigar up in its mouth, and run around appearing to be smoking the cigar. The medium's point: never interpret. One might also say, don't edit, since details might turn out to be important identifiers for the sitter. Part of the ideology of this spirit medium culture is that the message is for the sitter, not the medium.

Sometimes the sitter doesn't recognize the most obvious information. On one occasion my wife Penelope gave a man a message at a public service about somebody named William. The man just could not recognize who that was, although the rest of the message was OK, he said. A day or so later I was sitting in the picnic shelter at the Fire Department picnic when I saw the same man come up to us and say to Penelope: "Now I know who William is. That was my dad's name. We just called him Dad." Honest.

I should also point out some of the reasons why 12% of our sample said that confirmations were not very important, and 9% said "not at all important." Some of these mediums thought that it was important to trust what "spirit" says and not question it. Some assume that the message must be correct, even if interpreted incorrectly by the sitter (or the medium). It is also possible that these explanations are a defense against any disconfirmations of one's belief.

Although Spiritualist classes in how to develop one's mediumship do have certain cultural similarities to each other, such as encouraging meditation, saying a prayer of protection, and developing platform etiquette (such as not telling someone her grandmother is going to die next week), there is also quite a lot of variation in how mediums work (Emmons and Emmons, 2003, pp. 225-259). About 70% of our mediums reported being clairvoyant (getting visual imagery, usually only an internal image), 61% clairaudient (usually an internal rather than external sense of hearing something), and 40% clairsentient or "kinesthetic" (that is, getting "feelings," although sometimes the word is used as a catch-all for any sense other than vision or hearing).

Some mediums have difficulty explaining how they get the information, or just start talking, sometimes forgetting what they have said afterwards. Mediums who go into full trance, which is rare in the U.S. these days, typically do not remember what they have said. Some go into semi-trance, observing themselves talk as if they are not in control. It also appears that the longer someone has done mediumship, the less they focus on how they do it. It is as if they learn by biofeedback what it feels like to do mediumship, and then just do it without thinking.

Conclusion

These two traditions of spirit mediumship in Hong Kong and in the United States are instances of the cultural universal of humans attempting to communicate with the spirits of deceased humans. Although they share many common patterns in terms of the behavior of spirit mediums going into some type, and degree, of altered state of consciousness, for example, or in their use of spirit guides, there are also important differences. Chinese negotiate with their ancestors for the benefit of both parties in practical matters, whereas Americans seek mostly personal advice and grief reduction for the living.

Although there is much more to be said about the substantive content of these two studies (cf. Emmons, 1982; and Emmons and Emmons, 2003 for more details), the emphasis of this piece has been on research methodology and the controversial implications of these methodologies for the sociology of science and knowledge. I have argued that participatory science (getting directly involved with the phenomenon, a kind of extreme participant observation), and a phenomenological approach (getting into "the mind of the medium" for example), are especially useful when dealing with anomalous or "paranormal" phenomena like spirit mediumship.

One reason for this is that it helps to appreciate better the experiences of one's research subjects. For example, I don't think that I would have appreciated fully how important confirmations are to American spirit mediums if I had not felt the pressure myself to justify my apparently "crazy" behavior of allegedly bringing in messages from the spirit world, and if I had not actually had the amazing experience of seeing two mediums deliver the same messages I was preparing to give.

Another reason for using participatory science and phenomenological methods to investigate anomalous experiences is that these are ways of possibly learning more about their paranormal aspects, beginning with looking to see if there is evidence that they actually exist (one of the goals of parapsychology, of course). Certainly the social functions of spirit mediumship would still exist, even if it turned out to be completely invalid (as a way of actually talking to the dead), but surely the question of whether such communication is possible is not an uninteresting question to human beings who are curious about the nature of their existence. The only sensible reason for ignoring the latter question would be that mainstream normal science needs to defend its orthodox positions.

References

Emmons, C. (1982). *Chinese ghosts and ESP: A study of paranormal beliefs and experiences.* Metuchen, NJ: Scarecrow Press.

Emmons, C. (2003). The Spiritualist movement: Bringing the dead back. In C. D. Bryant (Ed.), *Handbook of death and dying* (Vol. I) (pp. 57-64). Thousand Oaks, CA: Sage.

Emmons, C., & Emmons, P. (2003). *Guided by spirit: A journey into the mind of the medium.* New York: Writers Club Press.

Garroutte, E. M. (1993). When scientists saw ghosts and why they stopped. In R. Wuthnow (Ed.), *Vocabularies of public life* (pp.57-74). New York: Routledge.

Hsu, F. L.K. (1967). *Under the ancestor's shadow.* Stanford, CA: Stanford University Press.

Lain, D. (1985). *Guns and rain: Guerillas and spirit mediums in Zimbabwe.* Berkeley, CA: University of California Press.

Lewis, I. M. (1966). Spirit possession and deprivation cults. *Man, 1,* 307-329.

McClenon, J. (2002). *Wondrous healing: Shamanism, human evolution, and the origin of religion*. DeKalb, IL: Northern Illinois University Press.

Rock, A.J., J. Beischel, & G.E. Schwartz (2008). Thematic analysis of research mediums' experiences of discarnate communication. *Journal of Scientific Exploration, 22* (2), 179-192.

Schwartz, G. E. (2002). *The afterlife experiments: Breakthrough evidence of life after death*. New York, NY: Atria Books.

A medium trancing the underworld deity Tua Ya Pek in Singapore. Photograph by Fabian Graham.

VESSELS FOR THE GODS: *TANG-KI* SPIRIT MEDIUMSHIP IN SINGAPORE AND TAIWAN

FABIAN GRAHAM

T he mind wearies swiftly when it tries to grapple with concepts of the infinite. However, ancient tribes must have questioned their own mortality, and sought to find intelligent purpose beyond their own lifespan. In one such tribe, located in the Henan region of China, the priests and shamans devised a ritual system that allowed for communication between their ruler and the souls of his ancestors, thus acknowledging the existence of life beyond death. The tribe was named after the ruling family, the Shang, which over time became the name of the dynasty.[1] The emperor was the secular and religious leader, and the Shang religion focused on the relationship between the emperor and his ancestors, who were by extension emperors in Heaven, therefore laying the foundations and initial framework for Chinese ancestor and deity worship.

The souls of ancestors were worshiped and offered sacrifices in exchange for blessings and favours, and were consulted for advice through elaborate forms of divination. The religion was practiced throughout the social hierarchy, and ancient divination bones both with and without inscriptions provide archaeological evidence that religious divination was employed by both the educated elite and illiterate alike. Primeval notions of a spirit world existing beyond death evolved that, in the fullness of time, would be developed to maturity, and in the terminology of more complex philosophies. However, in the Shang period, primitive concepts recognized the distinction between malevolent spirits, such as ghosts, demons or devils (*gui*),[2] and benevolent spirits (*Shen*); and between earthly (*po*) and spiritual (*hun*) components of the soul (Thompson, 1979). Male (*yang*) attributes were associated with the *hun* portion of the soul, and female (*yin*) attributes were allotted to the *po* section of the soul.[3]

Following death, the two portions of the soul would separate. The earthly *po* soul would remain in the grave so long as the body had been buried with correct ritual, and sacrifices continued to be offered to it. If these conditions were not met, the *po* soul would become restless, and transform into a malevolent spirit or vengeful ghost (*gui*) to haunt its descendants. This eventuality was to be avoided, so the importance of correct burial, continuing sacrifice and worship were integrated into the family cult from its inauguration. If an individual died an un-natural death, or had been seriously wronged in their lifetime, the *po* soul would become malicious and manifest as a ghost, demon or devil in the afterlife to seek revenge.

The spiritual (*hun*) component of the soul would ascend to the spirit world, Heaven (*Tian*), the dwelling place of the gods, and, if sacrificed to correctly, there it would remain, sending down blessings and acting as an intermediary between its descendants and higher deities. Thus, the spiritual (*hun*) soul of an individual was of the same nature as the deities, and the worship of gods by a family was almost indistinguishable in nature from the worship of their ancestors. A philosophical framework allowing for the deification of emperors and other meritorious individuals thus promoting them from ancestral spirit to deity was also established and became one of the foundations of folk religion in the Shang dynasty.

The system that evolved was fluid in nature, in which the soul of an ancestor could become a deity or a ghost, and a ghost, if sacrificed to, and worshiped, could become an ancestor or deity. Ancestors and deities are both comprised of spiritual energy, the distinctive difference being that deities have more spiritual power (*ling*) than ancestors, and while ancestors may affect the lives of their descendants, deities can affect the lives of individuals, communities, states or empires. The deceased thereby acquired more powers in ancestral form than they had possessed in life, ritualistic sacrifices were offered to them, and henceforth, ancestors, who had the power to influence the lives of their descendants, were attributed with powers similar to, but lesser than, deities (Thompson, 1979). Therefore, inherent to the belief system developed by the Shang was a mutual dependence between the living and the dead, the first requiring blessings and divine assistance and the latter requiring sacrifices for their welfare in the afterlife.

Folk Taoism and Spirit Possession

Later, these fundamental beliefs became incorporated into orthodox Taoism, and have been maintained in both the orthodox and folk Taoist traditions into contemporary times. However, trance possession is not practiced in orthodox Taoism, only by spirit mediums in the folk Taoist tradition. Folk Taoism is the religion of the masses, and anthropologists have coined a variety of terms to describe this religion including 'shenism' (Elliott 1955), 'popular religion' (Bell, 1992; Chan, 2009; Teiser, 1995), and the worship of 'Gods, Ghosts and Ancestors' (Jordan, 1972; Ahern, 1973), but these terms have become overused and do not relate to contemporary emic self-identity. While recognizing that 'folk Taoism' is not a universally accepted term, it is a useful academic term in that it distinguishes the religion practiced by the majority of Chinese religionists from the orthodox Taoism practiced by Taoist priests. However, it should be noted that within folk Taoist communities, this distinction is only made by a minority of practitioners, the majority simply identifying themselves as Taoists.

Folk Taoism is a complex mix of folk, Taoist and Buddhist beliefs, traditions, deities and rituals that have intertwined in a complex historic process occurring between the second century BCE and the present, which now constitutes a syncretic tradition commonly practiced by the majority of Chinese religionists today. Folk Taoist temples often contain an eclectic mix of deity statues on their altars, and it is not uncommon to find the Mahayana Buddhist Bodhisattvas *Guan Yin Pusa* and *Dizangwang Pusa* as well as deities that predate religious Taoism,[4] for example *Tudi Gong*, worshipped alongside Taoist deities in folk Taoist temples. Folk Taoism, although ancient, is still in the process of evolution, with new rituals and beliefs being developed in an on-going process to meet the needs of modernity. It is to this tradition that spirit mediumship belongs, and I have therefore adopted the term folk Taoism to apply to the religion practiced by traditional Chinese religionists including spirit mediums who identify themselves and their temples as Taoist. The concept of souls surviving death and subsequently being worshipped as deities, either as anthropomorphic images or manifested as deities incarnate through spirit mediums is intrinsic to this tradition.

Comber (1958) claims the origin of Chinese spirit mediums dates back to the Zhou dynasty (1125-255 BCE). Chan (2009), by linking some performance aspects of spirit mediumship, for example, the Wu step of King Yu the Great, and modern exorcism to *nuo* exorcisms in ancient China, dates the origins of Chinese spirit mediumship as far back as the Xia dynasty (1990-1557 BCE).[5] "*Nuo* rituals were processional and always led by a warrior exorcist known as the *fang xiang shi* who has been variously described as 'warrior of the four directions' or 'the manic general who clears the way'...[who was] armed with a lance and shield, and dancing wildly" (Chan, 2009, p.3). Chan points out the commonalities between this image and the image of the modern spirit medium: "In Zhou times, the *fang xiang shi* was a court position, but inevitably the idea of exorcistic rituals with a wild warrior clearing the way of evil spirits became popular among the common people who began to have their own versions of the *nuo*. The exorcisms began to take on a distinctive festive air" (Chan, 2009, p.4). Spirit mediumship has flourished over the centuries, especially so in the south-eastern provinces of China from where the tradition has spread to Chinese communities throughout Southeast Asia. Emigrants would commonly have taken deity statues or incense ash containing the spiritual essence (*ling*) of a deity in order to establish temples or altars in their new homes. In this way, both deities and spirit mediumship has spread, most notably to Singapore and Taiwan where the practices have thrived and have become integral to the contemporary religious landscapes.

Ling plays a central role in folk Taoism and is considered accumulative and diminishing in nature, thereby allowing a deity to increase in power relative to sacrifices and worship offered to them, or conversely, to lose their power if worship and sacrifice is lessened until, when their *ling* is finally exhausted, they may cease to exist. While a deity still retains spiritual efficacy, it may enter the body of a medium. The ontological construct on which spirit possession is posited relies on a spirit medium's *hun* soul leaving the body, thus creating a vacuum for the soul of the deity to occupy. Elliott (1955) reports the belief that the medium's own *hun* soul is taken care of by other spiritual beings, commonly deities or spirit armies protecting a temple, while the *po* element of the soul remains in the medium's body. When interviewing deities tranced by contemporary spirit mediums, they maintained that the medium's displaced soul had entered a sacred object such as a deity statue or command flag, or that it remained close in the temple guarded by spirit armies.

Until recent times, mediums were commonly chosen by the possessing deity against their own will. "Field researchers again and again stress the supposedly involuntary character of the process: prospective mediums suffer seizures, hallucinations, or strange ailments that are interpreted as a deity's call to surrender to it" (Clart, 2003, p.153). While the mediums that I interviewed in contemporary Taiwan and Singapore were aware of these traditional archetypes, the attitude commonly adopted now is one of, 'that was in the old days, it still sometimes happens like that, but times have changed', and either denied that these commonalities applied to them or portrayed their own experience in a very positive light. While the deity still chooses their medium, it is common nowadays for new mediums to be drawn towards a certain deity and to offer their services as a vessel for gods as an act of devotion. These mediums are warrior mediums, known in Hokkien[6] as *tang-ki*. The warrior mediums are associated with a theatre of pain including self-mortification and body piercing with sacred ritual objects performed as "a religious practice in which the *tang-ki* as warrior god, arms himself to do battle with evil demons" (Chan, 2009, p.1).

The *tang-ki* is considered to be a deity incarnate. As such, through the spirit medium, devotees can not only communicate directly in a conversational manner with a deity,[7] but also interact with other spiritual entities though ritual. In contrast, in the absence of a possessed medium, incense is employed to initiate communication between the human and spiritual realms. After the incense smoke has drawn the attention of a deity, *jiao*, two crescent shaped divination blocks having one flat and one convex surface are cast to answer questions put to a deity. If two flat or concave sides land facing up, the answer is interpreted as 'no', but one flat and one convex side indicates an affirmative answer. Therefore, in conducting transactions, a limited social connection is established between the devotees and deities utilizing the *jiao* to facilitate two-way communication. However, as the deity is limited to 'yes' or 'no' answers, this creates a different schematic from the conversational relationship enjoyed by devotees and deities tranced through spirit mediums.

Trance Possession and Temple Culture

Although spirit possession will vary between mediums, trance phenomena typically include a selection of the following stages which may be seen as comprising a polythetic class; where a member of the class need only hold a selection from the group of attributes to belong (Needham, 1975 & Southwold, 1978). Before going into a trance, a medium is supposed to vomit any food in their stomach, after which their body may become very cold and even icy to the touch. Drums and gongs start, and the medium makes their way to a dragon chair.[8] An evocation is chanted by assistants,[9] and the first noticeable signs of trance, in the form of yawns and stretches, occur. These may develop into combinations of quivering, shaking, swaying or rocking motions. Amid the incense smoke, the drums rise to a crescendo, and as the deity enters, the medium stands in a martial posture and allows their assistants to dress them in a costume prepared specifically for the possessing deity. These costumes are bespoke, often envisaged by the medium in dreams while in training, and crafted by skilled tailors. In general, once in trance, the medium behaves in a solemn manner unless trancing a deity known for their sense of humor, and only in an intoxicated manner if possessed by *Jigong*, a deity famed for his drunkenness. After they have been fully dressed, the medium leads their assistants and devotees in paying respects to the deities represented on the temple altar, and may then write several talismans which are burned over the main censers in the temple to alert Heaven that a deity has manifested in the human realm. Personal consultations then begin, each person having taken a number on arrival at the temple. The medium does not know in advance what will be asked of them. While possessed, the medium personifies the deity possessing them, portraying the characteristics of the possessing deity as, "when in a state of trance, the power of the spirit is said actually to be in the person" (Tong, 1989, p.79).

On important ritual occasions such as the birthday of a deity or anniversary of a temple, self-mortification with a selection of weapons and tongue cutting to let blood to daub on charm papers and personal objects may occur. This is because while possessed, the medium's blood carries the spiritual efficacy of the possessing deity, and the deity may choose to use this to produce long lasting protective talisman for their devotees. Pre AIDS, stamping clothing and household ornaments with blood as a form of protection or benefaction was a common practice, but is less prominent today. Deities perform various ritual functions after possessing their medium which may include summoning Heaven or Underworld armies to gather information and protect the temple premises, as well as performing healing, luck changing and protective rituals. Devotees converse freely with deities during consultations, the most common subjects being related to health, family, relationships and business. The medium may speak in deity language, which is usually unintelligible to the uninitiated, and must be translated by an interpreter. However, the use of deity language is becoming less common, and contemporary mediums more often speak in the local vernacular, or in Mandarin Chinese. When consultations and public duties are finished, the deity announces or signals that they are about to 'return', meaning to leave the medium, and then the medium may be propelled into the air as the deity leaves and fall into the arms of their assistants, or sit down to quietly de-trance. The medium then returns to a normal state of consciousness.

Trance Possession from a Clinical Perspective

I have chosen to report the findings of Ng (2000) who researched trance possession from the discipline of psychology so as to offer an alternate perspective on a phenomenon more often associated with anthropological and ethnographic research. It should be noted while that Ng's research was undertaken in clinical settings with patients suffering from involuntary possession and not in a religious environment, it confirms cases of spirit possession and xenoglossy [speaking in unlearned languages – e.g., see Gauld, 1982], and therefore lends support to the emic understanding of spirit mediumship.

Possession may or may not involve trance, and trance may or may not involve possession. When a trance possession occurs in a culturally authorised setting, such as a religious ritual, it is both expected and normative (Ng, 200, p. 565). Trance has been described as denoting "a psychophysiological transformation probably involving changes in brain–body chemistry and functioning, while possession involves cultural–religious conceptions defined via shared ritual practices and belief systems" (Halperin, 1996 in Ng, 2000, p.561). Among *tang-ki*, trance is usually followed closely by possession, or trance and possession may be simultaneous.

Ng (2000) states that possession-trance syndromes are culturally specific. By this, he means that there is some element of self-fulfilling prophecy, as in different cultures, correlated 'agents of possession' and the 'corresponding effects of their influence' are dominant, and people experience the "stereotyped behaviours characteristic of the possessing agent" (Ng, 2000, p.561). Similarly, spirit mediums from non-Chinese cultural groups are usually possessed by culturally specific deities, examples from Singapore being *Kali*, *Madurai Veeran* and *Hanuman* in ethnic Indians, and *Datuk Gong* in ethnic Malays. From an emic perspective this is consistent with the internal logic of trance possession in folk Taoism, and it would be suspect if a possessed medium were not to physiologically and psychologically take on the attributes of a possessing deity. For example, Elliott describes the mannerisms typical of a medium possessed by the monkey deity, 'The Great Sage Equal To Heaven,' *Sun Wu Cong*. "He raises his head, gazes around him, and begins to make scratching motions with his hands behind his ears. His lips quiver with a malevolent expression. Then, with a little leap, he jumps forward from the chair and lands on his toes in front of the offering table" (Elliott, 1955, p.85). Similarly, when possessed by the child deity *Nezha*, mediums may suck a pacifier, strike childlike kung fu poses, carry a wind-and-fire wheel[10] and often orate with a child's voice and vocabulary.

Clinical definitions of trance match the external appearance of spirit medium possession, which may be taken as evidence that while spirit medium possession contains elements of ritual performance, the trance state itself is genuine. 'Trance' implies a passage into another psychic state, derived from *transitus* and *transpire*, Latin for 'passage' and 'pass over.' During a trance, the individual becomes reflectively unconscious of their environment for a prolonged period of time. Bourguignon (1978) described trance as, "a state of functional, nonawareness, a detachment from the environment" (cited in Ng, 2000, p.560). Clinical features of trance include amnesia, emotional disturbance and loss of identity. A second definition of trance from the American Psychiatric Association (1994) includes three stages. First, an altered state of consciousness, which is inferred from the way in which the individual responds to and interacts with the environment. Second, partial or total amnesia after a trance state in that the individual has no recollections, or at most patchy ones, of the event. This of course makes researching spirit possession problematic as the spirit medium rarely remembers the period of time in which the possession occurred after exiting their trance state. On the issue of trance and memory loss, Ng reports, "the exit from trances was characterized by general unawareness (43.6%), total amnesia (54.5%), (and) partial amnesia (45.5%)" (Ng, 2000, p.573). The relationship between clinical amnesia following trance and the inability of spirit mediums to recall the whereabouts of their *hun* soul during possession, or their actions while possessed, may be a physiological result of trance. Therefore, from a methodological perspective, interviewing the possessing deity directly through the medium may be preferable to interviewing the medium after the fact. Nils Bubandt, in his study of spirits and possession in eastern Indonesia, makes a credible case for considering spirits as methodologically, if not ontologically, real. He argues that "spirits, when observed and engaged during possession rituals, are key informants who can be engaged, interviewed and analysed very much like the conventional key informant technique suggests" (Bubandt, 2009, p. 299). However, while Bubandt (2009) interviewed spirits to reveal the political role of mediums in regard to a sultanate within the political arena, the research on which this chapter is based focussed on interviewing *tang-ki* during a trance state to ascertain their experience of trance possession itself from the perspective of the possessing deity.

There are further relationships between clinical trance states and trance possession. A typical trance state lasts between 0.5-3 hours as does a spirit medium popssession, either in parade or for the purpose of personal consultations (Heinze, 1993; Ng, 2000). Prodromal symptoms of both include dizziness and light-headedness (Comber, 1958; Ng, 2000), feeling cold (Elliott, 1955; Ng, 2000), twitching movements of extremities (Comber, 1958,[11] Ng, 2000; Tong, 1989), and changes in body image or perception (Heinze, 1993; Ng, 2000). During trance states, Ng noted that 58% of the people that he observed had multiple shifts from ordinary consciousness to an altered state and back to ordinary consciousness, which is similar to descriptions of mediums who begin a possession in a deep state of trance, may go through a lighter stage, then deeper again during self-mortification, and then into a more shallow trance while answering divination questions, though these stages do depend on external factors including duties and rituals to be performed (Comber, 1958; Elliott, 1955; Heinze 1993). This is not to suggest that the possessing deity leaves the *tang-ki* during these periods.

Also in trance, a small percentage of people are able to speak, or understand, unlearned languages. Ng (2000) noted that one individual used a Javanese dialect which had been out of use for several generations and that he hadn't previously learned (Ng, 2000). Another, this time a soldier, claimed to have seen a female Japanese ghost and, according to eye witnesses from the garrison, while in a trance, spoke fluent Japanese in a female voice. According to both witnesses and himself, he was unable to speak Japanese when not in a trance state (Ng, 2000).

Possession is usually by lower order deities,[12] the reason most commonly offered being that a higher deity considers it undignified to possess a human body. For Ng, the medical and cultural inferences of this are thought provoking. If someone claims to be possessed by high ranking deities, they would probably be considered deluded, as this would be outside of the accepted cultural norm, and would not, therefore, be accepted by the person's own culture. Ng concludes that as a therapeutic intervention for those frequently possessed by lower order deities, one can advise them to pray to a higher ranking deity "for assistance to abort the (unwanted) trance states" (Ng, 2000, p.575), or, request the higher deities to intervene on the behalf of the human to pressure the lower deity to stop possessing them. In cases of spirit possession where a spirit medium is summoned to perform an exorcism, if the deity possessing the medium is higher in the celestial pantheon than the spirit to be exorcised, the higher order deity will demand that the lower order deity leave. Such intervention is 'culturally sensitive' and likely, as a first measure, to be successful in both instances.

Ethnographic Accounts of Mediumship

Returning to the relevant anthropological literature, academics who have contributed to the dialogue have portrayed folk Taoist spirit mediums on a variety of different interpretive levels, and with different degrees of reverence or skepticism.

At one end of the anthropological spectrum are the depictions of village mediums in Taiwan whose daily lives have been described by Ahern (1973), Diamond (1969) and Jordan (1972) who interpreted their actions as containing the malicious entities thought to negatively influence the lives of villagers. Prior to the modernizing effects of the Taiwan Miracle, spirit mediums lived in village communities and were unpaid for their services, and when not performing religious duties for neighbors, held regular jobs to provide their income. Village mediums of the 1970s fulfilled the traditional expectancy of reluctant individuals who battled against their fate before submitting to the seeming inevitability of serving a deity (Diamond, 1969; Jordan, 1972; Ahern, 1973). In many cases, a deal had been struck between a deity and a prospective medium whereby the deity cured them of an illness in return for future service.

Self-mortification was, and still is, common practice, using an assortment of five traditional weapons: sword, axe, ball of nails,[13] rostrum of a sawfish, and a spiked club. During processions including an annual inspection of the borders of a temple's territory and birthday celebrations for a deity, spirit mediums may mortify their flesh with one or more of the weapons, producing a dramatic effect. Lacerations of the skin causing bleeding are common, but it is believed that the wounds inflicted in trance leave no scars. Harrell (1979) relates this to taboos relating to the soul (*ling hun*) of a foetus during pregnancy, in that harming its *ling hun* will inflict actual physiological injury on the unborn child. There is therefore a taboo around hammering nails into particular walls on specific dates during a pregnancy as this may injure the foetus spirit, and cause the child to be born with a hair lip. In the case of trance possession, as the *ling hun* of the spirit medium is absent from their body to make room for the spirit of the possessing deity, their *ling hun* cannot be harmed by self-mortification, and therefore no permanent physical damage is endured.

Elliott's claim that the underlying assumption behind spirit medium practices is that "a spiritual being of vast and undefined powers possesses the body of a human medium and enables him to inflict injury upon himself without feeling pain, and to speak with divine wisdom, giving advice to worshippers and curing their illness" (Elliott, 1955, p.15), clearly illustrates an alternate perspective on the *tang-ki* phenomenon to that of anthropologists researching in Taiwan. Likewise, Comber (1958) saw spirit mediums as the most important religious specialists within folk Taoism in Singapore as "they become, in effect, the reincarnation of the god concerned, and their very words and actions are vital" (Comber, 1958, p.194). Comber, in common with other researchers in Singapore (Clammer, 1993; Comber, 1958; Elliott, 1955; Ju, 1983; Tong, 1989), saw acts of self-mortification performed to "amply demonstrate in the eyes of the cult's devotees the power of the deity to render him impervious to pain" (Comber, 1958, p.198).

At the opposite end of the anthropological spectrum, Margaret Chan (2006, 2008, 2009) has approached mediumship from a Taoist cosmological perspective and has applied specialist Taoist knowledge to folk Taoist traditions. The resulting exegesis is that of warrior gods and demi-gods incarnating though spirit mediums to do battle with demonic forces for the benefit of mankind. The demonic forces take four basic forms: ghosts (*gui*), monsters (*yao*), strange beings (*guai*) and demons (*mo*) (Chan, 2009). Mediums use a selection of weapons, including a range of articles for self-mortification, whips and swords for exorcism, and talismans and sacred choreographies, all of which are empowered to do battle with forces of evil (Chan, 2009). Chan explains that, "the *tang-ki* does not operate as a lone knight errant, but as a general at the head of spirit armies. The parish of a temple is protected by the thirty-six celestial armies under the command of *Bei Ji Shang Di*, The North Pole Emperor, also known as *Xuan Tian Shang Di*, Emperor of the Dark Heavens ... The *tang-ki* has a covenant with *Bei Ji Shang Di* and his celestial armies ... *Tang-kis* pierce their bodies with swords and skewers in order to take on the spirit power imbued in these weapons; driven into the very flesh of the *tang-ki*, the weapons super-charge the *tang-ki* with spirit power" (Chan, 2009, p.9-12). Self-mortification by spirit mediums is, therefore, inherently violent as it is a brutal form of combat against powerful dark forces. In essence, "every single performance element in the *tang-ki* repertoire is an act of war magic" (Chan, 2009, p.17) and hence war magic is "the operative principle of Chinese Popular Religion" (Chan, 2009, p.8). Her exegesis therefore provides an underlying metaphysical framework to explain the self-mortification practices and healing capacities of Chinese spirit mediums.

Conclusion

This chapter began looking back into the Neolithic past to the origins of the Chinese spiritual belief system. The practice of spirit mediumship in Chinese culture is clearly ancient, dating back at least as far as the Zhou dynasty, and based on earlier philosophical constructs from the Shang dynasty entailing contractual relationships between the people and their gods. Deities are dependent on their followers to increase their *ling* through worship and offerings, and upon spirit mediums through which they incarnate in a living body, and the possessed *tang-ki* are believed to be deities incarnate. Evidence suggests that the trance states achieved are both genuine, and of a physiological intensity that should be unattainable without severe trauma, suggesting paranormal activity as the catalyst to trance states in folk Taoist spirit mediumship.

The Chinese belief system has consistently attributed illness and misfortune to the actions of malevolent spirits. In order to relieve illness and misfortune, these spirits must be defeated or exorcised in spiritual battle. Therefore, *tang-ki* enter into a ritual trance when there is a need, and in trance, it is the spirit of the deity and not that of the medium who performs the various ritual acts. The rituals performed by spiritual entities through their mediums are therefore seen to affect material reality in the form of curing illness, exorcising malevolent spirits, changing an individual's luck, dispelling misfortune, divining the future and so forth. The deities themselves may be categorized depending on the source of their original *ling* as belonging to one of three broad groupings.

The first category of deities that possess mediums is that of historic characters that later became deified, for example, the deified Han dynasty general Guan Gong, and the twelfth century monk *Dao Ji Shan Shi* more commonly known as *Ji Gong*. The ontological link between spirit mediumship and life after death research is therefore evident. This is one class of spirits that people appeal to, and bargain with as if dealing with humans, and this relationship may have acted as a catalyst for the creation of a pantheon of other anthropomorphic deities.

The second category of deities are manifestations of inanimate objects, for example, stars and constellations which have been anthropomorphized into human form, examples being Nandou Xingjun and Beidou Xingjun, the Lords of the Southern and Northern Dippers. Chan (2008) argues that anthropomorphized spirits are 'Double nature-beings', i.e. human in form but spirit in essence, and their icons "are sacral portals that permit spirits access into the mortal world" (Chan, 2008, p. 1). The inanimate nature of these deities suggests that, while spirit possession may occur, this cannot be associated with life after death experiences, rather, with the unification of cosmic spirits and the human consciousness. Chan (2008) claims that an anthropomorphized form is necessary in order to worship and bargain with deities, and as Paper notes, "nature and other spirits over time became transformed into dead humans so that they too can possess us" (Paper, 2009, p. 344). Perhaps anthropomorphization is necessary before a deity can enter a human form, and Paper suggests that this may be because a human spirit is more likely to fit into a human body than a spirit with a different shape (Paper, 2009, p. 334). Chan (2008) suggests, "the anthropomorphic image, as against the aniconic, gives a spirit the body it needs for an existence in the human world, but the soul is not tied to the body" (Chan, 2008, p. 23).

The third variety of deities that possess spirit mediums are mythologized characters from oral folk-lore, later immortalised in popular novels, before becoming anthropomorphized and worshipped as deities. An example is *Sun Wu Kong* from *Wu Cheng en's* 16th century novel *Journey to the West*: "There was a rock that since the creation of the world had been worked upon by the pure essences of Heaven and the fine savours of Earth, the vigour of sunshine and the grace of moonlight till at last it became magically pregnant and one day split open, giving birth to a stone egg, about as big as a playing ball. Fructified by the wind it developed into a stone monkey, complete with every organ and limb. At once this monkey learned to climb and run; but its first act was to make a bow towards each of the four quarters" (Waley, 2005, p.11). In contemporary Singapore and Taiwan, *Sun Wu Kong* is one of the deities that most frequently possess spirit mediums.

This third category raises an exciting ontological supposition, namely, that in folk Taoism, a spiritual entity can be created through the accumulation of direct spiritual energy (*ling*), manifested through worship and offerings under circumstances where there was no original living or inanimate nature spirit. This would inverse the equation of God creating humans, to humans, through their concentrated efforts, projecting *ling* from their own internal spiritual reserve and creating deities, spiritual beings which are capable of possessing a spirit medium in trance.

Folk Taoist spirit mediumship is a fascinating area of study, and the practices play an integral and evolving role in contemporary folk Taoist landscapes. However, I would suggest that if the complex interactions between the spiritual and social worlds are not to remain an enigma within the academic world, a complete exegesis of *tang-ki* trance possession will require extensive future research. This may be from a paranthropological (the anthropology of the paranormal) perspective, and would ideally entail experiential research of trance states and spirit possession supported through long-term cooperation and friendships between researchers and spirit mediums. Most importantly, future research must be based on mutual cooperation and respect between the international academic and local Taoist communities.

Glossary of Chinese Characters

Beidou Xingjun - 北斗星君
Bei Ji Shang Di - 北极上帝
Dao Ji Shan Shi - 道濟禪師
Dizangwang Pusa - 地藏王菩薩
Fang xiang shi - 方向士
Fuxi - 伏羲
Guai - 怪
Guangong - 關公
Guan Yin Pusa - 觀音菩薩
Gui - 鬼
Huangdi - 黃帝
Hun - 魂
Jiao - 筊
Jigong - 濟公
Ling - 靈
Ling hun - 靈魂
Mo - 魔

Nandou Xingjun - 南斗星君
Nezha - 哪吒
Nuo - 傩
Po - 魄
Shang - 商
Shen - 神
Shennong - 神農
Shun - 舜
Sun Wu Cong - 孫悟空
Tian - 天
Tian Shi Tao - 天師道
Tudi Gong - 土地公
Xia - 夏朝
Xuan Tian Shang Di - 玄天上帝
Wu Cheng en- 吳承恩
Yang - 陽
Yao - 堯
Yao - 妖
Yin - 陰
Yu - 禹
Zhang Daoling - 張道陵

Notes

1. 1766 - 1122 BCE.

2. Pinyin Romanization has been used to identify Chinese names and concepts, with the Chinese characters presented in a glossary at the end of the chapter.

3. A fuller system of *yin* and *yang* attributes and of the nature of the soul was developed and systemized before the end of the Han dynasty (Adler, 2002, p. 62).

4. Religious Taoism (as opposed to earlier schools of philosophical Taoism) is generally accepted to have originated with the Way of the Celestial Masters (Tian Shi Tao) movement which was founded by *Zhang Daoling* in 142 CE.

5. The first sovereign *Fuxi* is said to have lived in the 29th century BCE Documented history began in the 18th century BCE with the Shang dynasty. Between these two dates, lived two sovereigns, *Shennong* and *Huangdi*; the three sage kings *Yao*, *Shun* and *Yu*; and the Xia dynasty. Cited from: Adler (2002) All of these are worshipped as deities in contemporary folk Taoism.

6. Hokkien is the language spoken in Fujian province in the southeast of China. The majority of residents who now live in the regions where spirit mediumship is most commonly practiced including Singapore, Taiwan and Chinese communities in Thailand, Malaysia and Indonesia emigrated mostly from Fujian Province and are still predominantly Hokkien speakers.

7. Chan (2008) suggests that one way in which the power of the ruling elite was infringed on was through spirit mediums, as this brought the gods directly into the community and allowed common people to "interact face-to-face with their deities" (Chan, 2008, p.4).

8. An ornate throne like chair, usually painted red with gold decoration. There may be a trigram containing a yin yang symbol in the centre. The arm rests and sides of the chair are tipped with dragon heads as a symbol of power.

9. In some cases, the medium sits in the dragon chair and chants an invocation to the deity themselves.

10. A mythological weapon also used as a means to fly.

11. "The temple assistants will start beating gongs and drums faster and faster, louder and louder, until a crescendo is reached after a few minutes when the medium's head, arms, legs and body begin to jerk and quiver in a strange, uncontrollable fashion. He is possessed" (Comber, 1958, p.199).

12. Guan Yin and Guan Gong usually being the highest. The Jade Emperor, Lao Zi, and Buddha for example are not thought to possess humans.

13. Referred to in literature from Singapore as a 'prick ball'.

References

Adler, J. (2002). *Chinese religion (Religions of the world)*. London: Routledge.

Bell. C. (1992). *Ritual theory, ritual practice*. New York: Oxford University Press.

Bourguignon, E. (1978). Spirit possession and altered states of consciousness: The evolution of an enquiry. In G. D. Spindler (Ed.), *The making of psychological anthropology* (pp. 479–515). Berkley: University of California Press.

Bubandt, N. (2009). Interview with an ancestor: Spirits as informants and the politics of possession in North Maluku. *Ethnography, 10*, 291-316.

Chan. M. (2006). *Ritual is theatre, theatre is ritual: Tang-Ki; Chinese spirit medium worship*. Singapore: Singapore Management University.

Chan. M. (2008). *Bodies for the gods: Image worship in Chinese popular religion.* Unpublished manuscript.

Chan. M. (2009). *Warrior gods incarnate of Chinese popular religion.* Unpublished manuscript.

Chun Fang-yu. (2001). *Kuan-yin. The Chinese transformation of Avalokitesvara.* Columbia, OH: Columbia University Press.

Clammer. J. (1993). Religious pluralism and Chinese beliefs in Singapore. In Cheu Hock Tong (Ed.), *Chinese beliefs and practices in Southeast Asia*. Malaysia: Pelanduk Publications.

Clart. P. (2003). Moral mediums: Spirit-writing and the cultural construction of Chinese spirit mediumship. *Ethnologies, 25*, 153-189.

Comber. L. (1958). Chinese temples in Singapore. In L. Comber (Ed.). *Through the bamboo window: Chinese life and culture in 1950s Malaya & Singapore*. Talisman: Singapore Heritage Society.

Degroot. J. J. M. (1897). *The religious system of China (vol 3)*. Leiden: E. J. Brill.

Diamond. N. (1969). *K'un Shen: A Taiwanese village*. New York, London, Sydney: Holt, Rinehart and Winston.

Elliott. A. J. A. (1955). *Chinese spirit medium cults in Singapore (LSE monographs on social anthropology)*. London: Berg Publishers.

Gauld, A. (1982). *Mediumship and survival: A century of investigations*. London: William Heinemann.

Halperin, D. (1996). Trance and possession: Are they the same? *Transcultural Psychiatric Research Review, 33*, 33-41.

Heinze, R. I. (1993). The dynamics of Chinese religion: A recent case of spirit possession in Singapore. In Cheu Hock Tong (Ed.), *Chinese beliefs and practices in Southeast Asia*. Malaysia: Pelanduk Publications.

Jordan D. K. (1972). *Gods, ghosts and ancestors: The folk religion of a Taiwanese village*. Berkeley, CA: University of California Press.

Ju. S. H. (1983). Chinese spirit mediums in Singapore: An ethnographic study. In Clammer (Ed.), *Studies in Chinese folk religion in Singapore and Malaysia*. Singapore: National University of Singapore.

Needham. R. (1975). Polythetic classification: convergence and consequences. *Man, New Series, 10* (3), 349-369.

Ng. B. Y. (2000). Phenomenology of trance states seen at a psychiatric hospital in Singapore: A cross-cultural perspective. *Transcultural Psychiatry, 37*, 560-579.

Paper. J. (2009). The role of possession trance in Chinese culture and religion: a comparative overview from the Neolithic to the present. In *The people and the Tao: new studies in Chinese religions in honour of Daniel L Overmyer*. Institut Monumenta Serika, Sankt Augustin.

Southwold. M. (1978). Buddhism and the definition of religion. *Man, 13*, 362-379.

Teiser. S. F. (1995) Popular religion. *Journal of Asian Studies, 54* (2), 378-395.

Thompson. L.G. (1979). *Chinese religion*. Belmont, CA: Wadsworth Publishing Company.

Tong, C. K. (1989). Child diviners: Religious knowledge and power among the Chinese in Singapore. *Southeast Asian Ethnography, 8*, 71–86.

Wu Ch'eng En. (1590). *Monkey: Journey to the West*. Translated by A. Waley (2005). New York: Penguin Classic.

Biographies

Fiona Bowie, PhD, studied Anthropology at the Universities of Durham and Oxford. She has taught in departments of Theology and Religious Studies and Anthropology in the Universities of Wales, Bristol, Linköping in Sweden and Virginia. She is a member of Wolfson College, Oxford and Visiting Senior Research Fellow in the Department of Theology and Religious Studies at King's College London. She is founder of the Afterlife Research Centre and is currently working on ethnographic approaches to the study of mediumship and the afterlife.

Charles Emmons, PhD, is a sociologist at Gettysburg College, U.S. His research is mainly on science, religion and the paranormal. He has coauthored with his wife, Penelope Emmons, *Science and Spirit: Exploring the Limits of Consciousness* (2012) and *Guided by Spirit: A Journey into the Mind of the Medium* (2003). Other publications include *Chinese Ghosts and ESP: A Study of Paranormal Beliefs and Experiences* (1982), and *At the Threshold: UFOs, Science and the New Age* (1997). He is active in Exploring the Extraordinary, an honorary member of the Board of Reviewers of Paranthropology, and member of The Society for Scientific Exploration.

Hannah Gilbert has a BA (Hons) in Anthropology from the University of Durham, and a PhD in Sociology from the University of York. Her doctoral project looked at representations and experiences of the spirit world in British spirit mediumship. She is the director of Compassionate Wellbeing and co-director of Exploring the Extraordinary, and is currently writing a book about grief and the emotional characteristics of the dead.

Fabian Graham has been researching Chinese religion in Southeast Asia since 2005. Intrigued by the on-going creation of new deities and methods of communicating with them, he felt that anthropology offered the most dynamic research methodologies and analytical tools for his field of study. Having completed an MA in Taiwan Studies at National Chengchi University in Taipei, he returned to England to study Social Anthropological Analysis at Fitzwilliam College, Cambridge. After graduating, he joined Bristol University where, with encouragement from Dr. Fiona Bowie, he focused his research on spirit mediumship in Taiwan and Singapore before transferring to The School of Oriental and African Studies in London to complete his PhD. Adopting an experiential approach where possible, he spent eighteen months interviewing mediums in trance states, participating in rituals, and attempted to enter trance states himself with the intention of experiencing spirit possession first hand. His academic research into spirit mediumship and esoteric Taoist practices is on-going, and, while pursuing his interests in palaeontology, history, Asian civilisations, and religious architecture, looks forward to further explorations into the metaphysical dimensions of religious experience.

Jack Hunter, MLitt, is a PhD candidate in the Department of Archaeology and Anthropology at the University of Bristol. His research takes the form of an ethnographic study of contemporary trance and physical mediumship in Bristol, focusing on themes of personhood, performance, altered states of consciousness and anomalous experience. In 2010 he established *Paranthropology: Journal of Anthropological Approaches to the Paranormal*, as a means to promote an interdisciplinary dialogue on issues relating to paranormal beliefs, experiences and phenomena. He is the author of *Why People Believe in Spirits, Gods and Magic* (2012), a beginner's introduction to the anthropology of the supernatural.

Stanley Krippner, PhD, is Alan Watts Professor of Psychology at Saybrook University. He was the 2002 recipient of the American Psychological Association Award for Distinguished Contributions to the Advancement of International Psychology and is the co-author of several books including *Personal Mythology, Dream Telepathy,* and *The Voice of Rolling Thunder.* He co-edited *Varieties of Anomalous Experience: Examining the Scientific Evidence,* and *Debating Psychic Experience: Human Potential or Human Illusion?*

David Luke completed his PhD on the psychology of luck in 2007, and is now Senior Lecturer in Psychology at the University of Greenwich where he teaches an undergraduate course on the Psychology of Exceptional Human Experience, and is also guest lecturer on the MSc in Transpersonal Psychology and Consciousness Studies at the University of Northampton. He was President of the Parapsychological Association between 2009-2011 and as a researcher he has a special interest in transpersonal experiences, anomalous phenomena and altered states of consciousness, having published almost 100 academic papers in this area. He is coauthor of the undergraduate textbook *Anomalistic Psychology* (2012, Palgrave Macmillan), director of the Ecology, Cosmos and Consciousness salon at the institute of Ecotechnics, London, and is a cofounder and director of Breaking Convention: Multidisciplinary Conference on Psychedelic Consciousness. He has studied techniques of consciousness alteration from South America to India, from the perspective of scientists, shamans and Shivaites, but increasingly has more questions than answers.

Fatima Regina Machado has a PhD in psychology from the University of São Paulo (USP) and a PhD in Communication and Semiotics from the Pontifical Catholic University of São Paulo (PUC). She holds a master degree in Science of Religion from the same institution. She works as a researcher at the Laboratory of Social Psychology of Religion, University of São Paulo. She is a founder (with Wellington Zangari) and scientific director of Inter Psi – Laboratory of Anomalistic Psychology and Psychosocial Processes, Brazil.

Everton de Oliveira Maraldi, MSc, is a psychologist and a graduate student at the Institute of Psychology of the University of São Paulo, Brazil, and is a member of the Inter Psi - Laboratory of Anomalistic Psychology and Psychosocial Processes, USP, Brazil. His research interests include topics such as dissociation, mediumship, anomalous creative experiences, and paranormal beliefs. He is currently working on a PhD dissertation about dissociative experiences and related variables among religious and non-religious Brazilian respondents (acknowledgements to FAPESP - Foundation for Research Support of São Paulo, Brazil).

Deirdre Meintel, PhD, is professor of anthropology at the Université de Montréal. She is cofounder and editor of a journal called Diversité urbaine and directs an interdisciplinary research group of the same name. She is also one of the two directors of the Centre de recherches en études ethniques des universités montréalaises. She has worked on ethnicity, migration and family, ethnic identity, transnationalism and mixedness and has done fieldwork in Mexico, the Cape Verde Islands, the U.S. and Québec. In recent years her work has focused on religion and modernity and she has been studying a Spiritualist congregation in Montréal. Since 2006 she has been directing a team project on religious and spiritual currents that have developed in Quebec since the 1960s.

Tamlyn Ryan, PhD, is Academic Skills Coordinator at the University of York, working with Widening Participation, student transition and progress. She graduated from the University of Liverpool in 2006 with a BA (Hons) (First Class) Sociology and Social Policy, before commencing an ESRC- funded 1+3 Studentship at the University of York. Her research interests have focussed on alternative spirituality, the Psychic-Spiritual Milieu and the internet. Tamlyn's doctoral research, completed in 2012: *Virtual Spirituality: The Negotiation and (Re)-Presentation of Psychic-Spiritual Identity on the Internet*, is an autoethnographic approach to alternative spirituality on the internet. This is available here: http://etheses.whiterose.ac.uk/3794/

Diana Espírito Santo wrote her PhD in social anthropology at University College London on concepts of Self in Cuban Creole spiritism, known as 'espiritismo cruzado.' She returns often to Havana to follow up her research through varied foci – dreams, spirit biographies, divination, the experience of witchcraft and transgression, politics and religion. Since 2009 she has been a postdoctoral researcher – most recently at the Centre for Research in Anthropology (CRIA), based at the New University of Lisbon. She currently works and writes on notions of ontological plasticity in the theology and phenomenology of Brazilian Umbanda. She has co-edited two books and her monograph, provisionally entitled *Developing the Dead*, is under review at a US press.

Bettina E. Schmidt, PhD in cultural anthropology at Philipps-University Marburg, is senior lecturer in the study of religions at University of Wales Trinity St David. She has published extensively on Caribbean and Latin American religions, identity, cultural theories and migration. Her academic interests include the anthropology of religion, diaspora identity, religious experience, urban studies, medical anthropology and gender issues. Her main fieldworks were conducted in Mexico, Puerto Rico, Ecuador, New York City, and, more recently, in São Paulo, Brazil. She is the author of *Caribbean Diaspora in the USA: Diversity of Caribbean Religions in New York City* (2008, Ashgate) and co-editor of *Spirit Possession and Trance: New Interdisciplinary Perspectives* (2010, Continuum).

Dr. Barbara Stöckigt, MD, PhD, is a physician with several years of medical experience in psychiatric hospitals. One of her interests is the extent of human consciousness, where it can lead to and how to deal with it. Having travelled widely, getting to know various cultures, she has explored cross-cultural healing systems within medical anthropology. In her doctorate she combined these interests in the field of transcultural psychiatry, conducting her research in East Africa. Currently she is working as a scientist in the Institute for Social Medicine, Epidemiology and Health Economics, Project Division Complementary Medicine, at the Charité Universitätsmedizin in Berlin, Germany.

Wellington Zangari has a PhD in psychology from the University of São Paulo (USP), Brazil, and holds a master degree in Science of Religion from the Pontifical Catholic University of São Paulo (PUC). He did an internship at the Division of Perception Studies – University of Virginia during his postdoctoral research. Wellington is professor of anomalistic psychology and social psychology of religion at the University of São Paulo. He is one of the founders (with Fatima Machado) and coordinators of Inter Psi – Laboratory of Anomalistic Psychology and Psychosocial Processes, University of São Paulo, Brazil.

INDEX

259-261, 265, 270, 302, 308-309, 316-317, 321-322, 335
Experiential Source Hypothesis (ESH) 105, 124
Extrasensory Perception (ESP) 106, 134, 208, 259-261, 265-266, 268, 271, 293, 309, 312
Extraterrestrials 213

Fang 241, 245
Fasting 235
Favret-Saada, J. 86
Felix Experimental Group (FEG) 13, 28-30, 50
Feminism 318
Fenwick, E. 34
Fenwich, P. 34
Fertility 165, 198
Festinger, L. 37-38
Folk-psychology 99, 104, 105, 124
Fontana, D. 63, 109
Fox Sisters 57, 70, 106-107, 306
Foy, R. 26
France 187, 258
Frankfurt 29
Fraud 23, 27-28, 29, 30-32, 36, 50, 57, 108, 276, 278, 289
Functionalism 101-104, 248

Gabon 238
Gabriel da Costa, J. (Mestre Gabriel) 233
Garrett, E.J. 108
Gatekeeper 28, 79-80, 84-85
Geertz, C. 117
Gender 60, 78, 159, 250, 318
General Extrasensory Perception (GESP) 268
Genie 239, 311
Geomagnetism 262, 280-281
Germany 29
Gestures 162, 200, 287
Ghosts 100, 140, 201, 301, 303, 305, 308-310, 314, 326-327, 336, 338

Giesler, P. 263-269, 291
Gift Exchange 150
Gilbert, H. 12
Giras 258, 263
Globalization 92
God 78, 144, 164, 166-167, 172, 192, 216, 217, 341
Goddess 85, 224, 310
Guan Yin Pusa 328, 342
Gui 326, 338, 342
Guthrie, S. 103
Gypsy Kings, The 196

Hallucinations 40, 162, 172, 330
Hamilton-Parker, C. 136
Hamilton-Parker, J. 136
Hanuman 333
Harmaline 239
Harner, M. 50, 94, 231, 239-240, 247
Harner Foundation 231
Harrison, M. 109
Hatha Yoga 263
Havana 177, 181, 185-186, 190-193, 197-198
Hawking, S. 111
Healing 9, 21, 31, 50, 77, 79-82, 83, 87-88, 89, 146-147, 157-161, 163-165, 169, 171-172, 189, 212, 217, 230, 235, 237, 239, 246, 248-249, 258, 263, 267-270, 272, 273-278, 290, 291, 307, 332, 339
Healing Spirits 163, 165, 167-171
Heaven 188, 216, 236, 241, 325, 326, 331-332, 341
Hekura 238, 239-240
Hell 188, 241
Hell Bank Notes 305
Henan 325
Henbane 240
Herbal Medicine 160
Hinduism 132
Histocytopathological analysis 275
Hofmann, A. 242-243

Milton Keynes UK
Ingram Content Group UK Ltd.
UKHW011313300624
444945UK00017B/58